Creating Research and Scientific Documents Using Microsoft Word

Alexander V. Mamishev, PhD
Murray Sargent, PhD

PUBLISHED BY
Microsoft Press
A Division of Microsoft Corporation
One Microsoft Way
Redmond, Washington 98052-6399

Library of Congress Control Number: 2013945002
ISBN: 978-0-7356-7044-0

Printed and bound in the United States of America.

First Printing

Microsoft Press books are available through booksellers and distributors worldwide. If you need support related to this book, email Microsoft Press Book Support at mspinput@microsoft.com. Please tell us what you think of this book at http://www.microsoft.com/learning/booksurvey.

Microsoft and the trademarks listed at http://www.microsoft.com/en-us/legal/intellectualproperty/trademarks/en-us.aspx are trademarks of the Microsoft group of companies. All other marks are property of their respective owners.

The example companies, organizations, products, domain names, email addresses, logos, people, places, and events depicted herein are fictitious. No association with any real company, organization, product, domain name, email address, logo, person, place, or event is intended or should be inferred.

This book expresses the author's views and opinions. The information contained in this book is provided without any express, statutory, or implied warranties. Neither the authors, Microsoft Corporation, nor its resellers, or distributors will be held liable for any damages caused or alleged to be caused either directly or indirectly by this book.

Acquisitions Editor: Devon Musgrave
Developmental Editor: Devon Musgrave
Editorial Production: Online Training Solutions, Inc. (OTSI)
Copyeditor: Denise Bankaitis (OTSI)
Indexer: Jan Bednarczuk
Cover: Twist Creative • Seattle

Contents

What do you think of this book? We want to hear from you!

Microsoft is interested in hearing your feedback so we can continually improve our
books and learning resources for you. To participate in a brief online survey, please visit:

microsoft.com/learning/booksurvey

Chapter 7   **How to work with citations**   **169**

What do you think of this book? We want to hear from you!

Microsoft is interested in hearing your feedback so we can continually improve our
books and learning resources for you. To participate in a brief online survey, please visit:

microsoft.com/learning/booksurvey

Foreword

I am delighted to introduce this book by Alex Mamishev and Murray Sargent on writing technical papers in Microsoft Word. This is a book I have wanted to see for some time, and I believe it will be of great assistance to technical authors in academia, research, and business. The idea of commissioning such a book came to me on hearing a seminar by Alex on his STREAM Tools while at the same time learning about Murray's wonderful work on mathematical equations in Word.

I started my academic life in the 1970s as a theoretical particle physicist. The research papers and books I wrote then were littered with complex mathematical equations, multiple integrals, and arcane symbols. My first papers were, of course, produced with a typewriter but, with the advent of mini-computers like DEC's famous VAX, I progressed to using the UNIX troff typesetting system. When I moved into computer science in the mid-1980s, I switched to LaTeX, written by Leslie Lamport and based on Donald Knuth's TeX typesetting system, and still beloved within the computer science and particle physics communities. But with the arrival of the IBM PC in 1981, I also found myself using WordStar and later WordPerfect to write collaborative project proposals that did not require mathematical notation. A decade or so later, as a university department chair, I found myself switching to Word for compatibility with others in the department and university administration. My complete conversion to Word came with my leadership of the multidisciplinary eScience Initiative in the UK in the early 2000s. I now found myself regularly collaborating with diverse communities of scientists who either did not know or want to use LaTeX!

We live in a world of collaboration in which working as part of a team to solve a complex problem or to undertake a specific task is a necessity, be it in business or in academia. In science, multidisciplinary collaboration between scientists of many disciplines is fast becoming the new norm. Similarly, project proposals and technical reports frequently involve many different parts of an organization or multiple organizations. Capturing the output of such diverse teams in a professional and attractive looking document is now more important than ever. In large part, this book was written to assist the many Word users who have not yet stepped up to using the advanced features of Word to more easily produce long documents with equations, tables, references, and footnotes. The template techniques described in this book will enable distributed teams to collaborate on documents using a common platform.

So I very much welcome this book and congratulate Alex and Murray for producing such an accessible text. I certainly know that using such templates and the other advanced features explained here would have made writing my latest book a whole lot easier!

Tony Hey
Vice President, Microsoft Research
October 2013

Acknowledgments

We would like to thank many individuals for their participation in various stages of this project.

At the University of Washington, several generations of students were the first adopters of the techniques described here. While it is impossible to name them all, some of the most active ones were Nels Jewell-Larsen and Kishore Sundara-Rajan. Overall, more than fifty people contributed to this project in different ways, and we would like to thank all of them here.

Joshua Hutt did a tremendous job setting up the text of this book in Word, updating the contents of the manuscript as he went along. Aaron Zielinski meticulously proofread and copyedited the text before it went to the publisher.

Several Microsoft employees greatly contributed to this project. Microsoft VP for Research, Tony Hey, recognized the value of this method and supported the project early on. Devon Musgrave directed the production process.

Introduction

The goal of this book is to teach the reader how to use the powerful features of Microsoft Word 2013 to develop complex technical documents. Writing long documents that are filled with equations, tables, cross-references, and literature citations requires the proper use of the advanced features in Word 2013; otherwise, the productivity and output quality of the writer or group are diminished.

The intended audience for this book is engineers, scientists, graduate students, and technical professionals. Typical readers from these groups have good working knowledge of Word. They have used it to write reports, resumes, and cover letters, and they know how to format text and look up online help. However, when it comes to writing a longer document, for example, a PhD dissertation, or a document that takes input from a dozen authors, for example, a multi-disciplinary research proposal, the basic techniques become insufficient.

A common recourse for this audience is to use LaTeX or TeX for their typesetting needs. In some specialties, it is possible to rely exclusively on LaTeX. However, most of those using LaTeX will sooner or later face the challenge of developing a document in Word, because of the requirements of a project leader or funding organization, or just because there is no chance that some of the team members will use LaTeX in their collaborative writing effort. When this situation occurs, it's time to learn about the advanced features of Word, which allow matching nearly every functionality of LaTeX-based software, while also being accessible to less sophisticated computer users. Moreover, even the most proficient users of LaTeX will find that collaborating on documents produced in Word is quicker and more efficient, provided they follow the guidelines explained in this book.

This book is based on STREAM Tools methodology. STREAM Tools is a writing system based on using efficient processes to produce quality content and attractive documents. STREAM Tools seeks to enable and automate parts of the writing process, but it does not substitute for the process itself. More about STREAM Tools can be found in "Appendix B: About STREAM Tools."

Who this book is for

This book has been designed for use by anyone in academia, industry, or commerce who needs to produce complex, high-quality technical documents, such as research papers, grant proposals, books, or doctoral dissertations. The methods in this book are, for the most part, also applicable to earlier versions of Word; you simply have to find the alternative locations of buttons in the user interface.

How this book is organized

Ideally, you should read this book once, completing the recap sections at the end of each chapter. This will familiarize you with the principles and best practices of template use. When you are finished with this book, you will be proficient in the use of templates, and you will have the skills necessary to expand your use of templates as you desire. We recommend that you keep this book nearby and continue to refer to it as you write. Before long, you will also be able to create templates of your own, for any purpose.

If you work on documents with others, it's important that they use the same system and the same template-centered approach. Consolidating your methods will save you countless hours of modifying your document's formatting and organization, and help you avoid visual and stylistic inconsistencies along the way.

It is also worth noting that any portion of a document built with such templates can be instantly and effortlessly imported into any other template-based document. In this way, you can greatly improve your efficiency as you escape the tradition of meticulously scrutinizing document numbering, formatting, and other small details.

 Note The Word 2013 program is not available from this website. You should purchase and install that program before using this book.

Terminology

This book uses various terms with which you may be unfamiliar. The following table provides a short list of some key terms, their definitions, and where they are first described.

Term	Definition	First introduced
Template	Any document with pre-made headings, sections, styles, and fields.	Page 2
Element	Headings, equations, figures, tables, and references.	Page 3
Cross-Reference	Text in Word 2013 that refers directly to other text in the document. Will update when the source text is changed (generally requires pressing Ctrl+A and F9).	Page 16
Field Codes	Text that is automatically generated by Word. Includes cross-references.	Page 40
Yellow Text	Filler text that describes the type of text that belongs in a section of the document.	Page 2
Styles	Feature in Word 2013 that can be applied to quickly change the appearance and layout of text, both per character and per paragraph.	Page 6
STREAM Tools	Collaborative writing system developed by Alexander Mamishev and Sean Williams. See *http://www.streamtoolsonline.com*.	Page 13

Symbols and notations used in this book

Throughout the book, you will encounter many instructions on how to perform various tasks in Word 2013. These tasks will often involve navigating through menus and using keystrokes, in addition to following along with examples. The formatting conventions used in this book are described in the following sections.

Formatting of menu operations

Menu options and button clicks will appear in bold. When you are required to click multiple menu options in short succession, they will be separated by double-bar arrows, like so:

Menu ⇒ Menu ⇒ Menu Option

Formatting of keystroke operations

Keystrokes will also appear in bold. Those that are meant to be pressed simultaneously will be separated with plus signs:

Keystroke + Keystroke

Keystrokes that are meant to be pressed in succession will be separated with single-bar arrows:

Keystroke → Keystroke

Formatting of notes

> **Note** Notes will appear formatted like this.

Formatting of good examples

Good example.

Formatting of bad examples

Bad example.

Errata

We've made every effort to ensure the accuracy of this book and its companion content. Any errors that have been reported since this book was published are listed here:

http://aka.ms/670440/errata

If you find an error that is not already listed, you can report it to us through the same page.

If you need additional support, email Microsoft Press Book Support at *mspinput@ microsoft.com*.

Please note that product support for Microsoft software is not offered through the addresses above.

We want to hear from you

At Microsoft Press, your satisfaction is our top priority, and your feedback our most valuable asset. Please tell us what you think of this book at:

http://www.microsoft.com/learning/booksurvey

The survey is short, and we read every one of your comments and ideas. Thanks in advance for your input!

Stay in touch

Let's keep the conversation going! We're on Twitter at *http://twitter.com/MicrosoftPress*.

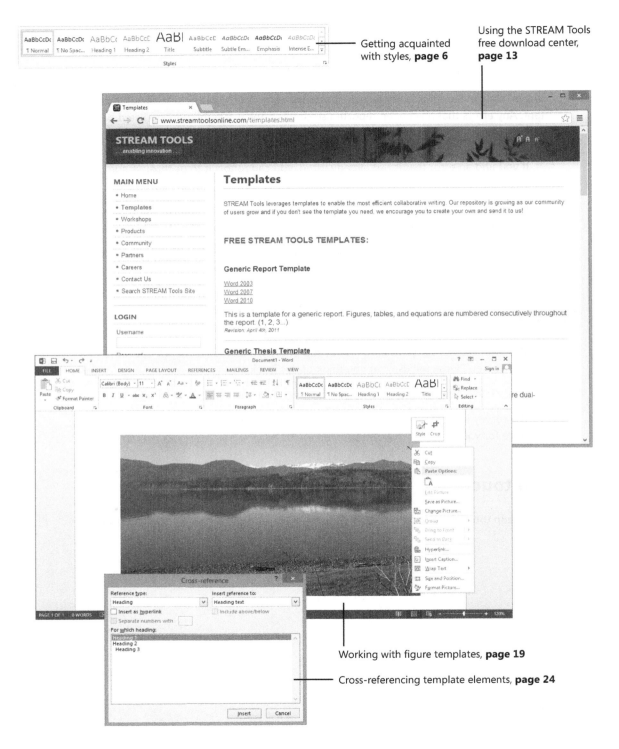

Getting acquainted with styles, **page 6**

Using the STREAM Tools free download center, **page 13**

Working with figure templates, **page 19**

Cross-referencing template elements, **page 24**

CHAPTER 1

Using templates in Word 2013

In this chapter, you will learn how to

- Improve your productivity through three key features of templates

- Speed up formatting and template creation by using styles

- Identify and use the five basic elements of templates

- Create any basic element by using an existing template

- Automate your document through the use of cross-references

This chapter will introduce you to styles and templates. If you learn one thing from this book, it should be that when you work with long and complex documents, it is important to pay attention to styles. Styles are the ultimate solution when it comes to saving time, effort, and your sanity, and their usefulness will grow exponentially with the length of your documents.

When you use styles, you can easily modify the appearance of your document to more effectively express its structure and to standardize and modify the appearance of your document with little effort. Styles will also help you get the most out of advanced cross-referencing features available in Microsoft Word 2013, and they are required for editing in the *Outline view*, using the *Navigation pane*, and automatically generating a table of contents.

 Practice Files The template file for this chapter can be found on the STREAM Tools website, at *www.streamtoolsonline.com/htwrp/templates/chapter1.docx*.

Word 2013, templates, and you

You are probably reading this book because you write research papers often, either as part of your job, or for your studies. It is also likely that you do not take full advantage of the features available in Word 2013 to more expeditiously handle this task.

What you might not know is that the advanced features of Word are both easy to use and quite powerful. In fact, the latest versions of Word have been so effective at automating document design that they are a perfect tool with which to write research papers and similar documents. With this book in hand, you are well on your way to creating high-quality research papers with minimal effort.

The most important thing you will learn from this book is to rely on templates for every document that you write.

You should begin writing with an outline of your document, using filler we refer to as yellow text, which includes descriptions of what each section will eventually contain. You should use styles to format the yellow text and each element of the template. This will help you to quickly format your document to conform to the requirements of any publisher, journal, or funding source.

A minor but necessary distinction

One thing you should understand is the difference between traditional Word templates (files with a .dotx extension) and the templates referenced in this book. The templates described in this book can be thought of as *documents by example*. What this means is that instead of worrying about file extensions, complicated field codes, and other minutiae commonly associated with .dotx templates, you will be creating templates as standard Word 2013 documents, complete with example elements such as headings, figures, and tables.

This approach is commonly used by publishers, conference organizers, and businesses. The only difference is your templates will include styles and other field-based features, and will thus be much more responsive and easy to use.

 Note For an extensive guide to organizing your workflow when writing technical documents and collaborating with multidisciplinary teams, see *Technical Writing for Teams: The STREAM Tools Handbook*, by Alexander Mamishev and Sean Williams (Wiley-IEEE Press, 2010).

Why use templates?

When properly used, templates will help you by automatically numbering and formatting the headings, tables, figures, equations, and literature citations in your document. For example, if you change the format of a single heading in a template-based document, the remaining headings can be updated with the click of a button. Additionally, an index and a table of contents can be automatically generated on the fly—allowing you to more effectively preview your document as it evolves.

Two key document authoring features in Word, *Outline view* and the *Navigation pane*, are made available through the use of styles. With Outline view, you can view your document with the level of detail you choose—you can view all of the content at once, just top-level headings, or anything in between. The Navigation pane offers an auto-generated list of your document's headings, which can be used for quick traversal, making navigating your document fast and efficient. Therefore, by using properly designed, style-enabled templates, you gain instant access to advanced document creation tools that will further accelerate your writing process.

Never start at the beginning

The greatest aspect of using templates is that they save you from having to design your documents from scratch. Instead of spending up to several hours creating and maintaining your document's formatting, numbering, and structure, you can use templates to jump straight into creating content. Additionally, the templates that you develop can be quickly adapted for use with future publications, and your previous work can be easily imported into new template designs. Most importantly, using templates will make your papers easier on the eyes, and will let you focus on what matters—the content.

Important fundamental concepts

Because templates are so powerful, the core rules of this book can be reduced to four easy-to-remember steps:

Step 1

Use template files to create your new manuscripts.

Step 2

Copy existing elements—headings, equations, figures, tables, and references—and paste the copy into a new location in the document to create a new element that maintains automatic numbering.

Step 3

Edit the elements.

Step 4

Cross-reference elements, especially equations, figures, tables, and references, to ensure your references update automatically.

These practices apply across the entire system, regardless of the particular type of document or place in the document.

Basic elements of templates

The templates you create in this book will include the five elements mentioned previously, namely: (1) headings, (2) tables, (3) figures, (4) equations, and (5) citations. They are as follows:

Headings

This is a chapter heading

This is a section heading

This is a mid-section heading

Tables

TABLE 1-1 Basic table layout and format

Column A	Column B	Column C	Column D
Row 1A	Row 1B	Row 1C	Row 1D
Row 2A	Row 2B	Row 2C	Row 2D
Row 3A	Row 3B	Row 3C	Row 3D
Row 4A	Row 4B	Row 4C	Row 4D

Figures

FIGURE 1.1 *This is a photo of the University of Washington campus. The figure numbering is automatic.*

Equations

$$F = G\frac{m_1 m_2}{r^2} \tag{1}$$

Literature citations

Each journal, conference, and publisher has its own requirements for literature citations. A citation can look like this:

... as described in [23]...

...

23. A. V. Mamishev, Breaking Barriers: Breaking Barriers: A Practical Guide to Getting into Graduate School in the United States, Lulu Press, 2011.

or like this

... as described in Mamishev et. al. ...

...

A.V. Mamishev and S.D. Williams, "Technical Writing for Teams: The STREAM Tools Handbook," Wiley-IEEE Press, First Edition, May 3, 2010.

or in many other ways. Chapter 7, "How to work with citations" is dedicated to handling literature citations.

Basics of effective template use

First of all, with any properly designed, premade template, you will need only to download the template, open it, and replace all of the indicated filler text.

To create new figures, tables, or equations

1. Locate an existing figure, table, or equation, select it (and its caption and number), and press **Ctrl+C**.

2. Place the cursor where you would like the new figure or equation to be located, and press **Ctrl+V**.

3. Replace the text and image.

If the figure or equation is in a table, simply copy the entire table. To ensure that you use templates properly, you should understand how styles work in Word 2013, and you should know how to create references. The following sections will walk you through using a basic template, and how to properly reference equations.

All about styles

In general, you should be able to use templates without having to modify or create styles. You should learn how to change and select styles, because it is inevitable that you will encounter a situation in which simple copy and paste techniques fail to achieve the results you want.

First, understand that Word 2013 views your document as a series of paragraphs, each with its own style. In many cases, two paragraphs will have the same style, as in body text. However, every heading and caption also counts as a *paragraph* in Word, and therefore each is styled separately.

In addition to the standard *paragraph* styles that are applied per paragraph, *character* styles can be applied per word (or character), allowing you to further modify the formatting while maintaining the link to a common style. For the vast majority of the techniques in this text, you will not need to use character styles, but you should be aware of their existence.

Note The styles for the notes in this book make use of both *paragraph* and *character* styles. First, the paragraph style is applied and the note is typed, after which the character style, which includes the black color, is applied to the word *Note*. This way, the formatting is quick and easy to apply, and all of the notes in the book can be modified with just a few clicks.

Finally, you should know that styles are incorporated into your document's hierarchical structure. As previously mentioned, Word offers an Outline view and a Navigation pane, both of which require the use of heading styles. The default heading styles can be incorporated into a multilevel list, which extends their hierarchy with a host of optional complementary numbering schemes. To learn how to use multilevel lists to organize the numbering scheme and structure of your document, see Chapter 3, "How to work with headings."

Using styles

To apply a style to your text, place the cursor within the paragraph you want to change. Then locate and click the desired style in the **Style** gallery, on the **Home** tab.

The Style gallery is the foundation of proper template design and use.

If none of the styles you see are quite right, click the button in the lower-right corner of the **Style** gallery (⊽) to see more. You can also click **Options** in the lower-right corner of the **Styles** pane to access the full list of styles embedded in the document. Right-click any style in the list and click **Add to Style Gallery** to make that style accessible from the ribbon.

Show the Style Inspector
Open the Manage Styles dialog box

The Styles pane gives you complete access to all of the current document's styles, and it allows you to permanently delete any of them.

To remove a style from the **Style** gallery, simply locate the style, right-click it, and click **Remove from Style Gallery** (▣). The style can be recovered at any time by clicking the **Options** button in the lower-right corner.

You can also permanently delete styles from your document. To do so, click the button at the bottom of the **Styles** pane to open the **Manage Styles** dialog box.

Open the Manage Styles dialog box

Then, select a style from the list and click **Delete**.

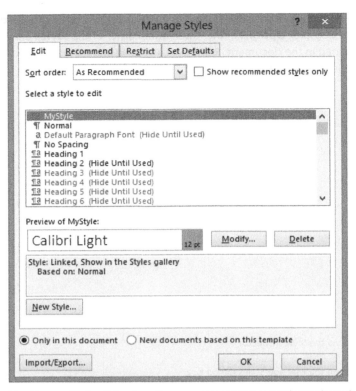

The Manage Styles dialog box gives you even greater control over the styles in your document. From here, you can permanently delete any of the styles in your document.

 Note Some of the styles you create can be deleted through the **Styles** pane. Right-click the style and click **Delete *MyStyle***, where ***MyStyle*** is the style name. Some of the default styles, such as Normal and Heading 1, are required by Word and cannot be deleted.

When you are deleting a style from your document, Word 2013 will ask you to confirm. Be careful! You can undo this action with **Ctrl+Z**, but only while the document remains open.

Creating and modifying styles

To create a style, first type some text and apply some formatting. Select the text, then click the flyout button in the lower-right corner of the **Style** gallery (⊽) to expand the gallery . Then in the lower-left corner of the gallery, click **Create a Style** (🏊), which will display the **Create New Style from Formatting** dialog box.

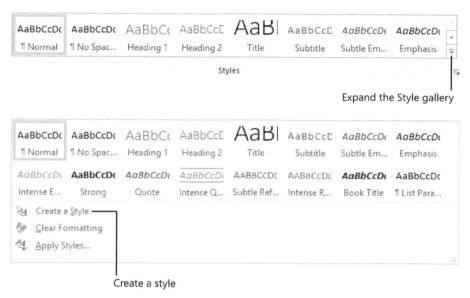

Expand the Style gallery

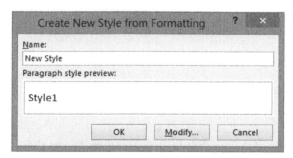

Create a style

To create a style, click the button in the lower-right corner of the Style gallery, and click Create A Style.

Type a name for the style and click **OK** to save.

You can choose any name that is not in use. To further customize your style, click Modify.

You can also click **Modify** to open a window that will enable you to further customize your new style. For advanced formatting like indentation and line spacing, click **Format** and choose the relevant menu option. When finished, click **OK**. The style appears in the **Style** gallery, ready to use whenever you choose.

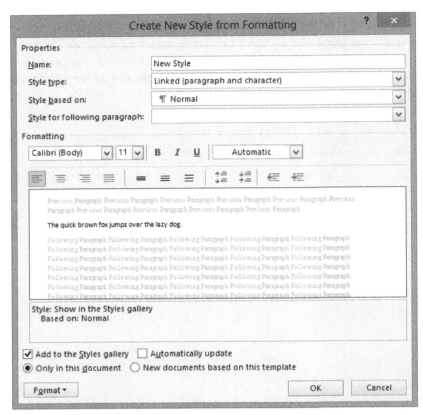

Choose the font and style options, and click Format to access advanced typesetting options, such as line spacing, borders, and shading.

You might sometimes want to modify the text in your document directly by using the tools on the left side of the **Home** tab. When you do this, you can easily update the corresponding style to match the change.

To update a style to match changed text

1. Select the text you have changed.

2. In the **Style** gallery or **Styles** pane, right-click your style (such as **Heading 1**), and click **Update Heading 1 to Match Selection**.

This will work with all styles, but it is recommended that you use care, because it only works predictably when the text you select has uniform formatting.

Lastly, styles are governed by inheritance. That is, the **Normal** style is the blueprint for all other styles; if you modify it, your other styles might change, as well. To prevent an element of a style from changing, such as the font, you must explicitly specify your choice in that style. Right-click the style, click **Modify**, and choose the font you want to use. Now, when you modify one of that style's parent styles, the font of that child style will not change.

> **Note** It is recommended that you use the settings on the **Design** tab to manage the global fonts and colors for your document, rather than changing the **Normal** style. For more information, refer to Chapter 2, "How to design templates."

The Style Inspector

Sometimes, you might find that the processes for applying and modifying styles are not functioning as expected. Perhaps applying a style will change certain elements of the text, such as color or size, but not others such as fonts or borders. To work through this quickly, you can use the **Style Inspector**. It will show you the paragraph and character styles (called "Text level formatting") applied to text, in addition to any non-style formatting applied on top of that.

To access the Style Inspector

1. Click the dialog box launcher (⌐) in the lower-right corner of the **Style** gallery.

2. In the **Styles** pane that appears, click the middle button at the lower-left side of the pane.

3. Use the **Style Inspector** by placing the cursor on a selection of text.

4. (Optional) Pin the style selector to the side of the window by clicking it and dragging it to the edge.

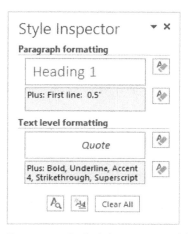

You can use the Style Inspector to quickly isolate and identify the styling of any text, no matter how complex. It will also allow you to completely remove all styles from a selection.

The Reveal Formatting pane

A more powerful alternative to the **Style Inspector** is the **Reveal Formatting** pane, which you can use to view even more detailed data about a selection. To access the **Reveal Formatting** pane, press **Shift+F1**.

You can use the Reveal Formatting pane to view the properties of a selection of text. Click Distinguish Style Source to show from which styles the properties are derived.

How to work with templates

As previously mentioned, the templates described in this book do not refer to traditional .dotx files, the design of which often requires additional steps and formatting to get right. Instead, you can use regular .docx files as "example documents," complete with placeholders for headings, figures, tables, equations, and more. The benefits of this approach are twofold. First, you save time in designing your templates, because you need only configure styles and create placeholder elements. Second, because these templates are based on styles, they are more flexible than a .dotx file designed for a singular purpose.

The approach outlined in this section is powerful enough to handle everything from short research papers to doctoral dissertations. To create consistent, professional documents with minimal effort and frustration, you should always begin with a proper template. If you do not have a suitable template, and you cannot find one online, you should adhere to the standards outlined in Chapter 2 to create a template to suit your needs.

Step 1: Find a template for your document

In general, you should be able to find a template for any document that you want to create. Many such templates are available online, and a growing collection of STREAM Tools–compatible templates can be found at the STREAM Tools website, at *http://www.streamtoolsonline.com*. Moreover, many journals provide Word templates for the submission of manuscripts in their required format. Similarly, universities often provide templates for their theses. If the template you find does not make proper use of styles and reference features, the chapters that follow will show you how to make them STREAM Tools–compatible.

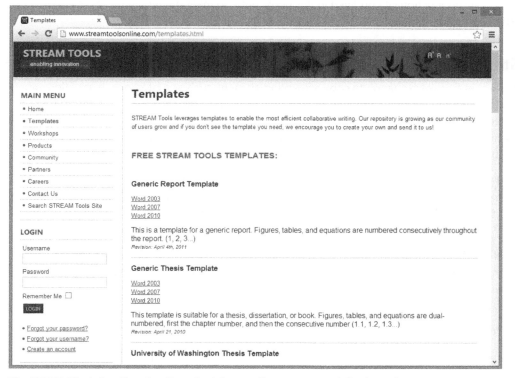

The STREAM Tools Free Template Download Center offers many user-defined templates.

In the event that you cannot locate a template that meets your needs, you should create one. For some special cases, you might find that a "dumb" template exists—that is, one created without the use of styles and field-based features. In this case, you can modify the template to include this advanced functionality. For an in-depth guide to creating templates, in addition to updating "dumb" templates, refer to Chapter 2. The following three standard templates have been designed explicitly for this purpose.

TABLE 1-2 Basic templates available with this book

File name	Description
BasicTemplateSingleColumn.docx	A single-column template for short reports and papers, typically up to 20 or 30 pages.
BasicTemplateDoubleColumn.docx	A double-column template for camera-ready double-column papers, typically up to 10 pages.
BasicThesisOrBookTemplate.docx	A single-column template for long manuscripts, such as theses, books, or long reports. Main differences from the other two templates are: ■ Chapter number is included in the numbers of figures, tables, and equations, such as Figure 3.5 rather than Figure 15). ■ Templates for the front matter (preface, table of contents, and so on) and the back matter (appendixes, index) are included.

By altering these basic templates, writers can create new, derived templates that not only possess the advanced functionality outlined in this book, but also meet the requirements of a specific publisher, agency, or journal.

Step 2: Copy existing elements into new locations

It might at first seem strange to copy an existing element, such as a heading, an equation, or a figure, to create a new one, but templates make it easy to create a new element from an existing one. When you know exactly what happens as you create new elements and how styles and auto-formatting fields are affected by your actions, you can choose to create new elements from scratch. In the beginning, however, it is much safer and simpler to copy and paste.

If you copy an existing element and then paste the copy into a new location, this maintains the *auto-numbering* of the element so that every time somebody adds an element such as a new heading, the entire document automatically updates all the numbers of each element.

Note For elements with multiple parts, such as those with captions, this copy-and-paste method is virtually foolproof. It can save you the effort of reconstructing the element manually.

Procedurally, it looks like this:

To copy an existing element to create a new one

1. Copy and paste the existing element to a new location; for example, copy an existing figure and its caption, and then paste the copy into a new location.

2. Type new text into the copy; for example, type in the new caption for a figure.

 Note Do *not* type over the automatic caption number.

3. Press **Ctrl+A** to select the contents of the entire document, and then press **F9** to update the numbering and fields (for example, numbering of figure captions, table of contents, and headings).

When you follow these steps, the number attached to your element is updated to reflect its sequence in the document. For example, if you copy a figure into Chapter 3 of your document, and it is the second figure in that chapter, it is numbered Figure 3.2.

Step 3: Edit the elements

The next step of the process is editing the elements. Recall that to create new elements, you copy a prior instance and then paste that copy into a new location in the document. This process leaves you with a duplicate of a prior element, and so the new element still needs to be edited.

Consider a heading, which is the easiest element to create and alter. If you wanted to insert a "Step 4" heading, you could copy the "Step 3" heading at the beginning of this section, and then paste the copy somewhere later. That would give you the new heading, "Step 4: Edit the elements." Notice that the number of the heading has updated but the text has not. Therefore, to update the text, select the text of the heading, add some text like "Step 4: New step," and update the document by pressing **Ctrl+A** and then **F9**.

Conceptually, all elements work the same way: (1) copy an instance, (2) paste it into a new location, and (3) edit that particular instance. Naturally, editing tables and figures is more complicated, because each of these has additional steps for ensuring the quality of the table or figure itself, but in principle, the process remains the same: **Copy** ⇒ **Paste** ⇒ **Edit** ⇒ **Update**.

Step 4: Cross-reference the elements

The final step in the process is to ensure that the numbering in your document updates automatically by adding cross-references. Imagine that cross-referencing is like asking Word to link a piece of text to an element in the document. The cross-reference reads and prints as normal text, but when you update the document's fields (**Ctrl+A** → **F9**), the text of the cross-reference is updated to match that of the element it is linked to. For example, we could insert a cross-reference to the heading for this section, and it would look identical to the heading text: "Step 4: Cross-reference the elements."

And if the title of the heading is changed to something like "Step 4: Linking elements," the in-text reference would automatically change to match it when you update the document by pressing **Ctrl+A** and then **F9**.

In the following sections, you'll discover the process for adding cross-references to elements. The complete process is simple, and it looks like this:

Copy ⇒ *Paste* ⇒ *Edit* ⇒ *Update* ⇒ *Cross-reference*

How to create elements in a document

So far, we have outlined the general concepts and process for working with templates. Each of the sections in the following pages describes the complete process for each of the major elements, moving from *copying* an old element, *pasting* it at a new location, *editing* the element, *updating* the document, and finally adding *cross-references* to the element as they are needed.

> **Note** Occasionally, the formatting is not successful when you update your document after following steps 1–4. If this happens, try turning on the **Formatting** view in Word by clicking the paragraph symbol (¶) located on the **Home** tab. This view reveals hidden formatting commands in Word. From this view, confirm that you have selected all of the formatting elements, including those just before and just after the element you copied.

How to make headings

To create a new heading element

1. Copy an existing heading. (Double-click the heading to select it, and then press **Ctrl+C**).

2. Paste the heading at the new desired location (**Ctrl+V**).

To edit a new heading

■ Replace the heading text as desired, but do not modify the heading number.

See Also *For more detailed instructions about how to work with headings, including step-by-step screen shots, refer to Chapter 3.*

How to make figures

In Word, a figure graphic or picture is a separate object from a figure caption. The automatic numbering applies to captions, and the graphics are treated as objects that happen to be next to captions. Be sure that you keep specific graphics and their corresponding captions together, because a figure element is really the combination of the figure *and* the caption.

Make a new figure element

To make a new figure element

1. Copy an existing graphic and the corresponding caption.

2. Paste them into a new desired location.

Edit the new figure element

Because each figure consists of two parts (the graphic and the caption), editing a figure requires that you edit each of the two parts. Therefore, the process for editing the new figure consists of two stages.

This process assumes that your graphic has been created and is ready to be inserted into your document.

Stage 1: Editing the graphical element

1. Right-click the old graphic and click **Change Picture** (also available on the **Format** tool tab that appears on the ribbon when you select the graphic).

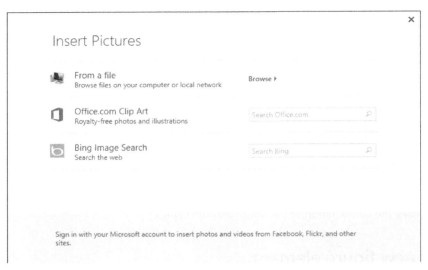

The Insert Pictures dialog box lets you quickly replace an existing graphic with a picture from your computer or online.

 Note When you use **Change Picture**, the new picture will keep the aspect ratio, formatting, and other properties of the old one. To discard those properties, you can delete the old picture, and click **Pictures** on the **Insert** tab.

2. Click **From a file**, locate the picture, and click **Insert**.

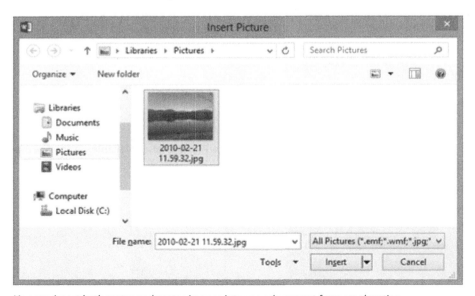

You can insert both raster and vector images into your document from any location.

Note If you would like to insert a picture that you have copied to the Clipboard, just delete the old graphic and paste the new one in its place. To avoid compatibility issues between versions and writers, do not use **Paste**. Instead, click **Home ⇒ Paste Special ⇒ Picture**.

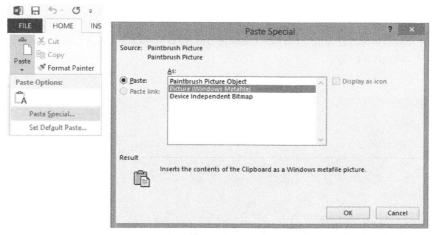

The Paste Special function ensures that your images and figures are stored properly.

3. Click the graphic to select it.

The Picture Tools group has many options to customize the look and layout of your pictures.

4. Adjust the size and centering of the graphic, as desired.

1. Delete the text of the prior caption.

2. Type the new text.

Note Remember to preserve the figure number, because it is a field. For example, in the caption, "Figure 14. Experimental setup," you can replace the words *Experimental setup*. Do not change the field *Figure 14*. The number will update automatically.

Figure 1: Discovery Bay, in Washington.

When the cursor is placed on the caption number, or when the caption is selected, it appears with a grey background. This signals that it is a field and should not be modified.

Note To easily locate all of the fields in your document, press **Ctrl+A**. The fields are highlighted with a darker shade of grey than the surrounding text.

For more detailed instructions about how to work with figures including advanced layout techniques, refer to Chapter 4, How to Work with Figures.

This text is an example of how Ctrl+A can help you find the fields in your document.

For more detailed instructions about how to work with figures, including advanced layout techniques, refer to Chapter 4, "How to work with figures."

How to make tables

The process for creating, editing, and cross-referencing tables is nearly identical to that of figures. For the purposes of this book, the table itself is equivalent to a graphic, because the table exists independently from the caption. One slight formatting difference is that table captions should appear *above* the table rather than below, as in the case of a figure. In other words, tables are labeled on top, whereas figures are labeled on the bottom.

Make a new table element

To make a new table element

1. Copy an existing table and its caption.

2. Paste them into a new desired location.

Edit the new table element

Because each table consists of two parts, the table array and the caption, editing likewise requires that you edit each of the two parts. Therefore, editing the new table occurs in two stages.

> **Note** There are three main methods for replacing the old table. You can (1) paste a new table in its place, (2) make a new table from scratch, or (3) reuse the old table.
>
> If you are using table styles, it might be easiest to create a new table from scratch. If you reuse the old table, you can preserve its formatting, including colors and borders.

Stage 1: Inserting the table

- Delete the old table in the new location and paste a new table in its place.

    Or

1. Delete the old table and click **Insert** ⇒ **Table** ⇒ **Insert Table**.

2. In the **Insert Table** dialog box, indicate how many columns and rows your table will contain. Alternatively, you can define up to a 10 × 8 table from the drop-down menu.

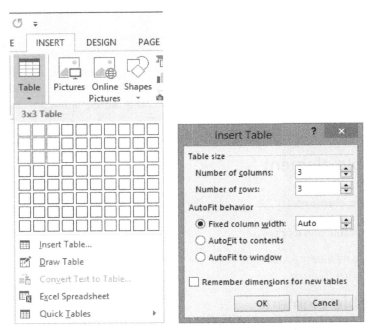

By using the Insert Table grid, you can create tables of up to 10 columns and 8 rows. By using the Insert Table dialog box, you can create tables that are even larger.

3. Click **OK**.

4. To quickly style the table, click it, navigate to the **Design** tab, and choose a style in the **Table Styles** group.

— Show all table styles

Table Styles

You can use the Table Styles gallery to quickly add color and other formatting to any table.

Or

1. Delete the text of the table (point to the table, click its placement square (⊞), and then press the **Delete** key).

2. If needed, add new rows or columns to the table by using the **Insert** buttons in the **Rows & Columns** group of the **Layout** tab.

You can use the buttons in the Rows & Columns group to restructure the tables in your documents.

3. Type or paste the new contents into the table.

Stage 2: Editing the caption

1. Delete the text of the prior caption.

2. Type the new text.

Note Remember to preserve the table number, because it is a field. For example, in the caption, "Table 14. Experimental setup," replace the words *Experimental setup*. Do not type inside the field *Table 14.* The number will update automatically.

For more detailed instructions about how to work with tables, including how to create table styles, refer to Chapter 5, "How to work with tables."

How to place equations

To create a new equation element

1. Copy the entire line of an existing equation.

2. Paste it to the new location.

To edit a new equation

1. Click the equation itself and edit it.

2. To reference the equation, you must create a bookmark. (This is covered in the following section, and in Chapter 6, "How to work with equations.")

Although the equation editor in Word 2013 is powerful and flexible enough to create equations for technical documents of virtually any size, you might still prefer to use third-party software. If this is the case, we recommend using MathType as your equation editor.

For more detailed instructions about how to work with equations, including advanced equation features, refer to Chapter 6.

How to insert cross-references

Cross-references are a fundamental element of well-written technical documents and are the key to making your templates scalable.

For more detailed instructions about how to work with cross-references, refer to the individual chapter in this book concerning the element you would like to cross-reference.

Headings

To cross-reference a heading

1. Identify a place in the text where you'd like to refer to the heading.

2. Click **Insert** ⇒ **Cross-Reference**.

3. Select **Heading** in the **Reference type** box.

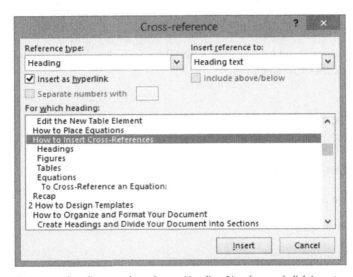

To insert a heading number, choose Heading Number and click Insert.

4. Choose **Heading number** in the **Insert reference to** box.

5. Clear the **Include above/below** check box.

6. Click **Insert**.

Now you will see the heading number in the text where you placed your cursor in step 1. Depending upon which type of reference suits your text best, you might also choose to include a cross-reference to the text of the heading as well. In this case, simply repeat the preceding process and then select **Heading text** in the **Insert reference to** box. To update your text, click **Ctrl+A** to select the entire text and then press **F9** to complete the update.

Figures

To cross-reference a figure

1. Click **Insert** ⇒ **Cross-Reference**.

2. In the **Reference type** box, click **Figure**.

3. In the **Insert reference to** box, click **Only label and number**.

4. Choose the desired figure from the list, and then click **Insert**.

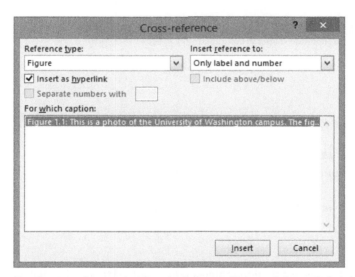

To reference a figure, select it under Reference Type, and choose Only Label And Number.

To update the document with the numbering for the figure, Press **Ctrl+A** → **F9**.

Tables

To cross-reference a table

Cross-reference

1. Click **Insert** ⇒ **Cross-Reference**.

2. In the **Reference type** box, click **Table**.

3. In the **Insert reference to** box, click **Only label and number**.

4. Choose the desired table from the list, and then click **Insert**.

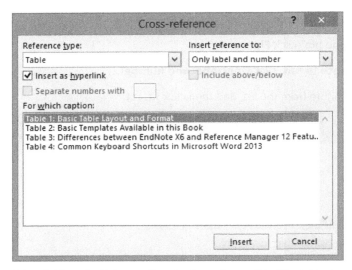

Select Table under Reference Type to choose from a list of the tables in your document.

To update the document with the numbering for the table, press **Ctrl+A** → **F9**.

Equations

Creating a cross-reference for a new equation requires two separate stages. First, you create a bookmark to the equation number. Then, you cross-reference the bookmark. There are other ways to number equations, but this is the most reliable. It works with the built-in Equation Editor and with Math-Type. The steps here assume you have already copied and pasted an existing equation. For detailed instructions on how to create new equations, refer to Chapter 6.

> **Note** If you use MathType to number your equations, your collaborators without MathType might have difficulty working with your document.

Stage 1: Create a bookmark

Bookmark

1. Select the equation number on the right in the equation line.

2. Click **Insert ⇒ Bookmark**.

3. Give this bookmark a name that starts with **eq**, such as **eqFourierSeries**.

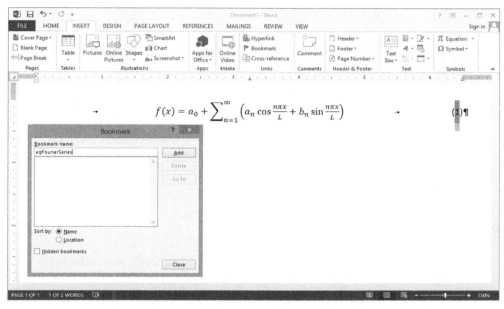

Creating a bookmark for the number will allow you to cross-reference the equation properly.

Stage 2: Cross-reference the equation by using the bookmark

1. Click **Insert ⇒ Cross-reference**.

2. In the **Reference type** box, click **Bookmark**.

3. In the **Insert reference to** box, click **Bookmark text**.

4. Choose the equation bookmark from the list, and then click **Insert**.

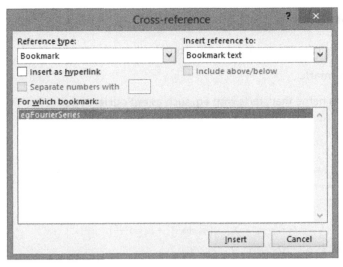

You can use bookmarks and cross-references to automate your equation numbering.

To update the equation, press **Ctrl+A** → **F9**.

Recap

In this chapter, you learned about templates, STREAM Tools, styles, and customizing Word 2013 to meet your needs. You also learned about finding and using templates, the basic templates that have already been created for you, and the proper techniques for using these templates.

By now, you should be able to

- Offer three reasons why templates can improve your productivity
- List the four stages of document development and describe the tasks associated with them
- Describe styles and how they are used, including their use in Outline view, the Navigation pane, and in automatically generating a table of contents
- Download a template from *http://www.streamtoolsonline.com*
- Explain the basics of template use:
  - Making headings
  - Making figures
  - Making tables
  - Making equations
  - Cross-referencing

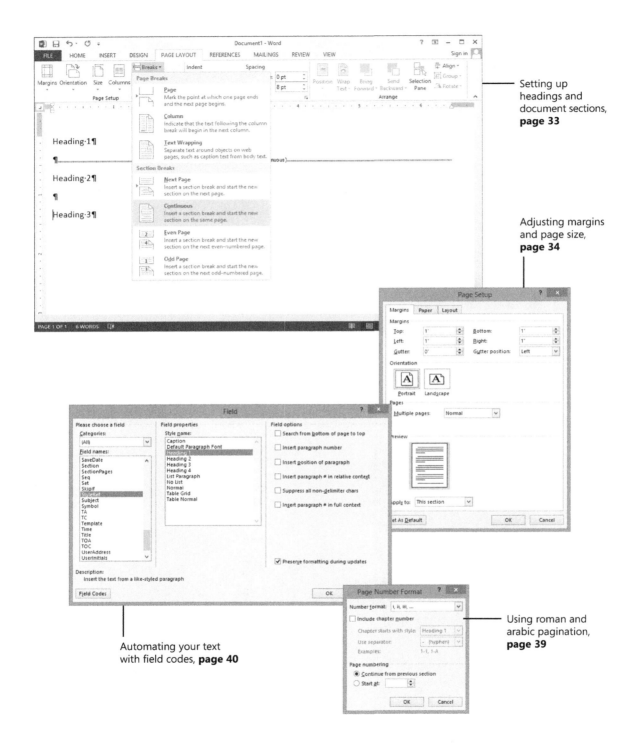

Setting up
headings and
document sections,
page 33

Adjusting margins
and page size,
page 34

Using roman and
arabic pagination,
page 39

Automating your text
with field codes, **page 40**

CHAPTER 2

How to design templates

In this chapter, you will learn how to

- Organize and format your documents

- Adjust default styles to match requirements

- Create generic headings, tables, and equations

- Insert generic figures

- Place generic gray text fields

Though it might seem daunting at first, designing templates for Microsoft Word 2013 is a straight-forward and easy task. Although there are a myriad of ready-made templates available online, you might not find the exact template you need, and existing templates might not suit your needs closely enough to be adapted to your purpose. In addition, the document you want to create might be in a format that you will need to use many times in the future.

If this is the case, your best course of action is to design your own template from scratch. This chapter will help you design powerful, adaptable templates that make use of the advanced cross-referencing and field-based features of Word 2013.

How to organize and format your document

You will need to decide upon the general organization of your document. Are you creating a research report or a master's thesis? Perhaps you want to write a book? For each type of document you create, there are a few specific layout and formatting choices that are suitable. This section will help you create and modify elements such as headings, sections, columns, color schemes, and page numbering.

Create headings and divide your document into sections

Before you modify any styles or formatting, it is important that you establish the conceptual structure of your document. After you have identified the order of the document and defined a rough skeleton, it will be easier to make more significant cosmetic changes.

Many formatting choices, such as whether to use roman or arabic numbers for pagination, how many columns to use, margin size, and page orientation, to name a few, can be made on a per-section basis. As a result, any time you want to change one of these options for only a portion of your document, you will need to create section breaks.

When you create a template, it is advisable to define the sections ahead of time, incorporating section breaks with your headings where appropriate.

To create headings

1. Type the section headings, leaving a blank line between each one.

2. Click the first heading to place the cursor, and then choose **Heading 1** from the **Style** gallery (**Ctrl+Alt+1**). Repeat for all headings.

To delineate the template's sections

1. Place the cursor where the break should be inserted. Generally, this is at the beginning of a heading.

2. Navigate to the **Page Layout** tab on the ribbon, and then click **Breaks** in the **Page Setup** group.

3. From the drop-down menu, select a section break; generally, a **Continuous** break will be appropriate.

4. Repeat this process for each section.

> **Note** To view the newly placed break, click the paragraph marker (¶) on the **Home** tab of the ribbon, in the **Paragraph** group.

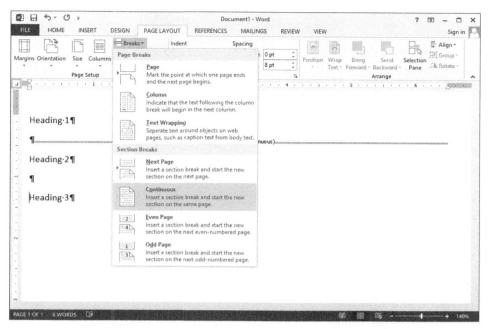

You should use continuous section breaks to ensure that your page numbering, dimensions, and other elements function correctly.

Note If your template does not require section breaks, but you would still like each Heading 1 to appear on a new page, you can set this through the style properties. Right-click the **Heading 1** style in the **Style** gallery and click **Modify**. Click **Format** ⇒ **Paragraph**, and on the **Line and Page Breaks** page, select the **Page break before** check box.

Adjust page dimensions and margins

The template you are designing might be for your own purposes, or it might be specific to an RFP (request for proposal), a class, or a supervisor's instruction. Whatever the case, you might find it necessary to specify page dimensions and margins that differ from the default.

To adjust your template's margins, dimensions, and layout

1. Navigate to the **Page Layout** tab on the ribbon.

2. Click the dialog box launcher (⌐)in the lower-right corner of the **Page Setup** group.

3. In the **Page Setup** dialog box, choose the margin sizes that you require.

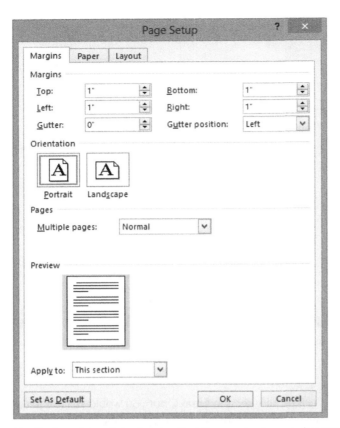

Use the Page Setup dialog box to adjust the margins for your document. Note that the Apply To drop-down list will let you choose different margin styles for each section.

> **Note** Make sure that **Whole document** is selected in the **Apply to** list. Otherwise, the changes that you make will be applied only to the current section. Alternatively, you can adjust the margins before inserting section breaks into your document.

4. On the **Paper** page, choose the dimensions for your document from the **Paper Size** drop-down list, or specify exact values in the **Width** and **Height** text boxes.

   You can modify additional settings on the **Layout** page. In most cases, this will not be necessary. However, you might find that for certain types of documents, **Section start** should be set to **Odd page** instead of **Continuous**. This automatically inserts blank pages between sections as needed, ensuring that new sections begin on odd pages; for example, for books, dissertations, and longer manuscripts.

5. Click **OK**.

Choose the appropriate number of columns

Setting columns in Word 2013 is a simple way to change the entire visual appeal of your document. Follow these steps to adjust the number of columns per page as well as the column spacing. In conjunction with the previously mentioned orientation and margin options, this technique can produce powerful and appealing templates. Do not forget that you can choose different column layouts for each section.

To adjust the number and size of your template's columns

1. Click the **Page Layout** tab.

2. In the **Page Setup** group, click **Columns**, and then click **More Columns**.

3. Choose your preferred column settings, and then click **OK**.

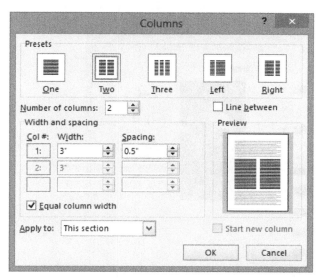

You can adjust the columns of your document in a number of interesting ways. For most journal articles and reports, you should choose Equal Column Width, and no line between.

> **Note** By default, changes to the column settings are applied to the current section. In the **Apply to** list, you can choose to modify the column settings for the entire document, or from the current section onward.

Choose a color scheme

If you are writing for academic purposes, you probably will not need to set up a color scheme, because the non-picture elements of research publications are generally printed in black and white. However, that does not mean that all of your documents will be formatted that way, and it might be useful for you to know how to manage your document's color scheme. In addition, the default color scheme has blue headings, which is more than likely unsuitable for your purposes. There is a built-in color scheme manager in Word 2013.

To change your color scheme or define your own

1. Navigate to the **Design** tab on the ribbon.

2. Click the **Colors** button in the **Document Formatting** group.

3. Choose a built-in color scheme, or select **Customize Colors** to define your own colors.

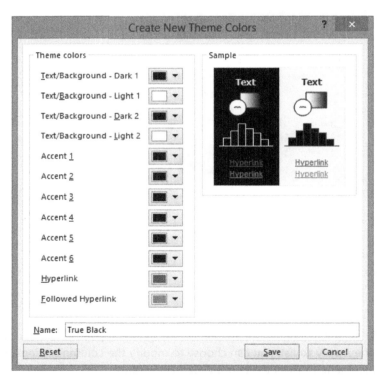

You can specify all of the colors for your theme. For a true black-and-white theme, you can set all of the Accent colors to black, resulting in all-black heading styles.

Choose a font scheme

In many scientific publications, the same font is used for the headings and the body text. For other publications, the heading fonts are sans-serif, whereas body text is serif. In general, your captions should always be sans-serif, to maximize readability, especially if they are italicized.

To choose your own fonts or select from the built-in sets

1. Navigate to the **Design** tab on the ribbon.

2. Click the **Fonts** button in the **Document Formatting** group.

3. Choose a built-in font set, or select **Customize Fonts** to define your own.

You can choose any fonts you would like for your headings and body text. Though it might seem unnecessary, this is a quick and simple way to make sure your fonts are all the same.

Use page numbering and other header features

Generally, you will not need to venture beyond the built-in page numbering styles in Word 2013. However, in more complex templates, you might need to use roman pagination, either in lieu of or in addition to standard arabic numerals. Additionally, you might want to include a context-sensitive title for the page, referring to chapter or heading text. In any of these cases, you will work within the headers, and you will use fields.

To choose from the built-in numbering schemes in Word 2013

1. Navigate to the **Insert** tab on the ribbon.

2. Click the **Page Number** button in the **Header & Footer** group.

3. Select a position (**Top of Page** 🖺, **Bottom of Page** 🖺) and a numbering style.

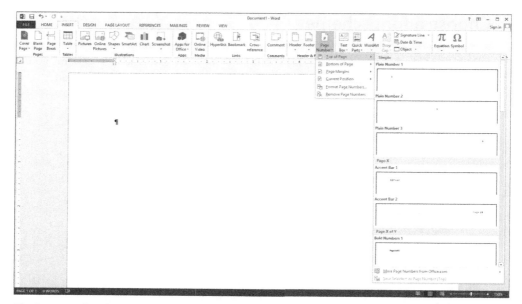

The Page Number drop-down menu contains an assortment of alignments and styles, all of which you can further modify to suit your needs.

To use roman pagination

1. Navigate to the **Insert** tab on the ribbon.

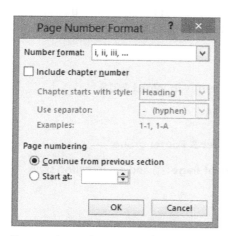

2. Click the **Page Number** button in the **Header & Footer** group.

3. Click **Format Page Numbers** (image).

4. Choose a page number style from the **Number format** drop-down list.

   Optional: Choose to include the chapter (heading) number, as well.

You can choose the page numbering format in this box, and include a chapter number as well.

5. Click the **Page Number** button in the **Header & Footer** box again.

6. Select a position (**Top of Page**, **Bottom of Page**) and a numbering style.

To use both roman and arabic numbering

1. Follow the previous section's instructions to create at least two sections in your document.

2. Navigate to the first section of your template.

3. On the **Insert** tab of the ribbon, click the **Page Number** button, and then click **Format Page Numbers.**

4. Choose the roman numbers, and then click **OK**.

5. Click the **Page Number** button in the **Header & Footer** group again.

6. Select a position (**Top of Page**, **Bottom of Page**) and a numbering style.

7. Navigate to the next section of your template, click the **Page Number** button once more, and then click **Format Page Numbers** (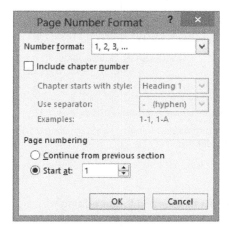).

8. Choose the arabic numbers, and then in the **Start at** box, choose **1**.

Remember to choose 1 in the Start At box. This resets the page numbers for the new section. You can also use this process in each chapter, in conjunction with the Include Chapter Number option, to create chapter-based page numbering.

9. Click **OK**.

10. Click the **Page Number** button in the **Header & Footer** group again.

11. Select a position (**Top of Page**, **Bottom of Page**) and a numbering style.

To add a context-sensitive title for the page

1. Double-click the header area.

2. Navigate to the **Insert** tab of the ribbon.

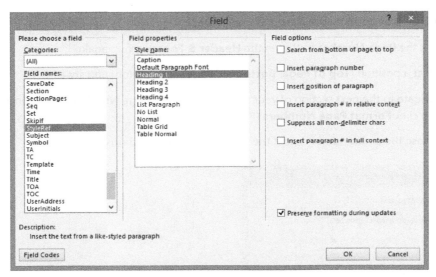

3. Click **Quick Parts** in the **Text** group.

4. Click **Field** (▣).

5. Select **StyleRef** in the **Field names** box, and **Heading 1** (or your preferred style) in the **Style name** box.

Fields are powerful elements that can automate your templates in many ways. By using a StyleRef field, you can insert text that updates as you change the original text.

6. Center the title (**Ctrl+E**).

7. Double-click the body of the document to exit header and footer editing.

To add a page number to the context-sensitive title

1. Left-align the title (≡ or **Ctrl+L**).

2. Insert tabs on the left and the right side of the title (**Ctrl+Tab**).

3. Insert a center tab stop (⊥) for the title and a right tab stop (⌐) for the page number.

Note To insert a tab stop, click the tab stop selector ( L) (under the ribbon, to the left of the ruler) and select the type you need. Then, click in the gray margin directly underneath the ruler, and drag to place the tab stop.

Click in this area to create tab stops,
and draft left or right to place them

A left tab stop resembles a short L. Tab stops can be placed anywhere on the ruler. A dotted line will appear below the tab stop during placement to facilitate proper alignment.

Alternatively, you can place tabs through the **Paragraph** dialog box. Simply right-click the line you would like to align, choose **Paragraph**, and then click **Tabs** to access the dialog box.

Tab stops can be inserted through the Tabs dialog box with greater precision.

This method is more exact, but generally less intuitive. You can also access the **Paragraph** dialog box through the **Home** tab on the ribbon. Place the cursor on the line in question and click the dialog box launcher in the paragraph group.

4. Place the cursor at the far right position after the tab.

5. Click **Insert** ⇒ **Page Number** ⇒ **Current Position** ⇒ **Plain Number**.

6. Select the entire header and save it as a new style (click the **More** button in the **Styles** group of the **Home** tab (⩔), and click **Create a Style**).

7. Add a bottom border if desired (**Modify** ⇒ **Format** ⇒ **Border**).

8. Click **OK** in all dialog boxes.

9. Double-click the main portion of the document to exit the header.

To make even page numbers appear on the left

1. Navigate to an even-numbered page, and double-click inside the page header area.

2. On the **Header & Footer Design** tool tab, select the **Different Odd & Even Pages** check box.

3. Select the header text on an odd-numbered page, copy it (**Ctrl+C**) and paste it (**Ctrl+V**) to the even-page header.

4. Select the page number, cut (**Ctrl+X**) and paste (**Ctrl+V**) it in the upper-left position.

5. Double-click the main portion of the document to exit the header.

How to adjust default styles to match requirements

The next thing you will need to do is modify the default Word 2013 styles to suit the requirements for your template. To do this is quite simple.

To modify styles

1. Navigate to the **Home** tab of the ribbon.

2. Find the style you want to change in the **Style** gallery. Click the small gray button (⩔) to reveal more, or click the dialog box launcher (⌐) in the lower-right corner to reveal the **Styles** pane.

> **Note** To add a style from the **Styles** pane to your **Style** gallery, simply right-click the style and click **Add to Style Gallery**.

3. Right-click the style, and click **Modify.**

4. Choose the basic formatting options, including font, size, and color.

5. Click the **Format** button in the lower-left corner to access advanced formatting options.

6. Click **OK** to save your changes.

> **Note** If **Automatically Update** is selected, any changes you make to text that uses this style will immediately be applied to all other text that uses the style.

How to create generic headings

For any given template, you should include at least one generic heading for each heading level that will appear in the final document. For templates with more specific purposes, you might want to include headings for each section that will appear in a document. For instance, if you are creating a template for a funding proposal for submission to a particular agency, you should include all of the headings that the agency's RFP suggests.

To create top-level headings in your document

1. Type the heading text.

2. Navigate to the **Home** tab on the ribbon.

AaBbC(3. Click **Heading 1** in the **Style** gallery (or press **Ctrl+Alt+1**).

Heading 1 4. Repeat for all remaining headings.

The Style gallery allows you to quickly switch styles, as well as modify existing styles.

To create subheadings in your document

1. Type the subheading text.

2. Navigate to the **Home** tab on the ribbon.

AaBbCcD 3. Click **Heading 2** in the **Style** gallery (or press **Ctrl+Alt+2**).

Heading 2 4. Repeat for all remaining subheadings.

How to insert a generic figure

It is probably safe to assume that the majority of documents you create for research publications will include figures. Therefore, it is best to include at least one generic figure and a figure caption in your template, for easy cut-and-paste functionality.

Many journals require that figures be included at the end of the document, and some even require them to be submitted as separate files. The best practice is to follow these procedures and make sure to keep the source files for your figures. If you must include your figures at the end of your document, it will still be a matter of copy-and-paste.

To insert a generic figure and caption

Pictures

1. Either copy the image to the Clipboard (**Ctrl+C** in most applications) and use **Paste Special** (see Chapter 1, "Using templates in Word 2013") to paste it directly into your template, or navigate to the **Insert** tab, click **Pictures**, select the picture you want to use, and then click **OK**.

2. Resize the picture as necessary (click the picture and drag the small dots on the corners).

You can resize pictures by right-clicking the dots on the corners and sides, by right-clicking and then clicking Size And Position in the menu that appears, or by using the size options on the Format tab of the ribbon.

3. Click the picture, and navigate to the new tool tab that appears, **Format** (with the fuchsia **Picture Tools** heading).

4. Click **Picture Border** and **Picture Effects** and select a border style and shadow or embossing effects, if desired. Alternatively, you can select from the presets in the **Picture Styles** box.

5. Right-click the picture, point to **Wrap Text**, and make sure that **In Line with Text** is selected.

6. Press **Ctrl+E** to center the picture, or click the **Center** button (≡) in the **Paragraph** group on the **Home** tab.

7. Create a new line under the picture, making sure it is centered, and then on the **References** tab, in the **Captions** group, click the **Insert Caption** button.

8. In the **Label** drop-down menu, make sure that **Figure** is selected, and click **New Label** if you need different text such as *Fig.* rather than *Figure*.

9. Click **Numbering** to define different numbers if needed, and then click **OK**.

10. Type some placeholder text for the caption and modify the style, if necessary.

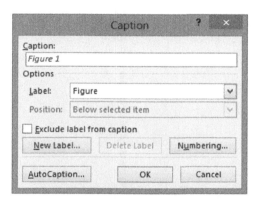

You can choose the specific format and wording for your labels, and specify different numbering schemes such as chapter-based numbering, for longer documents.

How to create a generic table

Generally speaking, you will rarely have tables with the same number of cells, so it will usually be more efficient to create your tables from scratch. In addition, Word 2013 offers a great table styling mechanism, which will allow you to define the alignment, formatting, and design of your tables once so that you can use them as many times as you need them. For designing your templates, it is highly recommended that you use this method, which is covered in this section, as well as in Chapter 5, "How to work with tables."

However, it is not uncommon to need to create a single table for a document. The following procedure describes how to create and format tables quickly and easily.

Create a generic table

To create a generic table

1. Click the **Table** button on the **Insert** tab of the ribbon.

2. Choose the dimensions of your table; 3 x 4 is probably a safe choice.

3. The table will appear, filling the active width of the page. Right-click the icon above the upper-left corner of the table (⊞), and then click **Table Properties**.

4. Choose **Center** for the **Alignment**, and **None** for **Text wrapping**, and then click **Options**.

You can align your table just as you would align text, and you can also choose how to wrap text. For a normal table, which will appear with a caption, it is advised that you choose not to wrap the text.

Note If you would like to wrap text around your table, you will need to add an additional row for the caption. To place the caption above the table, place the cursor in a top-row cell, navigate to the **Layout** tab, and click **Insert Above**. Drag through all the cells of the new row to select them, and then click **Merge Cells**. Finally, navigate to the **Design** tab and click the arrow next to the **Borders** button. Click the **Top Border**, **Left Border**, and **Bottom Border** buttons to remove the borders around the caption.

5. Determine your preferred cell margins and click **OK**.

Shading

6. Click **Borders and Shading**.

7. From here, you can customize the borders and shading for the entire table. To create a stylized table, choose **2 ¼ pt** for **Width**, and choose a light color. Click the top and left side border icons once to remove the current border, and a second time to apply the new border.

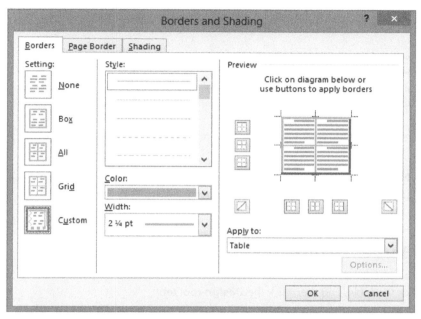

You can specify border widths, colors, and styles for inner and outer borders separately in the Borders And Shading dialog box. You can also choose to apply them per cell, or to the whole table.

8. Choose a darker color, and click the bottom and right border icons twice.

9. Set **Width** to **1 ½ pt**, select the lighter color (or a color between the two shades), click the two middle border buttons twice, and then click **OK**.

10. Now select the top row of your table (click in the upper-right cell and drag to the upper-left cell), navigate to the **Design** tab, click the **Shading** paint bucket button, and choose a color. Alternatively, you can right-click the selected cells and click the small paint bucket icon that appears.

Insert Caption

11. Click the table, and on the **References** tab, click **Insert Caption**.

12. In the **Label** box, make sure that **Table** is selected. Click **New Label** if you need different text, click **Numbering** to define different numbers if needed, and then click **OK**.

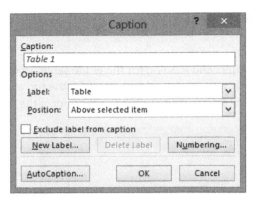

As in the other caption dialog boxes, you can customize the appearance of your caption text. You can also choose to place the caption above or below the table.

13. Type some placeholder text for the caption and modify the style, if necessary.

 Note If you elected to wrap text around your table, simply cut (**Ctrl+X**) and paste (**Ctrl+V**) the caption into the borderless cell above the table.

Use the Border Painter tool

You can also use the Border Painter tool to style and color your table borders. To use it, first create a table, then click the table, and then click the **Design** tool tab.

To use the Border Painter tool

1. Choose style, thickness, and color for the border. Alternatively, you can choose a preset style from the **Border Styles** drop-down menu.

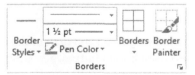

The Border Painter lets you style table borders directly. Click the Border Painter button, or choose a style in the drop-down menus on the left to activate the Border Painter.

2. Drag along any of the borders of the table to style that border with the properties you chose.

3. When you are finished, click the **Border Painter** button to turn off the Border Painter mode.

4. Use the **Shading** button to add color to the table cells. Drag across multiple cells to select them.

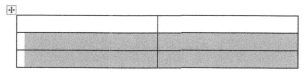

Drag across multiple cells to select them. You can apply border and shading changes to the entire selection.

Create a table style

In most cases, it might be possible for you to create one table template for your document that you can adapt for each table. However, it might be advisable for you to create a table style to govern the appearance of your document's tables, especially if the document you are creating will be very long (for example, a thesis or dissertation). Unfortunately, there is no way to save the style of an existing table, but new table styles can be created without much difficulty.

To create a table style

1. Click the **Table** button on the **Insert** tab of the ribbon.

2. Create a table of 3 x 3 or larger.

3. Navigate to the **Design** tool tab, and click the **More** button ( ) next to the gallery in the **Table Styles** group.

4. Click **New Table Style** ( ) below the gallery.

5. In the dialog box that appears, chose font and formatting options for your table. Notice that the **Apply formatting to** drop-down menu will allow you to change the styling of the whole table or just a subset, such as the header row.

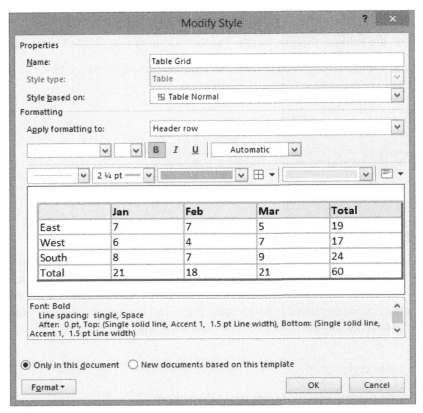

In the Modify Style dialog box, you can customize the colors and formatting of your table based on row, column, corner, and more. By using these options, you can create fully customized and unified tables for your document with only a few clicks.

6. To change the outlines, make sure **Whole table** is selected under **Apply formatting to**, click **Format**, and then click **Borders and Shading**.

7. Choose the borders to suit your preferences, and click **OK**.

8. To achieve a shaded first column, as in the picture, select **Header row** and choose a color under the font options, on the right.

9. If you need more explicit customization, select additional menu items under **Apply formatting to**, and modify their appearance as needed.

How to create a generic equation

There are two recommended ways to create equations in Word 2013, and Chapter 6, "How to work with equations," deals with both methods in full detail. Use the following procedure to create a generic equation template with the built-in equation editor in Word 2013. If you prefer to use MathType, please refer to Chapter 6.

Note that neither of the methods recommended in the book uses the seemingly natural Word function **Insert** ⇒ **Caption** ⇒ **Equation**. This function acts as a direct analogue to the other automatic captions. Though it might be useful for non-scientific documents, it is not recommended for research documents. Instead, use bookmarks to achieve proper equation numbering and cross-referencing.

Create a generic numbered equation

To create a numbered equation

1. Create a new line for the equation, and insert a tab on the line (**Ctrl+Tab**).

2. On the **Insert** tab, click the bottom half of the **Equation** button.

3. Click one of the generic equations such as Fourier Series.

4. Insert a tab (**Ctrl+Tab**) on the right side of the equation, outside of the equation box.

> **Note** If the ruler is not visible below the ribbon, navigate to the **View** tab and click **Ruler** in the **Show** group.

5. Insert a center tab stop (⊥) in the middle of the ruler (at about the 3.25" mark for letter-sized paper) for the equation and a right (⅃) tab stop at the right margin for the page number.

Note To insert a tab stop, click the tab stop selector (L) (under the ribbon, to the left of the ruler) until it changes into the type that you want to place. Next, click the bottom border of the ruler (and drag left or right, as needed) to place the tab stop.

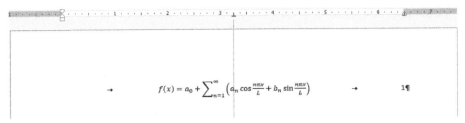

$$f(x) = a_0 + \sum_{n=1}^{\infty} \left(a_n \cos \frac{n\pi x}{L} + b_n \sin \frac{n\pi x}{L} \right)$$

A left tab stop resembles a short L. Tab stops can be placed anywhere on the ruler. A dotted line will appear below the tab stop during placement to help with alignment.

Alternatively, you can specify tab stops with exact measurements. Simply right-click the line you would like to add a tab stop to, click **Paragraph**, and then click **Tabs** to access the dialog box.

Tab stops can be inserted through the Tabs dialog box with greater precision.

This method is more exact, but less intuitive. You can also access the **Paragraph** dialog box through the **Home** tab on the ribbon. Place the cursor on the line in question and click the dialog box launcher in the **Paragraph** group.

6. Select the entire line, and on the **Home** tab of the ribbon, click the **More** button to the lower right of the **Styles** group (⯯) and click **Create a Style**.

7. Name the style **Equation**, and click **OK**.

Insert
Caption

8. Place the cursor at the right side of the equation line, and then click the **Insert Caption** button on the **References** tab.

9. On the **Label** menu, choose **Equation**.

10. Make sure the **Exclude label from caption** is selected, and then click **OK**.

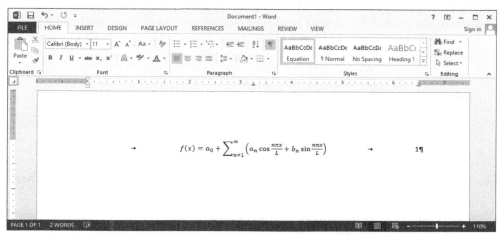

$$f(x) = a_0 + \sum_{n=1}^{\infty} \left(a_n \cos \frac{n\pi x}{L} + b_n \sin \frac{n\pi x}{L} \right)$$

Your equation should appear centered with the number aligned to the right margin.

Bookmark

11. Select the number and click the **Bookmark** button on the **Insert** tab.

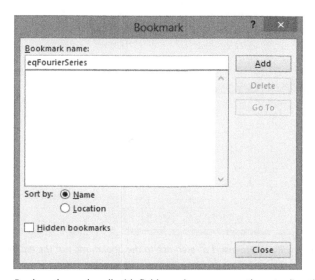

Bookmarks work well with fields, and you can use them to directly quote text, whether or not the source material changes.

12. Type a name for the equation, such as **eqFourierSeries**, and click **Add**. If you will use bookmarks for other purposes, it is advisable to begin every equation name with *eq*.

13. Insert parentheses around the number.

14. Make sure the cursor is on the equation line and click the **Equation** style in the **Style** gallery.

Create a cross-reference to an equation

Because the method for creating equations requires the use of bookmarks and additional caption options, the approach for cross-referencing them is unique among the methods in this book. Therefore, to introduce the proper procedure into your skill set, we will reproduce it here.

To cross-reference an equation

Cross-reference

1. Click **Insert** ⇒ **Cross-reference**.

2. Under **Reference Type**, click **Bookmark**.

3. Clear the **Insert as hyperlink** check box, unless you have a strong reason to have a hyperlink in your document.

4. Under **Insert reference to**, click **Bookmark text**.

5. Choose the desired bookmark from the list, and then click **Insert**.

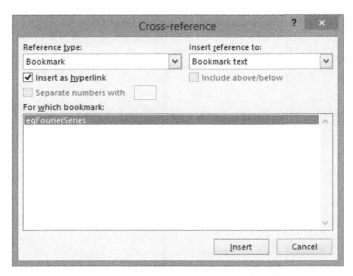

To cross-reference equations, you will need to insert a reference to the bookmark, not the equation caption.

To update the equation, press **Ctrl+A** and then press **F9**. Be sure to save your document as well.

How to place generic gray text fields

Many pre-made templates will make proper use of gray placeholder text. What makes this type of text so useful is that it can be selected in its entirety with a single click. In addition, it can only be replaced, not modified, and you can use special highlighting to make it stand out so that it is not easily missed. The highlighting will disappear automatically when you replace the text with actual content.

To create generic gray text fields

1. Navigate to the **Insert** tab of the ribbon, click **Quick Parts** in the **Text** group, and then click **Field**.

2. Click the **Field Codes** button in the lower-left corner.

3. Replace the equal sign with **MACROBUTTON DoFieldClick *TemplateText***, substituting the text you want to use for ***TemplateText***.

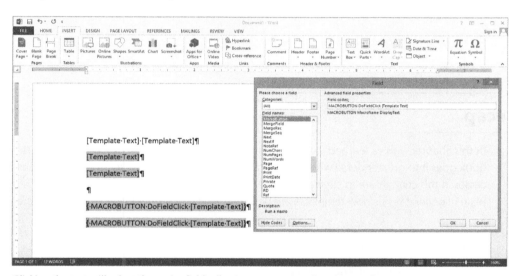

Clicking the text will select the entire field, allowing you to type directly over the text.

> **Note** The standard format includes braces. For a name field, you would type: **MACROBUTTON DoFieldClick [*Name*]**.

4. Click **OK**.

1. Highlight the field code in gray, if you want.

2. To remove the space at the end of the code, right-click it and click **Toggle Field Codes**.

3. Delete the space behind the square brace, right-click, and click **Toggle Field Codes** again.

Common template design errors

There are several common mistakes that you should watch out for while designing your templates. They include:

- Not using styles for formatting.

- Not defining all of the necessary styles.

- Relying on features present in external software.

- Using a text box feature.

- Failing to provide optimal figure-positioning features.

Recap

In this chapter, you've learned various ways for customizing and designing templates. The rest of the book goes into greater detail with full illustrations of each important step to ensure that all of the processes in this chapter are as clear as possible. After completing this chapter, you should be able to explain in general terms how templates are designed, and you should know your way around the ribbon.

By now, you should be able to

- Create and duplicate headings

- Logically structure a document with sections

- Adjust typography details such as margins, orientation, and columns

- Modify default styles

- Insert generic items (figures, tables, and equations)

- Create generic gray text fields

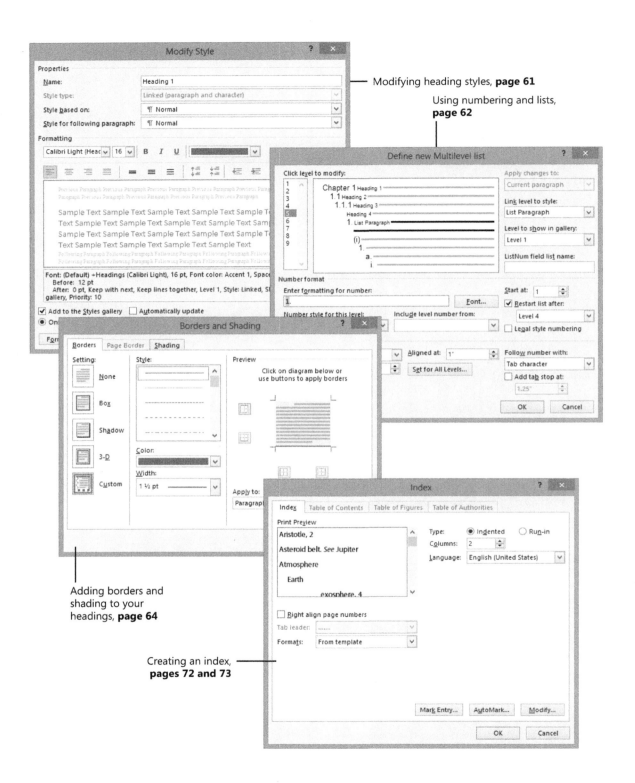

Modifying heading styles, **page 61**

Using numbering and lists, **page 62**

Adding borders and shading to your headings, **page 64**

Creating an index, **pages 72 and 73**

CHAPTER 3

How to work with headings

In this chapter, you will learn how to

- Create and cross-reference headings

- Use multilevel lists to organize your headings

- Enhance your headings with borders and shading

- Create page numbers and adjust their format

- Create tables of contents and limited, section-based tables of contents

- Create front matter, such as acknowledgments and forewords

- Create back matter, including appendices and indexes

Headings are the titles of chapters, sections, and subsections. You can use headings to give your document logical structure. In addition to generic, black-and-white headings, you can also create colorful, artistic headings. The effects are easy to create. This chapter will walk you through all aspects of heading creation, ensuring that your headings will be functional, powerful, and attractive.

How to create and cross-reference headings

There are two ways to make headings:

- Copy an existing heading.

- Create a new heading.

Note Because headings do not require cross-references, you might find it simpler to create them from scratch.

To create a new heading

1. Type the heading text where you want it in the document.

2. Click a **Heading** style in the **Style** gallery on the **Home** tab. Alternatively, you can press **Ctrl+Alt+#**, where # is the heading level you would like to create.

3. Press **Ctrl+A**, and then press **F9** to update the numbering and table of contents.

To cross-reference a heading

1. Click **References** ⇒ **Cross-Reference** in the **Captions** group.

2. In the **Reference type** drop-down list, select **Heading**, and then select a heading for cross-referencing.

3. In the **Insert reference to** drop-down list, select what you would like to cross-reference, and then click **OK**.

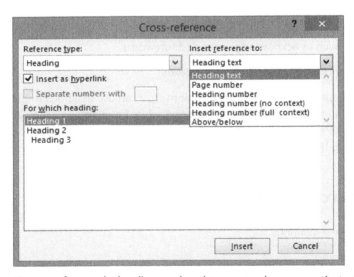

You can reference the heading number, the page number, or even the text of the heading.

How to alter headings

Writing teams will often need to change the appearance of headings to meet the needs of a particular writing situation. The two most common changes include altering style (font and size) and altering format (numbering schemes). In the procedure that follows, you will learn how to modify the style of a single heading level. To change the fonts, colors, and other properties for all the headings in your document, refer to Chapter 2, "How to design templates."

To alter the heading style

1. Click the **Home** tab on the ribbon.

2. Right-click the **Heading 1** style, and then click **Modify**.

3. In the **Modify Style** dialog box, alter the font, size, and spacing for your heading.

4. Adjust additional style properties by clicking the **Format** button, choose an element to change, and then click **OK**.

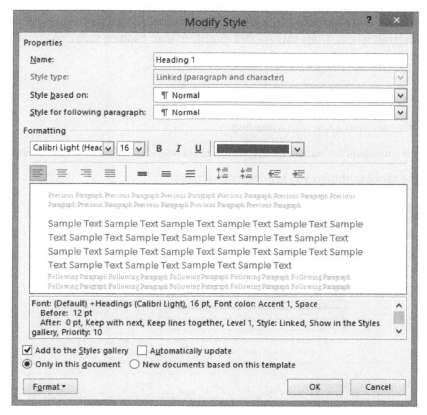

By using the Modify Style dialog box, you can alter a style without losing the manual adjustments you have made. Make sure the Automatically Update check box is cleared.

Note To avoid having to modify the style directly each time, you can select **Automatically update**. Word will then update the formatting for all your headings whenever you modify the attributes of a single one. This can be useful for specialized styles, such as headings. For more general styles, such as the Normal style, it is recommended that you not select this setting to avoid unnecessary complications.

Also note that if you use the **Update Style to Match Selection** menu item, you will lose any formatting changes that you made to text that uses the same style. To avoid this, it is recommended that you use the **Modify Style** dialog box instead.

How to use numbering and multilevel lists

Numbered lists, particularly multilevel lists, are an important part of chapter and section organization. When used properly, these lists help you organize your documents, and create automatically numbering and updating references. These lists are tied directly to your heading styles, so it makes sense to adjust them at the same time.

To create a multilevel list

1. Place the cursor on a line with a heading.

2. Click the multilevel list button on the **Home** tab, and click **Define new Multilevel list**.

3. Click the **More** button to access important settings.

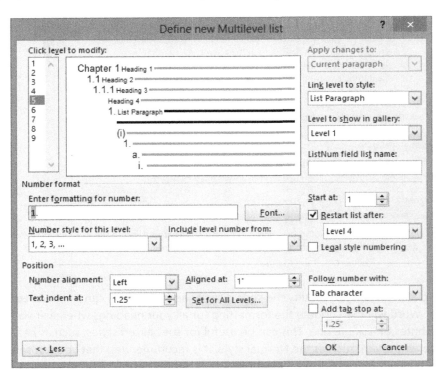

Use a multilevel list to create a cohesive numbering system by linking your styles to list levels. You can also remove the numbers for a level or include custom text.

4. Click a level to specify its settings.

5. You can choose a word for the prefix or use none at all; here, *Chapter* has been chosen. Simply type it in the **Enter formatting for number** box.

6. If you would like to use letters or roman numerals for a level, choose a different numbering scheme in the **Number style for this level** box.

7. Finally, if you want to hide the number for a particular level, simply click **Font** and make sure the **Hidden** check box is selected.

8. Click **OK** when you are finished.

By default, the numbers are linked to the heading styles, but you can choose other styles if you like. When you insert one of the corresponding styles in your document, it will be numbered automatically. If you chose to hide the number for a level, you might want to align it flush with the margin. To do so, insert the style in the document, and then click the bottom half of the ruler marker and drag it to the left.

You can chose the default indentation for any style by dragging the ruler marker that appears at the bottom of the ribbon. After adjusting it, update the style in the Style gallery.

How to set borders, shading, and special formatting

If you are designing something other than a standard research report or proposal, you might consider using fancy borders and formatting for your headings.

To set up borders and shading

1. Right-click the **Heading 1** style in the **Style** gallery, and click **Modify** ( ).

2. Click the **Format** button in the lower-left corner, and then click **Border**.

3. Choose a border color, width, and style, and click the border buttons to choose where to place the border. You can use different border styles for each side; just change the line settings and click a different border button. Click the **Options** button to adjust the padding and make the shaded region larger.

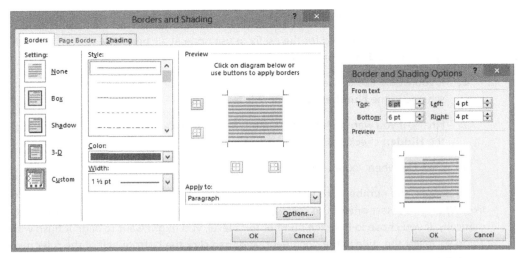

In the Borders And Shading dialog box, you can create borders and change their placement relative to your text. To ensure that the shading extends to fit the padding you choose, add a white border (to the top, in this example).

4. To modify the shading, click the **Shading** tab. To use a pattern, select one under **Patterns**, and choose a color, if you like.

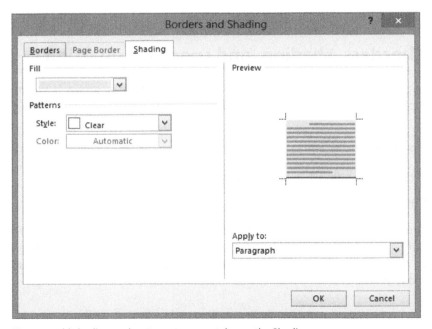

You can add shading and patterns to your styles on the Shading page.

5. Click **OK** in all dialog boxes.

6. To make your border extend to the edge of the page, simply drag the parts of the ruler marker to the edges.

When you align the ruler markers to the edges of the page, your newly designed style will fill the page.

> **Note** This method does not work well with headings of more than one line. The heading text will extend to the edge of the page. Therefore, you should use soft line breaks (**Shift+Enter**) to begin a new line before your line enters the margin, as depicted in the preceding graphic. Unfortunately, this will cause the line breaks to appear in your cross-references, and you must manually remove them before printing.
>
> To view formatting marks such as those shown in the previous graphic, click the **Paragraph** button on the **Home** tab (¶).

How to make headings work with fields

Create front matter

A long document such as a thesis or book often requires front matter, such as a preface, acknowledgments, or a table of contents. The headings for these sections are treated differently from the main document headings, because they are numbered in roman numerals whereas the main text is numbered with arabic numerals.

Control page numbers

To insert page numbers

1. Click the **Insert** tab, and in the **Header & Footer** group, click **Page Number**.

2. Choose your preference; for example, **Bottom of the Page**.

3. Choose your desired appearance.

4. To number the beginning of your document in roman numerals, click **Page Number** again, and then click **Format Page Numbers**(🖳).

5. Under **Number Format**, choose a numbering style.

6. Click **OK**.

To create section breaks

1. Place the cursor where you would like roman numbering to end.

2. On the **Page Layout** tab, click **Breaks**.

3. In the **Section Breaks** group, select **Next Page**. This inserts a section break between the two pages.

To restart numbering after a section break

1. Place the cursor after the section break (⊞), in the section you want to renumber.

2. On the **Insert** tab, click **Page Number**, and select **Format Page Numbers**.

3. Under **Number Format**, choose arabic numerals.

4. In the **Page Numbering** text box, select **Start at: 1**.

5. Click **OK**.

> **Note** You can manage your page numbering scheme in greater detail on the **Header & Footer Design** tool tab. To access it, double-click the page header and click the **Design** tab that appears.
>
> From here, you can check **Different First Page**, and delete the page number that appears on the first page of the section. Additionally, you can use **Different Odd & Even Pages** to align your page numbers to the outside, for a book-like layout.
>
>
>
> *The Header & Footer Tools Design tab will let you fully customize the behavior and appearance of your headers.*

Insert a table of contents

Sometimes you want to add entries to the table of contents that are not numbered Chapter 1, Chapter 2, and so on. For example, the preface, acknowledgments, and abstract should be listed in the table of contents, but wouldn't be sequentially numbered headings. In order to include these entries, you first have to create a new style, and then modify the table of contents to include the new style.

Stage 1: Create a new style for front matter

1. Manually change the front matter heading to look the way you want (for example, Arial, 20 pt, bold, centered).

    Note Alternatively, you could base the front matter heading on your **Heading 1** style. This will allow the front matter heading to inherit any changes that you make to the **Heading 1** style.

   To do this, create a front matter heading and apply the **Heading 1** style to it (**Ctrl+Alt+1**). Then, complete the following steps, making sure to remove the numbering from the style. In the **Modify Style** dialog box, click **Format**, then **Numbering**, and choose **None**.

2. Place the cursor on your newly formatted heading and click the button in the lower-right corner of the **Style** gallery (⏷).

3. Choose **Create a Style** at the bottom of the drop-down menu, and type in the style name; for example, **Front Heading**.

4. Click **Modify**, and choose **Normal** under **Style for the Following Paragraph**.

5. Click **OK**.

6. Apply this style formatting to all other front matter headings by using the **Style** gallery, as with any other heading style.

Stage 2: Add front matter sections to the table of contents

1. Place the cursor where you would like the table of contents to appear (or on the existing table of contents, if there is one).

Table of Contents ▾

2. On the **References** tab, click **Table of Contents**, and then click **Custom Table of Contents** ().

3. Click the **Options** button.

4. In the **Available styles** section of the dialog box, add a **1** in the **TOC level** box for **Front Heading**.

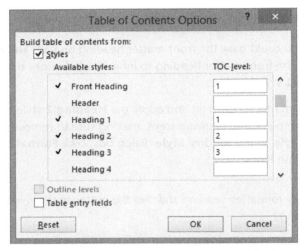

You can specify which styles are included in your table of contents in addition to the hierarchy.

> **Note** If you are using a style (such as **Appendix**) for back matter, at this point remember to put a **1** in the corresponding box as well. Detailed procedures for the back matter are discussed in the next section.

You should now have a new table of contents with the headings from your front matter listed with their respective page numbers. If you completed the first portion of the process listed in this section, then the numbers should be roman numerals for the front matter and arabic numerals for the remaining chapter and section headings.

How to create and format back matter

In addition to front matter, large documents also have back matter, such as appendices, an index, or a glossary. You can create and use an **Appendix** style for your appendices. The STREAM Tools template file *BasicThesisOrBookTemplate.docx* already contains appendices preformatted in this manner, but you can use the process described here to create new back matter in your document.

Create appendices

To create an appendix in your document, there are two stages.

Stage 1: Create the appendix

1. Type a title for the appendix in a new line where you want it to appear.

2. Change the style of the line to **Heading 1** (**Ctrl+Alt+1**).

3. Click the button in the lower-left corner of the **Style** gallery (⬇), and click **Create a Style**.

4. Name your style (**Appendix**, for example), and click **Modify**.

5. Under **Style for following paragraph**, choose **Normal**.

6. Click **Format** ⇒ **Numbering** ⇒ **Define New Number Format**.

7. Under **Number Style**, select capital letters, and under **Number format**, type **Appendix A**, where the A is the field value already in place.

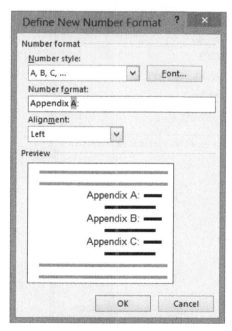

You can use the Define New Number Format dialog box to create a numbering scheme for any style.

8. Click **OK** in all three dialog boxes.

9. Now, reformat the appendix heading as necessary, including correcting the indentation and placing tab stops.

10. With the cursor on the appendix heading, right-click the **Appendix** style in the **Style** gallery, and click **Update Appendix to Match Selection**.

Stage 2: Add the appendix to the table of contents

If you followed the previous instructions, your appendix should appear in the table of contents automatically, at the same level as the **Heading 1** style. Simply press **Ctrl+A** → **F9** to update the fields, including the table of contents, and select **Update entire table** in the dialog box that appears.

If you did not base the **Appendix** style on **Heading 1**, you will need to manually add it to the table of contents hierarchy. In addition, you might want to add other styles to your table of contents. To do so, place the cursor on your table of contents, and follow these steps:

Table of Contents ▾

1. Click **References** ⇒ **Table of Contents**.

2. Click **Custom Table of Contents** (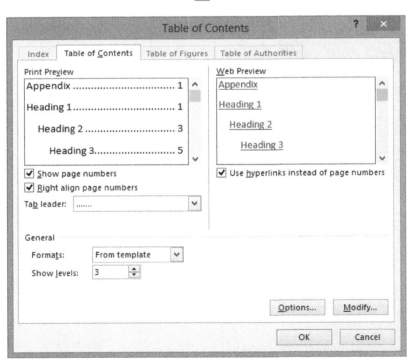).

Here you can adjust several basic elements of your table of contents, including how many levels to show and what type of tab leader to use.

3. Click the **Options** button.

4. In the **TOC level** box for **Appendix**, type **1**. If you would like to add another style to your table of contents, find it in the list, and enter a number for its **TOC level** setting.

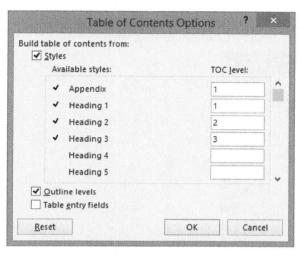

By adjusting the TOC Level setting for each style, you can select which styles to include. Their properties will be automatically adjusted to suit the table of contents hierarchy.

5. Click **OK** in all dialog boxes.

Create indexes

An index at the end of a book allows the reader to find the pages that mention specific words. Indexes are most frequently encountered in textbooks or manuals. Word Help provides a comprehensive description of the process of creating an index, should you need it.

However, we want to describe briefly how to create an index, because the process is relatively straightforward. First, it is best to save creating an index until near the very end of your writing project, because this step will add inline code to your document on every word that is indexed, and this code will make the text difficult to read. However, you can hide these marks by clicking the **Home** tab and then selecting **Show/Hide Paragraph Markings** (¶).

When you are ready to create an index, you need to mark the entries for it and then build the index at the end of the manuscript, much like you would build a table of contents at the front.

To mark entries for the index

1. Highlight the word you want to include in your index.

2. On the **References** tab, in the **Index** group, click **Mark Entry**.

3. In the dialog box that appears, choose the options that correspond to your needs.

You can customize the index entry to include a subentry, and use Mark All to mark every instance of the selected text.

To insert the index

1. Place the cursor on the page and line where you would like the index to appear.

2. On the **References** tab, in the **Index** group, click **Insert Index** (📄).

   Just like with any other automatically generated list, the index will be updated when you press **Ctrl+A → F9**.

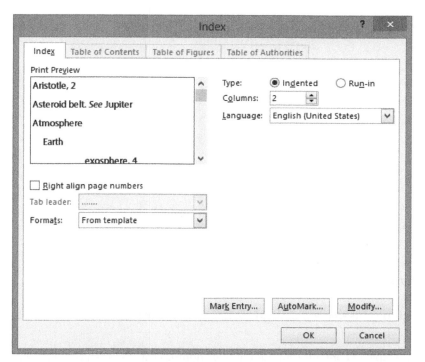

In the Index dialog box, you can choose the indentation, columns, and tab leaders for your index.

Use bookmarks for limited tables of contents

In some cases, you might want to include only a portion of text in your table of contents. For example, you might want to include a table of contents for each section of your document. You can achieve this with the table of contents feature available in Word 2013, by using bookmarks to include only a single chapter.

To create a section-based table of contents

1. Select the section of text that you want to use.

2. On the **Insert** tab, in the **Links** group, click **Bookmark**.

3. Type a name for your section, click **Add**, and then click **OK**.

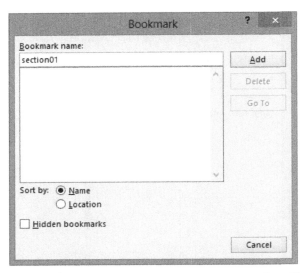

It is recommended that you choose descriptive names that will sort easily.

Table of
Contents ▾

4. Insert a table of contents where you would like it to appear (**References** ⇒ **Table of Contents**).

5. Select the entire table of contents (but not the title), right-click it, and then click **Edit Field**.

Make sure to select the entire table of contents, without the title.

6. If **TOC** is not selected, close the window and make sure you have selected the entire table of contents (including the space at the end).

7. Click the **Field Codes** button in the lower-left corner.

8. Click the **Options** button.

9. In the **Field Options** dialog box that appears, select **\b** from the **Switches** list, and then click the **Add to Field** button.

10. In the **Field codes** box, type the name of the bookmark you created (replacing **BOOKMARKNAME**, in the example).

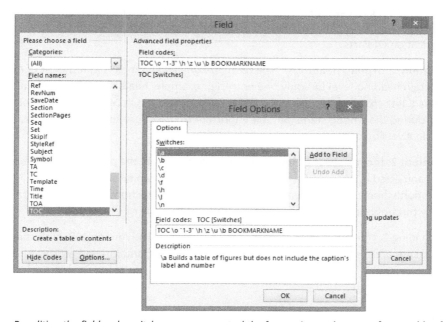

By editing the field code switches, you can control the formatting and source of your table of contents.

11. Click **OK** in all dialog boxes.

Common formatting mistakes in headings

The most common typesetting mistakes pertaining to headings include:

- **Manually numbering headings instead of creating automated templates**   Although this approach works for short documents, it defeats the idea of automatic generation of the table of contents and automatic heading numbering. It also eliminates the ability to cross-reference the heading in text.

- **Excessive switching of fonts**   In most technical and scientific manuscripts, the font of the headings is the same as the font of the main text. Mixing serif and sans serif fonts in the same manuscript is generally not a good idea. Of course, if your publisher expects mixed fonts, follow the instructions.

Common stylistic mistakes for headings

The following example contains several common stylistic mistakes. An analysis of these mistakes is described after the example. This example contains intentional errors.

Design
1.1. Mechanical Design
    1.2. Electrical design
        1.2.1. Wiring
Software Design
Fabrication Of Parts

- **Problem 1: orphan headings**   The term *orphan heading* means that the list of headings on a certain heading level has only one entry. For example, heading 1.2.1 in the example is an orphan. If there is no 1.2.2, then 1.2.1 should not exist. It is acceptable to have orphan headings during the writing stage, but it is important to make sure that no orphan headings exist in the final version of the manuscript.

- **Problem 2: inconsistent or incorrect capitalization**   In the previous example, both words are capitalized in heading 1.1, but only the first word is capitalized in heading 1.2. Both capitalization schemes are frequently used, but writers should choose one and maintain consistency throughout the document by following a *style guide*.

  In heading 2 of the example, the word *Of* is capitalized. The American English standard is to lowercase prepositions and conjunctions (such as *and*, *of*, and *for*) and articles (such as *a* and *the*).

Tips and tricks

Collapse headings

If you use heading styles, you can hide the content below a heading by clicking the triangle next to the heading. This feature can be a quick and easy alternative to Outline view.

◢ Heading 1
> This is a test sentence.

▷ Heading 1.1

Click the triangle next to a heading to collapse the heading and hide the text after it.

Maintain the table of contents until the last moment

Long journal papers and research proposals usually do not require tables of contents. However, your team might want to keep a table of contents in the manuscript until submission time. Doing so can help develop the structure of the manuscript as it evolves by presenting a navigation view of the document. You can delete the table of contents right before submission.

Alternatively, of course, you can use the Navigation pane, in addition to the Outline view, which are both easily accessible from the **View** tab of the ribbon.

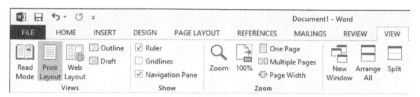

The Outline view and the Navigation pane can help you (and your team) manage long and complex documents.

Alter the automatic spacing before and after headings

Normally, the heading styles include a certain amount of top and bottom padding. If the defaults do not suit your template, you should adjust the style settings to create the spacing you want. (You should avoid creating extra spacing by inserting blank lines.) By relying exclusively on your styles' before and after spacing, you can create a consistent and professional template that will maintain its look throughout its usage.

To adjust the spacing for the heading style

1. Click the **Home** tab.

2. Right-click an entry in the **Style** gallery corresponding to the heading of interest.

3. Click **Modify** ⇒ **Format** ⇒ **Paragraph**, and then change spacing as desired in the **Spacing** selection boxes.

4. Click **OK** in the open dialog boxes to return to editing mode.

> **Note** Occasionally, formatting is not successful when you update your document. If this happens, try turning on the **Formatting** view in Word by clicking the paragraph symbol (¶). This view reveals hidden formatting commands in Word. From this view, confirm that you have selected all appropriate formatting elements, including those just before and just after the element you copied.

Recap

After completing this chapter, you should be quite proficient in several important aspects of document design. As you have seen, headings are tied to the structure and organization of documents, and using them properly is the key to making sure your front and back matter are assembled correctly.

By now, you should be able to

- Create headings

- Cross-reference headings

- Modify heading styles

- Use multilevel lists to organize your headings

- Enhance your headings with borders and shading

- Create page numbers and adjust their format

- Create tables of contents and limited, section-based tables of contents

- Create back matter, including appendices and indexes

Creating table-based figure templates, **page 84**

Creating dual-figure templates, **page 89**

Using styles to regulate caption spacing, **page 90**

Creating and formatting cross-references, **page 93**

CHAPTER 4

How to work with figures

In this chapter, you will learn how to

- Produce a variety of figures for different styles and layouts

- Create automatically updating cross-references for your figures

- Modify the numbering, style, and format of figure captions

- Use size, position, and alignment options to adjust figures

- Import figures from various sources

- Maintain consistent figures throughout your document

This chapter will introduce you to the fundamentals of figure templates, beginning with the most important choice of whether to use table-based or inline layouts. Although both of these layouts are powerful and work well with this system, your choice will be entirely dependent upon the greater layout of your document. You will also learn how to cross-reference your templates and alter them after they have been implemented. Finally, this chapter will point out stylistic mistakes you should be careful to avoid, and provide some miscellaneous tips and tricks to make your figure templates even more powerful.

How to conceptualize figures

Because nearly every technical document contains figures, learning how to create and edit them efficiently should be one of your primary document design goals. In the sections that follow, we discuss in detail methods for creating and cross-referencing figures as well as the process for altering figure templates.

Before beginning your work with figures, it's important to understand that what you might consider one figure actually consists of two independent objects that happen to be displayed above or below each other—the caption and graphic. Each of these are manipulated separately, but if you use the following methods, the graphic and the caption will "travel" together in your document as one linked unit. There are two ways to create figures:

- Copy a template figure (recommended for most cases).

- Create a new figure from scratch.

To reuse an existing figure by copying the template figure and caption, see Chapter 1, "Using templates in Word 2013." Chapter 1 lists the entire procedure for copying and pasting graphics, so it will not be repeated here. However, one point from Chapter 1 that bears repeating is to remember to use *Paste Special* for line art (as opposed to bitmaps), because using Paste Special gives you the opportunity to edit figures later without saving them to a separate file. Using *Paste Special* also increases the odds that your figure will remain compatible with the work of other writers. The most common selection that works well for Paste Special is *Picture (Windows Metafile)*, although this is not a foolproof selection. You might have to experiment with your pasting procedures to make the graphics look right.

Sometimes the fine features of line art become distorted with Paste Special, and this problem can be fixed by inserting a .png file created by a graphics package (Corel Draw, for example). To insert a .png file, place your cursor at the position at which you'd like the image to appear. On the **Insert** tab, select **Picture** (**Alt** → **N** → **P**), navigate to the image you'd like to use, and then click **Insert**. The selected image will be inserted at the desired location. Most likely, your file size will increase if you use .png source files rather than .wmf or .emf files.

How to choose a figure layout

Several basic layout choices are available to you for figure placement within your document. We do not recommend using text boxes for figures and captioning, so the following instructions will discuss only the use of tables and inline layouts. The next section will show you how to use these layout structures to create various figure templates for your documents.

Avoid using text boxes

For most technical documents, you should not resort to using text boxes for any aspect of your layout. Although text boxes can be convenient, and are even quite useful as a "quick fix" prior to printing, they can often do more harm than good. There are several important reasons to avoid text boxes, including the following:

- They do not allow you to properly use cross-references and fields within them because any text that you place within text boxes will require manual updating. Cross-referencing may work on your computer, but after you start working with collaborators, you will quickly discover the failure modes for this method.

- Their placement can be unpredictable. Placing a figure in a text box can cause it to jump to another page, or disappear completely; whereas placing a figure inline allows you to choose the exact location in which you'd like the figure to appear within your manuscript.

- They do not work with styles, so the padding and alignment options will be difficult to manage and maintain with any amount of consistency.

- They do not follow figures. If you decide to move or realign your figures, you must remember to do so for each text box as well.

Using table-based layouts

Many individuals choose to use tables to manage figure placement, and this style can be particularly useful in documents in which you need to manage figure placement with greater precision. Tables also make it easy to keep the caption and the figure together, as well as to keep two side-by-side figures together. Consequently, if you intend to wrap text tightly around your figures, it will be much easier to place your captions if you use tables.

Note If your document requires figures at fixed positions on the page, you should use a table-based layout. The only alternative is to use the alignment options, which necessitates the use of text boxes. This is unadvisable for the reasons already stated.

Inserting figures using inline layouts

The best way to place figures in most documents is by inserting them on their own line, and then placing the caption directly below them. This method ensures that your figure will appear in an exact location within your document, relative to your content, and not potentially end up at a point prior to it being introduced and referenced. Additionally, this method is easy to duplicate and modify.

How to create figures with table-based layouts

As previously mentioned, table-based layouts are essential when you would like to tightly wrap text around your figures, and when you would like to place your figures at fixed positions on the page (for example, at the top of the page). Of course, you could choose to use the text-wrapping options in Word to wrap text around your figures without tables, but you would quickly find that including captions necessitates other concessions, such as the use of text boxes. Therefore, if space is at a premium in your document, it's advisable to employ table-based layouts.

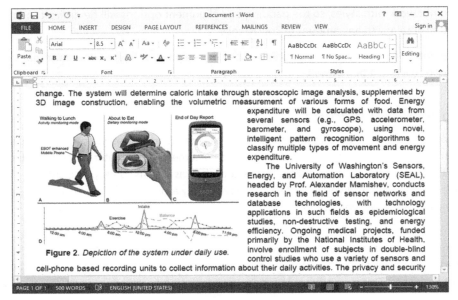

change. The system will determine caloric intake through stereoscopic image analysis, supplemented by 3D image construction, enabling the volumetric measurement of various forms of food. Energy expenditure will be calculated with data from several sensors (e.g., GPS, accelerometer, barometer, and gyroscope), using novel, intelligent pattern recognition algorithms to classify multiple types of movement and energy expenditure.

The University of Washington's Sensors, Energy, and Automation Laboratory (SEAL), headed by Prof. Alexander Mamishev, conducts research in the field of sensor networks and database technologies, with technology applications in such fields as epidemiological studies, non-destructive testing, and energy efficiency. Ongoing medical projects, funded primarily by the National Institutes of Health, involve enrollment of subjects in double-blind control studies who use a variety of sensors and cell-phone based recording units to collect information about their daily activities. The privacy and security

Figure 2. Depiction of the system under daily use.

A finished table template can be easily implemented within a text-heavy document.

Create a single-figure table-based layout

To create a generic table-based figure

Table

1. Navigate to the **Insert** tab and click **Table**.

2. Choose the table dimensions. For a single figure, choose a 1 x 2 table.

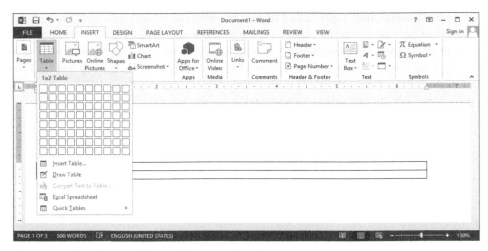

Choose a table with one cell for each figure and caption.

View Gridlines

3. To make the table easier to manage, place the cursor in the table, navigate to the **Layout** tab of the **Table Tools** portion of the ribbon, and then click **View Gridlines**.

4. Right-click the table's placement square (⊞) (point to the table, and it will appear in the upper-left corner), and click **Table Properties**.

Point to the table and right-click the square that appears in the upper-left corner.

5. Click the **Options** button and set **Default cell margins** to zero, and then click **OK**.

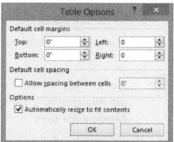

In the Table Properties dialog box, you can change alignment and other settings, including cell margins.

Note You might be tempted to use the top and bottom cell margins to fine-tune the spacing of the elements in your table, but we recommend that you use line spacing options, instead.

For example, you can increase the *before* spacing for the **Caption** style to draw the caption away from your figure. You can also use line spacing to ensure that all of your figures have the same spacing between the image and the accompanying caption.

Another less reliable alternative is manually adjusting the cell heights to achieve the desired padding. This can be done on a cell-by-cell basis, and, therefore, is very flexible. The downside is that it's a manual process and, thus, difficult to manage in a document with many figures. To adjust the height of a cell, point to its border, and then drag the cell until it's the size you want. Alternatively, you can access cell heights in the **Cell** tab of the **Table Properties** dialog box. Finally, right-click anywhere in the cell and choose one of the alignment options in **Cell Alignment** to more precisely control the positioning of your elements, at the expense of duplicability.

6. Set **Text Wrapping** to **Around**, and click **Positioning**.

7. Choose any exact positioning you would like for your table, and click **OK**.

Note If you would like the table to appear at the top of the page, under **Vertical**, set **Position** to 0", under **Relative to**, choose **Margin**, and clear the selection for **Move with text**.

To position the table by hand, point to the table, and then drag the placement square, releasing the mouse button to place the table.

8. Click **Borders and Shading**; under **Setting**, choose **None**; and then click **OK** in all dialog boxes.

9. Click the table's placement square to select the entire table.

10. On the **Layout** tab, in the **Alignment** group, click either the absolute center (▤), or the centered left-alignment (▤).

Pictures

11. Place the cursor in the upper cell. On the **Insert** tab, click **Pictures**, and then locate and select your picture.

12. In the **Size** group on the **Format** tab, resize and crop the picture as needed.

13. If the picture is smaller than the table cell, click the right border and drag it to the edge of the picture.

> **Note** Another foolproof method for resizing the table is to use the **AutoFit** feature. To do this, right-click the table's placement square, then click **AutoFit ⇒ AutoFit to Contents**. The table will automatically resize to fit the text and pictures in its cells. To lock the table at the new width, be sure to right-click the placement square again, and click **AutoFit ⇒ Fixed Column Width**.

14. Click the picture, and on the **References** tab, choose **Insert Caption**.

15. Click **OK**, and then type a caption for your figure.

16. Select the entire caption, copy and paste (**Ctrl+C → Ctrl+V**) or drag the caption into the cell beneath it, and delete the empty line below the picture.

Figure 1: A train in downtown Tacoma.

Figure 1: A train in downtown Tacoma.

Drag the caption to the bottom cell and drag the middle border to the top, flush with the figure.

17. If desired, select the entire caption, choose a non-bold font style, and then change the color of the font.

18. Click the **Line and Paragraph Spacing** ($\updownarrow\equiv$ ▾) button in the **Paragraph** group of the **Home** tab, and then click **Line Spacing Options**.

19. In the **Spacing** section, choose **Before** and **After** spacing (for example, 3 and 6).

20. Click the **More** button in the lower-right corner of the **Styles** gallery (▾), and click **Create a Style**. Name your new style **Figure Caption**, and use it for every figure that you create to ensure that all of your captions will have the same format.

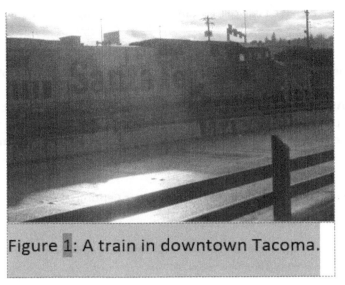
Figure 1: A train in downtown Tacoma.

By adding before and after spacing, you can ensure that the padding for your figures is consistent.

Create a dual-figure table-based layout

If you can create a single-figure layout with tables, creating a dual-figure layout with tables is easy. Simply create a 2 x 2 table and paste your figures and captions into the cells. You can space them appropriately with cell padding by selecting an entire row or column, and then adjusting the padding.

To create a dual-figure table-based layout

Table

View Gridlines

1. Navigate to the **Insert** tab and click **Table**.

2. Choose the dimensions you need. To place two figures next to each other, choose a 2 x 2 table.

3. To make the table easier to manage, place the cursor in the table, navigate to the **Layout** tab of the **Table Tools** portion of the ribbon, and then click **View Gridlines**.

4. Right-click the table's placement square (point to the table, and it will appear in the upper-left corner), and click **Table Properties**.

5. Click the **Options** button and set **Default cell margins** to zero, and then click **OK**.

6. Set **Text Wrapping** to **Around**.

7. Click **Positioning**, choose any exact positioning you would like for your table, and then click **OK**. Alternatively, you can position your figures by dragging the placement square (⊞).

8. Click **Borders and Shading**; under **Setting**, choose **None**; and then click **OK**.

9. Right-click in each of the cells, and under the **Cell Alignment** option, choose the absolute center (▦), (or the centered left-alignment ▤, for the lower, caption cell). You can also change alignment through the **Layout** tab on the ribbon.

Pictures

10. Place the cursor in the upper-left cell, click **Pictures** on the **Insert** tab, and then locate and select your picture.

11. Resize your figure as needed.

12. Click the border to the left of your figure and drag it to the edge of the figure to resize the cell to fit the figure.

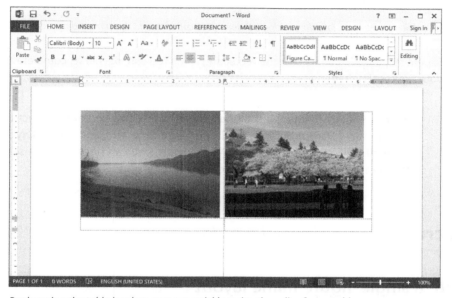

By dragging the table borders, you can quickly resize the cells of your table.

Insert Caption

13. Click the picture, and on the **References** tab, choose **Insert Caption**.

14. If you would like to use an abbreviation, such as "Fig.," click the **New Label** button, and type what you prefer in the box.

15. Click **OK**, and then type a caption for your figure.

16. Select the entire caption, copy and paste (or drag) it into the cell beneath it, and delete the empty line below the picture.

17. If desired, select the entire caption, remove the bold text formatting, and change its color.

18. Click the **More** button next to the **Styles** gallery (▼), and then click **Create a Style**. Name your new style **Figure Caption**, and use it for every figure that you create to ensure that all your captions will contain the same formatting.

| Figure 1: Discovery Bay in Washington. | Figure 2: The University of Washington. |

Use caption styles to dictate the spacing between your captions and the surrounding elements.

19. Repeat steps 10 through 14 for the remaining row. (You can, of course, complete the steps for both figures simultaneously.)

 Note If you are creating a multipart figure with a single caption, select the entire bottom row (drag through the cells, highlighting them), and on the **Layout** tab of the ribbon, click **Merge Cells.** Alternatively, you can right-click the selected cells and click **Merge Cells** in the context menu.

How to create inline figure layouts

Create a single-figure inline layout

To create an inline figure layout

1. Place your cursor on the line where you would like to insert your figure.

2. On the **Insert** tab, click **Pictures**.

3. Locate the picture or drawing you would like to insert, and click **Insert**.

4. On the **Home** tab, click the center button (≡) (or **Ctrl+E**).

5. Adjust the size of the picture by dragging the resizing handles, or by adjusting the width and height values on the **Format** tab of the ribbon.

6. Press **Enter** to create a new line.

Insert Caption

7. In the **Captions** box on the **References** tab, click **Insert Caption**.

8. If you would like to use an abbreviation, such as "Fig.," click the **New Label** button, and type what you prefer in the box.

9. Click **OK**, and then type a caption for your figure.

10. If you want, select the entire caption, remove the bold text formatting, and change its color.

11. With the cursor in the caption, click the **More** button next to the **Styles** gallery (⩡) , and click **Create a Style**.

12. Name your new style **Figure Caption**, and use it for each figure that you create to ensure that all of your captions have the same formatting.

13. Click **Modify** ⇒ **Format** ⇒ **Paragraph**, and adjust the line spacing as desired.

14. Click the **Line and Page Breaks** tab, and make sure that **Keep lines together** is selected.

15. Click **OK** in all dialog boxes.

Note Your pictures might occasionally become separated from their captions. To avoid this, it's recommended that you create a separate style for your figures, with **Keep with next** enabled to ensure that figure captions stay together on the same page. Remember to apply this style to each figure you create.

To access the **Keep with next** setting, right-click the **Figure** style, click **Modify**, and choose **Format** ⇒ **Paragraph**.

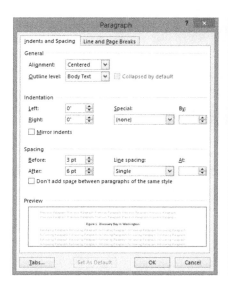

You can choose spacing for your figure style on the Indents And Spacing page. On the Line And Page Breaks page, make sure that Keep With Next is selected. All caption styles should have Keep Lines Together selected.

Create a dual-figure inline layout

To create a dual-figure inline layout

1. Complete the steps for creating a single-figure inline layout.

2. Select the figure and caption, and copy it to the Clipboard (**Ctrl+C** or **Right-click** ⇒ **Copy**).

3. Create a new line after the first figure and paste the copy there (**Ctrl+V** or **Right-click** ⇒ **Paste**).

4. Select both figures and captions and center them (≡ or **Ctrl+E**).

5. With both figures selected, navigate to the **Page Layout** tab, click **Columns**, and then select **Two** from the drop-down menu.

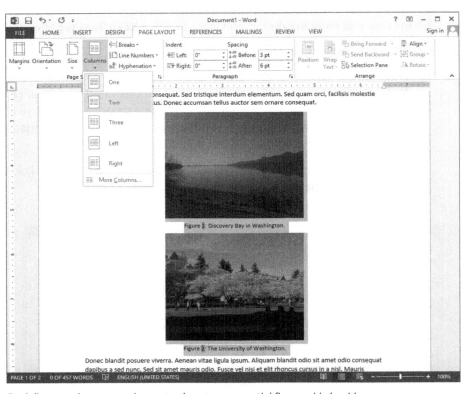

For inline templates, use columns to place two sequential figures side by side.

How to cross-reference figures

After you have created a figure, you can follow the same method to create cross-references as you've used with other elements of your document. You can copy and paste cross-references wherever you like, and they will automatically update to reflect the current ordering of your figures. So, for example, if you decide during the course of writing that Figure 4 should follow Figure 5, you need only to cut it, paste it into its new location, and press **Ctrl+A** → **F9**, and all of the numbering will be corrected automatically.

To cross-reference a figure

1. On the **Insert** tab, click **Cross-Reference**.
2. Under **Reference type**, click **Figure**.
3. Clear the **Insert as hyperlink** check box.
4. Under **Insert reference to**, click **Only label and number**.
5. Choose the desired figure from the list.
6. Click **Insert**.

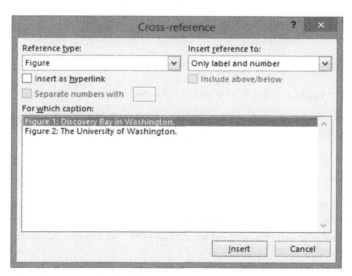

Using the Cross-reference features, you can quickly and easily update all of your references.

To update the document with the numbering for the figure, Press **Ctrl+A**, and then press **F9**, making sure to save your document after doing so.

How to alter figure captions

You might need to edit the caption or numbering style of a figure to match a new template. The steps for altering the caption styles for a figure template are listed in this section.

The most common change necessary is a change in the caption style. For example, you may need to change the figure caption style from *Figure 1* to *Fig. 1*. There are two general methods for changing figure captions, one that changes the figure template to automatically update, and another that relies on continual manual editing. Because each has limitations, we recommend you use them in the following appropriate cases.

To select a figure caption in one of your templates

Insert Caption

1. On the **References** tab, click **Insert Caption**.

2. Click **New Label**.

3. Enter the text for your label, such as **Fig**.

4. Click **OK** in all dialog boxes.

All of the figure captions for your template will be updated to the new caption; however, all references to the previous figures will be broken. Therefore, we suggested that you use this method in preexisting templates, but not in finished documents.

To change the caption style in an existing document

1. Manually change each caption's text from *Figure* to the desired text, such as *Fig.*

> **Note** Do not change the numbers. They will update automatically.

2. Press **Ctrl+A**, and then press **F9**.

All of the cross-references will be updated according to the new style. Unfortunately, you will have to change the text of every caption, manually. In addition, all new captions will use the previous label; therefore, we recommend that you use this method for documents that are nearly complete, but not for templates.

To change the numbering style in a figure template

Although many different reasons for changing a numbering style might occur, one of the most common is switching from a single number (Figure 2) to a dual number (Figure 2.1). This occurs most often when writers transition from a shorter document such as a journal article or stand-alone report to a thesis or longer document that has several major sections or chapters.

The easiest way to renumber your figures is as follows:

1. Select an existing figure caption.

2. Click **References** ⇒ **Insert Caption** ⇒ **Numbering**.

3. Choose the desired numbering scheme.

> **Note** If you need or want to include the chapter number in your captions, it's imperative that your document be set up with a multilevel list to number each heading. For in-depth instructions on how to set up multilevel list numbering, see Chapter 3, "How to work with headings."

To change the style of a figure caption

1. Select an existing figure caption (click the left margin, beside the caption).

2. On the **References** tab, click **Insert Caption**, and then click **Numbering**.

3. Select your preferences for the appearance of the caption in the dialog box. For section or chapter-based numbering, this includes selecting the **Include chapter number** check box.

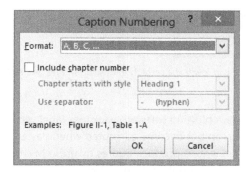

The caption numbering format that you choose will be used for every caption of that type.

4. Click **OK**, and then click **Close**.

5. Press **Ctrl+A** → **F9** to update the cross-references in the entire document.

6. Confirm that your changes have been applied in other parts of the document.

Common formatting mistakes in figures

- **Forgetting to reference and explain the figure**   Each figure should be mentioned in the text *before* its first appearance in the manuscript, and each figure should be explained in the text carefully to highlight the important points it illustrates. Finally, the figure should ideally be placed as closely as possible to the introductory and explanatory text.

- **Using excessive resolution**   Including a multimegabyte photo when a much lower resolution option would suffice is not a problem when the manuscripts includes only a couple of images; however, if a document contains hundreds of high resolution images, it will become a problem when working with the document. In general, try to keep your documents as lean as possible while retaining high enough image resolution for the printing needs.

  You can fix potential memory issues when inserting a picture. On the **Format** tab of the ribbon, click **Compress Pictures** ( ), and choose either a single image or all of the images in the document.

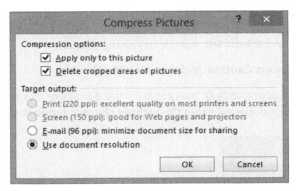

Through the Compress Pictures dialog box, you can lower the resolution of your images and reduce the size of your document.

- **Using corrupted fonts**   Many mainstream plotting software packages label vertical axes in such a way that they look good on the screen but become corrupted when pasted into Word. This problem most frequently occurs when writers produce figures by using Microsoft Excel. Why this happens is outside of the scope of this book, but we'll show you a procedure to fix this problem when it occurs.

Suppose the source inside your document is Excel, and you want to label the *x*-axis and the *y*-axis of a two-dimensional graph, add arrows and short comments to the picture, and paste the result into Word. In the process, you discover that your *y*-axis looks unattractive in Word, and the arrow pointers have inexplicably moved to different locations. The easiest solution is to fix the graphic by using a graphics software package.

To export a graphic to a .png file format by using Microsoft Paint

1. Generate your plot in Excel.

2. Right-click the chart, and then click **Copy** (**Ctrl+C**).

3. Open Microsoft Paint.

4. Resize the canvas until it's much smaller than your graphic (it will be automatically expanded to fit).

5. Click **Paste (Ctrl+V)**.

6. Click **File** ⇒ **Save As**.

7. Type a name for the figure under **File name**.

8. Under **Save as type**, select **PNG (*.png)**.

9. Click **Save**.

Pictures

10. Switch to Word and choose **Insert** ⇒ **Picture**.

11. Select your picture and click **Insert**.

12. Continue to incorporate the figure according to the instructions in this chapter.

> **Note** You do not have to save the figure in Paint. Alternatively, after pasting it into Paint, you can copy it immediately (**Ctrl+C**) and paste it into Word with **Paste Special**, as previously described. By using this procedure, you lose line art capability; it should be used when everything else fails.

To resize a figure

If the figure is too big or too small, change the size by pulling on the corner of the figure, not on the side, so that the height-to-width ratio is preserved. If you need to present several figures that are all exactly the same size:

1. Right-click the graphic.

2. Click **Format Picture** ( ).

3. Select the **Size** tab, and change **Scale** to the same dimensions for all figures.

4. Confirm that a check mark appears in front of the **Lock Aspect Ratio** menu line.

Common stylistic mistakes in figures

- **Graphic elements are too small**   As a general rule for figure elements, make sure that all elements in the figure are visible when the figure is shrunk to double-column paper format; in other words, when the figure spans only a half-page width. If all elements are easily distinguishable in the double-column format, they will also be large enough for Microsoft PowerPoint presentations and bold enough for making photocopies. For each element, specifically check the following items:

  - Line thickness.

  - Size of arrowheads.

  - Marker size (squares, dashes, triangles).

  - Font size in graphs. Notice that default settings in Excel and Matrix Laboratory (MATLAB) lead to font sizes that are too small for double-column display.

- **Using a serif font type**   Unless specified otherwise by the publisher, use Arial or a similar font for labels in your figures. Whatever you use, the font should be sans serif, common and recognizable, not too narrow, and easy to read. The default Times New Roman is not optimal for figures because the serifs (the small lines at the end of each letter-stroke) do not reproduce well at a lower resolution. An important exception is figures for patents—requirements for those differ from general requirements for figures for journal and conference papers and books. Refer to the patent guidelines for these specifications.

- **Using color inappropriately**   Remember that publications are mostly black and white so that even if the original document contains color elements, readers will often print or reproduce a manuscript in black and white. Therefore, red and blue lines in a graphic, which look great in PowerPoint, will be indistinguishable in print. For the same reason, referring to a *red line* in the text is meaningless if your graph is black and white in the printed copy of the manuscript. Rather than using color for manuscripts destined for print, consider using non-color–based markers in your figures, such as hash marks or triangles, which can distinguish features in a way that is easily reproducible in black and white. You should still use colors in addition to using markers, so that the graph will look its best when viewing in color is available.

- **Fuzzy images**   Lines must be crisp. Use line art, not bitmaps, whenever possible.

- **"As shown in Figure 1..."**   The preferred wording is "Figure 1 shows..." or "...explanatory text (see Figure 1)."

- **Mixing labels and caption styles**   It is recommended that you don't mix labels, such as *Figure* and *Fig.* in the same manuscript. This problem arises frequently, for example, when two conference papers are being combined into a journal paper.

- **Meaningless or repetitive captions**   The caption *Figure 12. Temperature vs. Humidity* is not a good caption if temperature and humidity correspond to the axes already indicated in the graph. Whenever possible, captions should be concise and informative rather than simply descriptive, because the caption can add meaning or interpretation to the text. In the previous example, a better caption might be *Figure 12. Glass transition consistently takes place earlier than predicted by theory.* A good caption briefly summarizes the importance of the figure.

- **Dual captions**   The default settings in plotting programs, such as Excel or MATLAB, often place captions or titles above figures, and these captions are then incorporated into the figures themselves when they are imported into Word. Figures in a manuscript should *not* be double-captioned. If this happens, touch up the figures by removing the captions in the native graphics. Additionally, the convention holds that figure captions should appear below graphics, not above them. So, unless your publication guidelines specify otherwise, place figure captions below the graphics. (Note that table captions, on the contrary, are usually placed above the tables.)

- **Showing a three-dimensional (3-D) plot from a bad angle**   Three-dimensional plots must show salient features of the data rather than simply functioning to make figures *pretty*. If a 3-D component does not add to the information value of the figure, then eliminate the 3-D aspect entirely. If, however, the 3-D aspect does help readers discern the meaning of a figure, the plot should be rotated into the most advantageous viewing position. Likewise, multiple 3-D plots with the same axes should be shown from the same angle for ease of comparison. In general, however, your team should seek to avoid 3-D plots when possible, because they tend to confuse readers more than they assist with understanding. With that said, there are many cases when 3-D representation is truly the most appropriate for the data.

Tips and tricks for figures

Word does not replicate some of the more powerful figure positioning capabilities of LaTeX, and some abilities might not be suitable for very long technical manuscripts. However, it is possible to overcome many limitations of Word with clever formatting. Several important features are discussed in the following section.

Orphan control

The figure and its caption should stay on the same page. If part of a caption runs over to the next page, it is called an *orphan*. The template file provided with this book is already formatted to prevent that from happening. However, if you've created a new template, and want to enable orphan control (and we recommend you do), force the caption to attach to the graphic above it this way:

1. Select both the graphic and the caption.

2. On the **Home** tab, click the dialog box launcher (⌐) in the lower-right corner of the **Paragraph** group, and then click the **Line and Page Breaks** tab in the dialog box that appears.

3. Make sure the **Keep lines together** check box is selected.

As a result, you may end up with a block of white space on the previous page. Unfortunately, there is no recommended elegant solution to this problem. Paragraph text can be moved around in the final version of the manuscript to optimize the figure placement. Despite this inconvenience, figure placement problems in Word do not propagate too far into subsequent pages.

> **Note** To ensure that your inline figures and captions all behave the same way, it is recommended that you modify the caption style as described previously, and apply the style to both your captions *and* your figures.

Figure positioning

The individual preferences (and publisher requirements) for figure positioning vary widely. The inline procedures described earlier work for figures that occupy most of the width of the page. In a single-column document, if the figure is narrow and page space needs to be conserved, a viable option is to use a double-column format. You can either group two figures together or wrap text on one side of a single figure. An equally convenient option is the table-based method described earlier in this chapter. This method makes it easier to keep the caption with the figure, but it does require more effort to use. In general, try to avoid mixing single and double-column layouts, because it can unnecessarily complicate the writing process.

> **Note** Some users place figures and captions inside text boxes. The advantage of this approach is that the text box can be pinned to a specific location such as at the bottom of the page, which allows the remaining text to wrap around the figure. Unfortunately, although text boxes allow for better control of figure positioning, they are not compatible with the figure caption auto-numbering feature.

Cross-referencing a remote figure

If the text refers to a figure that is located on a different page in the manuscript, help the reader find the figure by using the format "Figure 18 on page 132 shows...." Of course, the page number should be a field. You can create this by clicking **References**, **Cross-reference**, selecting **Figure** in the **Reference type** box, and selecting **Page number** in the **Insert reference to** box. Ideally, however, your figures should be located as close to the text that describes them as possible to assist readers.

Error! messages

Unfortunately, automatic cross-referencing of figures and tables in Word is far from foolproof. Often, the cross-references disappear during editing stages, and are replaced with text reading Error! Reference source not found. This happens most frequently when a field is copied to two locations and the references become ambiguous, colliding with each other. For example, suppose you begin with a piece of text that references Figure 4. You copy Figure 4 and its caption to a new location in the document, and after updating the cross-references, the new instance of Figure 4 becomes Figure 1. But what can you say about text references to the figure? Word has no way of knowing whether your intent is to reference the initial Figure 4 or the Figure 1 clone. Depending on the sequence of your text updating, you may get error messages. It is prudent to search the final version of the document for the **Error!** message so that you can repair any problems that have arisen during the final stages of editing.

> **Note** Occasionally, formatting is not successful when you update your document. If this happens, try turning the **Formatting** view in Word by clicking the paragraph symbol (¶). This view reveals hidden formatting commands in Word. From this view, confirm that you have selected all appropriate formatting elements, including those just before and just after the element you copied.

Recap

After completing this chapter, you should be able to handle all necessary aspects of implementing figures in Word 2013. As you know, figures are critical to the visual impact of documents, and using them properly can mean the difference between lacking appeal and making a strong impression.

By now, you should be able to

- Create figures

- Cross-reference figures

- Modify caption styles

- Use size, position, and alignment options to adjust figures

- Successfully import figures from various sources

- Avoid common formatting and stylistic mistakes

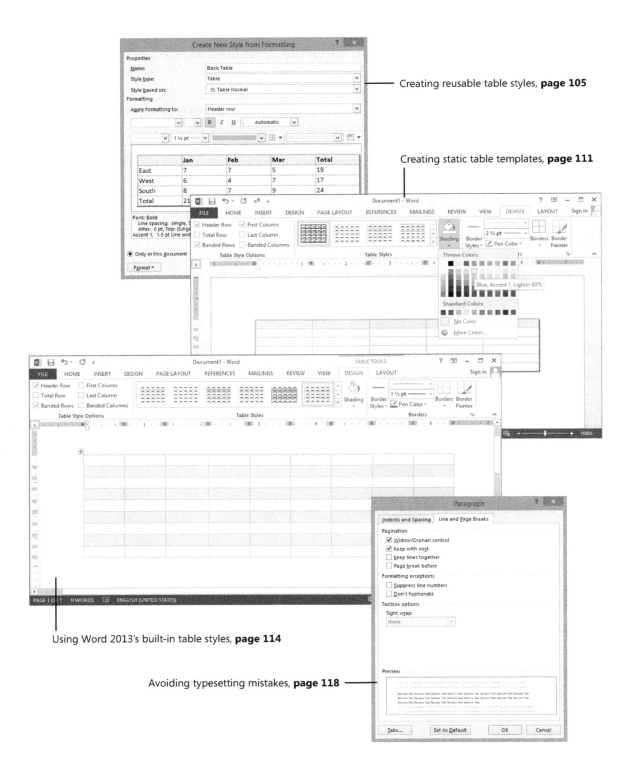

Creating reusable table styles, **page 105**

Creating static table templates, **page 111**

Using Word 2013's built-in table styles, **page 114**

Avoiding typesetting mistakes, **page 118**

CHAPTER 5

How to work with tables

In this chapter, you will learn how to

- Create stylish and flexible tables

- Create attractive and reusable table styles

- Add automatically updating cross-references for your tables

- Modify the table caption styles to accommodate document requirements

- Use various layout and positioning options to adjust your tables

- Import tables from Microsoft Excel, Google Docs, and other sources

- Avoid common formatting and stylistic mistakes

Like figures, tables are common and important elements in technical documents, and they need to be easily editable by all contributors. In this section, we describe the methods for creating and editing tables.

How to create tables

The logic behind creating and positioning tables is very similar to that of figures; therefore, before beginning your work with tables, it's important to understand that each table actually consists of two independent objects that happen to sit next to each other—the caption and the tabular information (table). Each of these objects are manipulated separately, but if you use the methods described in this chapter, the tabular information and the label will "travel" together in your document as one linked unit. There are two ways to create tables:

- Create a new table and apply a table style. (Recommended)

- Copy an existing table and modify its dimensions.

You can use either of these methods to successfully create and implement impressive and reusable tables in your documents. However, you might find that, despite the flexibility and extensibility of the first method, the second method will offer you more control over how your tables are presented. Using a modified existing table rather than creating a new table from scratch might be particularly useful when designing templates for use by others, and when implementing floating tables.

Create a table style

As discussed in Chapter 2, "How to design templates," you might be able to create a single table, which you can then adapt for each table in your document. However, you might find that a much more flexible option is to create a table style, which can be applied to any table and will dictate the appearance of your document's tables. Having a table style that you can easily apply is particularly useful if the document you are creating will be very long (for example, a thesis or dissertation). Unfortunately, there is no way to save the style of an existing table, but new table styles can be easily created. Finally, this approach works best when used with inline tables, for which text wrapping is disabled. To create floating tables that wrap text around the table, it is recommended that you copy an existing table.

Note If you do use table styles with a floating layout, you will have to manually modify the caption cell every time your style is modified or reapplied.

To create a table style

1. Click the **Table** button on the **Insert** tab of the ribbon.

2. Create a 3 x 3 table or larger.

3. Click the **Table Tools Design** tab, and then click the **More** button (⏷) next to the **Table Styles** gallery .

4. Click **New Table Style**.

5. In the dialog box that appears, choose your desired font and formatting options for your table. Notice that the **Apply formatting to** drop-down menu will allow you to affect the styling of the whole table, or just a subset, such as the header row.

6. To change the outlines, make sure **Whole table** is selected in the **Apply formatting to** drop-down menu, and then click **Format,** and then **Borders and Shading.**

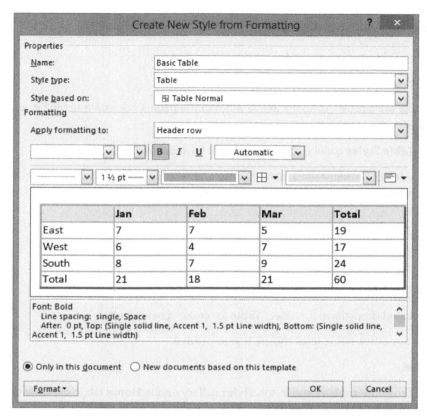

In the Create New Style From Formatting dialog box, you can customize the colors and formatting of your table based on row, column, corner, and more. By using these options, you can create fully customized and unified tables for your document with only a few clicks.

7. Choose the borders to suit your preferences, and then click **OK**.

8. To achieve a shaded first column, as in the screenshot, select **Header row** and choose a color under the font options, on the right.

9. If you need more explicit customization, select additional menu items in the **Apply formatting to** drop-down menu, and modify their appearance as needed.

To create a table with a table style

1. Click the **Table** button on the **Insert** tab of the ribbon.

2. Choose the dimensions of your table.

3. The table will appear, filling the active width of the page. Click within the table, and then click the **Design** tool tab on the ribbon.

4. In the **Table Styles** gallery, click the style you have defined.

5. Your table will be adjusted to match the style, at which point you can make any additional adjustments that you want for that specific table.

To create inline tables with no text wrapping

1. Create a new line above the table by pressing the **Enter** key.

2. On the **References** tab of the ribbon, click **Insert Caption**.

3. In the **Label** drop-down list, select **Table** (or create a new label).

4. Adjust any other elements of the caption as needed.

5. Click **OK**.

6. Select the entire caption, and in the **Styles** gallery on the **Home** tab, click the **More** button, and then click **Create a Style**.

7. Click **Modify**.

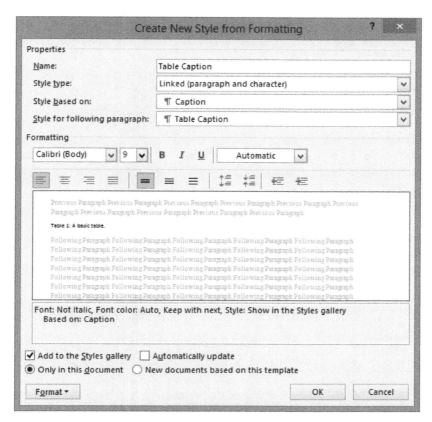

8. Change the text formatting and line spacing (under **Format** ⇒ **Paragraph**) to set the appearance of your caption.

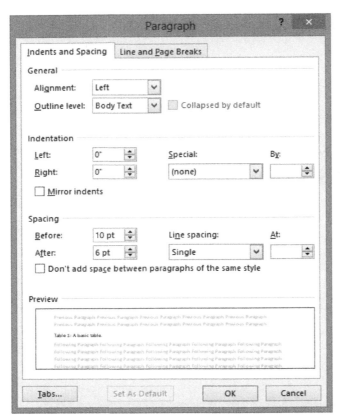

Make sure to change the formating as well as the line spacing to set the caption apart from the surrounding text (but not the table).

9. Click **OK**.

To create floating tables with text wrapping

> **Note** It is not recommended that you use table styles to create floating tables, because there is no reliable and consistent method for pairing the captions with the floating tables. If you must use styles, a workaround appears here.

Insert Caption

1. Click within the table.

2. On the **References** tab of the ribbon, click **Insert Caption**.

3. In the **Label** drop-down list, select **Table** (or create a new label).

4. Adjust any other elements of the caption as needed.

5. Click **OK**.

6. Select the entire caption, and in the **Style** gallery, click the **More** button, and then click **Create a Style**.

7. Click **Modify**.

8. Change the text formatting and line spacing (under **Format** ⇒ **Paragraph**) to set the appearance of your caption.

9. Click **OK**.

Create a table without a table style

Creating a table without a table style means that your table will not automatically update, and if you have more than one table, they will be unlinked from each other. This might be desirable in specific circumstances, such as short documents or documents with many varying tables; therefore, although it is not generally recommended, we have included the procedure for producing a "style-less" table here.

To create a "style-less" table

1. Click the **Table** button on the **Insert** tab of the ribbon.

2. Choose the table dimensions.

3. Point to the table and right-click the icon that appears over the upper-left corner (⊞), and then click **Table Properties**.

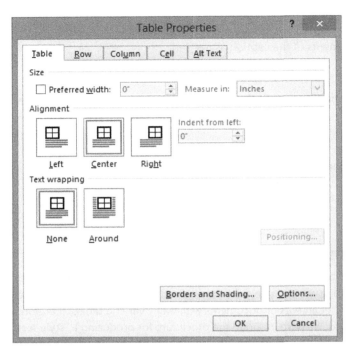

Choose alignment and margin options to suit your template. Remember that you can click the table's placement square to position it anywhere on the page. You can also use the Positioning dialog box for greater precision.

4. Choose an **Alignment** option, select **None** under **Text Wrapping**, and then click **Options**.

5. Choose appropriate cell margins, and then click **OK**.

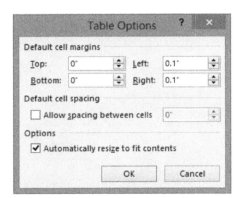

6. Click **Borders and Shading**.

7. From here you can customize the borders and shading for the entire table. Choose 2¼ pt for **Width**, and choose a light color. Click the top and left side border icons twice.

8. Choose a darker color, and click the bottom and right side border icons twice.

9. Set **Width** to 1½, select the lighter color (or a color in between the two shades), and then click the two middle border buttons twice.

10. Click **OK**.

Shading

11. Now select the top row of your table (click the leftmost cell and drag to the rightmost cell), click the **Design** tab that appears, click the **Shading** button, and then choose a color. Alternatively, you can right-click your selection, and then click the small paint bucket icon that appears.

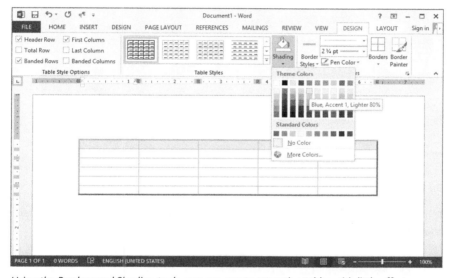

Using the Borders and Shading tools, you can create attractive tables with little effort.

Insert
Above

12. Right-click one of the shaded cells and click **Insert** ⇒ **Insert Rows Above**. You can also find the insert rows above button on the **Layout** tab of the ribbon.

Merge
Cells

13. Select the top row (click and drag from the leftmost cell to the rightmost cell), and then click **Merge Cells** (right-click or navigate to the **Layout** tab).

14. Right-click the table, click **Table Properties**, and then click **Borders and Shading**.

15. In the **Apply to** drop-down list, select **Cell**, and remove the top and side borders. Choose the lighter color and thicker border for the bottom border, and then click the bottom border icon twice to modify it.

16. On the **Shading** tab, in the **Fill** drop-down list, select **No Color**.

17. Click **OK**.

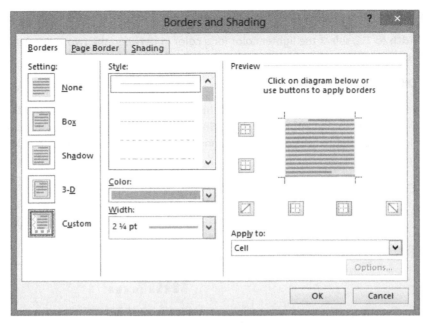

Remove the side and top borders and modify the bottom border to match the old top.

18. On the **References** tab, click **Insert Caption**.

19. In the **Label** drop-down menu, make sure that **Table** is selected, and in the **Position** drop-down menu, choose **Above selected item**, and click **OK**.

Make sure to select the Table and Above Selected Item options.

20. Select the caption and drag it into the topmost cell of the table.

21. Type placeholder text for the caption and modify its appearance as desired.

22. Right-click the caption, and then click **Paragraph**.

23. In the **Line and Page Breaks** tab, select the **Keep with next** box.

24. Select the entire caption, and on the **Home** tab in the **Style** gallery, click the **More** button (⤓), and then click **Create a Style**.

25. Name the style **Table Caption**, and then click **OK**.

Save your table caption as a style to unify and simplify your caption formatting.

How to use the built-in table styles in Word 2013

For many templates, you will not have to design your own table styles. Instead, you can rely on the collection of built-in table styles that Microsoft Word 2013 has to offer. More often than not, you can find a suitable style for your needs.

To use a built-in style

1. Create a table (**Insert** ⇒ **Table**).

2. On the **Design** tab, choose a style from the **Table Styles** group, or click the **More** button (⤓) to see all of the styles.

3. Create a caption for the table (**References** ⇒ **Insert Caption**).

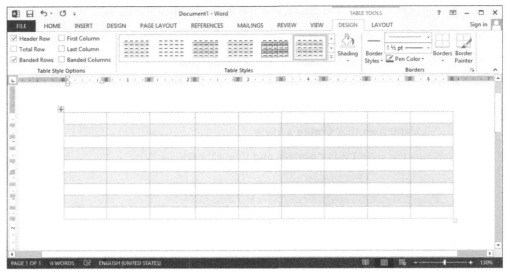

The built-in table styles can save you a lot of time when used to design your documents.

 Note If you use built-in styles, you should choose an in-line layout for your table. If you do use the styles with a floating layout, you will have to modify the caption cell manually every time your style is modified or reapplied.

How to cross-reference tables

After you have created a table, you can follow the same method to create cross-references as you used for figures and the other elements of your document. You can cut and paste the cross-references wherever you like, and they will automatically update to reflect the current ordering of your tables. Therefore, if during the course of writing you decide that two of your tables should be switched for organizational purposes, you need only to cut and paste them into their new locations, press **Ctrl+A** → **F9**, and all of the numbering will be corrected to reflect the new order.

To cross-reference a table

1. On the **References** tab, click **Cross-reference** (⬚).

2. In the **Reference type** drop-down list, select **Table**.

3. Clear the **Insert as hyperlink** check box.

4. In the **Insert reference to** drop-down list, select **Only label and number**.

5. Select the desired table from the list, and then click **Insert**.

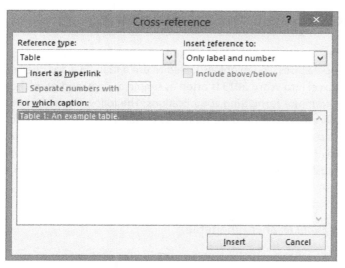

You can insert references to the table number as well as the number of the page on which the table appears.

How to alter tables

Aside from altering the actual content of the table, writers also frequently need to edit the caption style or numbering style. The steps for altering a table's caption style appear below.

Although there might be many different occurrences that necessitate changing a numbering style, one of the most common is switching from a single number ("Table 2") to a dual number ("Table 2.1") This change occurs most often when writers transition from a shorter document, such as a journal article or stand-alone report, to a thesis or longer document that has several major sections or chapters.

To change between numbering styles

1. Select one of the caption numbers that you wish to update.

2. On the **References** tab, click **Insert Caption**, and then click **Numbering**.

3. Select your preferences for the appearance of the caption in the dialog box.

4. Click **OK** in all dialog boxes.

5. Press **Ctrl+A** → **F9** to update the cross-references in the entire document.

6. Confirm that your changes have occurred in other parts of the document.

How to import tables from external programs

In order to create your tables, you might sometimes choose to produce them in an external program, such as Excel or Google Docs. You might also need to use a table that has been created for you. Importing tables from Excel into Word 2013 is often as simple as copy and paste; however, in some cases you might run into minor formatting complications. The following procedure will help ensure that you avoid complications and produce high-quality tables with minimal effort. We recommend that you avoid creating tables in the Google Docs Word Processor, as its formatting is generally not compatible with that of Word 2013. Additionally, be advised that if you create tables in Google Docs Spreadsheet, you will have to import the table into Excel before you can transfer it into Word 2013.

To import a table from Excel as an in-line table

1. Select the cells that you want to use in Excel and copy them to the clipboard (**Ctrl+C**).

2. Place the cursor on the line at which you would like to begin the table, and paste the cells (**Ctrl+V**).

 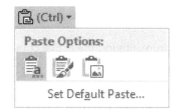

When you paste an object, such as a table, into a Microsoft Word document, a contextual paste dialog box will appear, allowing you to specify how the object is integrated into your document. The three choices that most commonly appear are: Keep Source Formatting (K), Merge Formatting (M), and Keep Text Only (T).

3. Point to the table, right-click the placement square that appears, and then click **Table Properties**.

4. Modify the table positioning, alignment, and borders as needed.

5. Create a new line above the table, and center the text (**Ctrl+E**).

6. On the **References** tab, click **Insert Caption**.

7. In the **Label** drop-down menu, make sure that **Table** is selected, click **New Label** if you need different text, click **Numbering** to define different numbers if needed, and then click **OK**.

8. Type placeholder text for the caption and modify the appearance as desired.

9. Right-click the caption, and then click **Paragraph**.

10. In the **Line and Page Breaks** tab, select the **Keep with next** check box.

11. Change the formatting of the caption text as needed.

12. Select the entire caption, and on the **Home** tab in the **Styles** gallery, click the **More** button ( ), and then click **Create a Style**.

13. Name the style **Table Caption**, and then click **OK**.

> **Note** The following procedure has been prepared as of August 2013. Due to continuous updates, the exporting process may be different in Google Docs Spreadsheet. The importing and transferring processes for Excel and Word 2013, however, will be the same.

To import a table from Google Docs Spreadsheet

1. Click **File** ⇒ **Download as** ⇒ **Microsoft Excel 97-2003 (.xlsx)**.

2. Open the file in Excel, and then click **Enable Editing**.

3. Follow the same steps as the previous procedure, making sure to use **Keep Source Formatting (K)** to preserve the formatting of your table.

Common typesetting mistakes

Prevent tables from running across multiple pages

Obviously, you want your tables to be as concise as possible and sometimes where you place a table in the text causes it to run across multiple pages. To prevent this from happening, follow the steps below.

To keep a table on one page

1. Select all but the last row of the table (click and drag from the top row).

2. On the **Home** tab of the ribbon, in the **Paragraph** group, click the dialog box launcher ( ).

3. On the **Line and Page Breaks** tab, select the **Keep with next** check box.

By selecting the Keep With Next check box, the rows of your table will not be split across multiple pages.

To keep a table on one page (alternative method)

1. Select the entire table (click the table's placement square ⊞).

2. On the **Page Layout tab,** click **Breaks**.

3. Under **Section Breaks**, select **Next Page**.

Occasionally, you might need to use large tables that travel across pages, in which case you should first figure out if the table can be divided into several, smaller tables to highlight salient features in greater detail. If the table must be longer, be sure to break the table at a new column/row rather than in the middle of a column/row.

To ensure that the heading row appears on the new page as well, right-click in the row, and then click **Table Properties**. Next, on the **Row** page, make sure the **Repeat as header row at the top of each page** check box is selected. The repeat as header row check box is useful in situations in which the pages of the table are somehow separated or users can't view them as a single larger sheet (as in a bound book).

You can also modify table styles to repeat the header row on new pages, which is described in the following procedure.

To modify a style to repeat the header row on new pages

1. Place the cursor in a table.

2. On the **Table Design** tab, right-click the style that you want to use here, and click **Modify Table Style**.

3. In the **Apply formatting to** drop-down menu, choose **Header row**.

4. Choose **Format** ⇒ **Table Properties**, and then click the **Row** tab.

5. Select the **Repeat as header row at the top of each page** check box.

6. Click **OK** in both the Table Properties and Modify Style dialog boxes.

Note Be judicious when selecting alignment options within the cell (right-justified, left-justified, or centered). The goal should be to make the table as readable as possible.

Common stylistic mistakes in tables

Omitting units and variable names in table headings

Remember to include the variable name, variable symbol, and the units of that variable in every table so that readers can be certain of the table's meaning.

Placing units in cells rather than in row or column headings

Although units are necessary, if the units are the same for all entries in the table column, you should place them in the heading of the column rather than after each entry. It makes the table more concise and much easier to read.

Using too many borders in a table

Writers typically include far too many borders in the interiors of the tables they create, thinking that the extra rules will help readers sort among items. In fact, the rules often create the opposite reaction, as readers get bogged down in searching the boxes. Instead, you should aspire to design elegant tables, with data that is presented completely and with as little intrusion as possible by non-data elements such as rules. Use rules only when absolutely necessary, such as for separating heading text from the columns/rows. For journal submissions, most publishers have guidelines about where borders ought to appear in a table.

Choosing type font size that is too small

Be sure that your table can be read when reproduced. Technical tables often contain a great deal of data and consequently writers frequently shrink type to fit more data into the table. Type that is difficult to read leads readers to become frustrated and can present problems when the table is reproduced. For example, after photocopying or shrinking a document, a six (6) might begin to look like an eight (8). Choosing the right font size will help your team as you strive to create smaller, clearer, more focused tables rather than larger, more expansive tables that attempt to cover too much data at once.

"As shown in Table 1..."

The preferred usage is "Table 1 shows..." or "... the text of the sentence ... (see Table 1).

Using meaningless or repetitive captions

Whenever possible, captions should be concise and informative rather than simply descriptive because the caption should add meaning or interpretation to the text. The caption "Table 12. Humidity Levels" is not a good caption if humidity corresponds to the rows (or more likely) the columns already indicated in the table. In this example, a better caption would be "Table 12. The humidity levels changed over time as predicted" because it briefly summarizes the importance of the table.

Placing captions at the bottom of the table

General convention states that table captions should be above the table and not below. Unless your publisher's guidelines suggest otherwise, place the table caption above the table. (Note that figure captions, on the contrary, are normally placed below the figure.)

Tips and tricks for tables

Orphan control

The table and its caption should stay together on the same page. If part of the table or the caption runs over to the next page, it's called an *orphan*. The template file is already formatted to prevent orphan captions.

To force the lines to stay together

1. Select both the graphic and the caption.

2. On the **Home** tab, on the lower right corner of the **Paragraph** group, click the button to open the **Paragraph** dialog box.

3. Select **Line and Page Breaks**.

4. Select the **Keep with next** and **Keep lines together** check boxes.

Table positioning

The individual preferences (and publisher requirements) for table positioning vary widely. For a document written in double-column format, it's acceptable to switch to a single-column format if the table is very wide. However, in general, you should avoid mixing single and double column format because it will complicate your process.

Cross-referencing remote tables

If the table is located far away from its reference in the manuscript, help the reader by using the style "Table 18 on page 132 shows..." Naturally, the page number should be a field. You can make this field by clicking **References, Cross-reference,** selecting **Table** in the **Reference Type** drop-down list, and then selecting **Page number** in the **Insert reference to** drop-down list.

Recap

After completing this chapter, you should be able to create and modify tables in Microsoft Word 2013. Additionally, you should be comfortable with importing tables from external programs, such as Excel and Google Docs Spreadsheet. Tables are powerful tools in the successful presentation of research publications, so it's critical that you format and reference them properly.

By now, you should be able to

- Create tables

- Cross-reference tables

- Modify caption styles

- Use size, position, padding, and alignment options to adjust tables

- Successfully import tables from other sources

- Avoid common formatting and stylistic mistakes

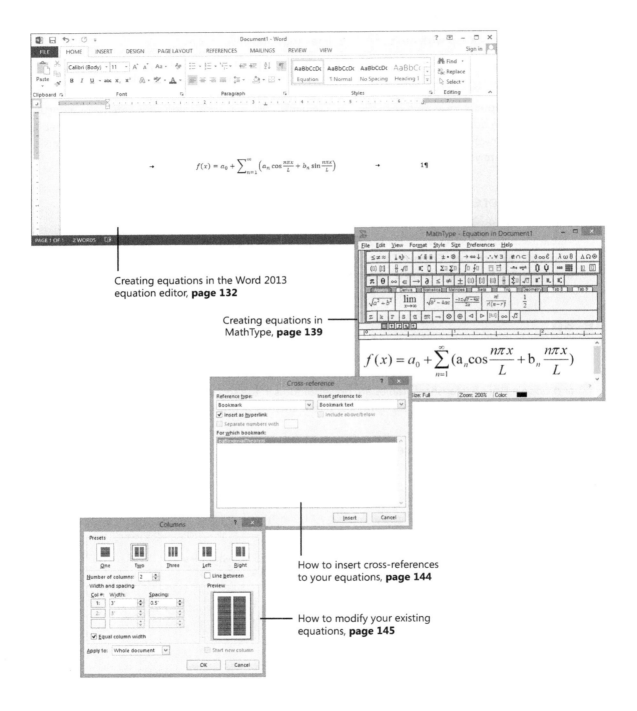

Creating equations in the Word 2013 equation editor, **page 132**

Creating equations in MathType, **page 139**

How to insert cross-references to your equations, **page 144**

How to modify your existing equations, **page 145**

CHAPTER 6

How to work with equations

In this chapter, you will learn how to

- Create properly formatted and consistent equations

- Use the Word 2013 built-in equation editor

- Create automatically updating cross-references for your equations

- Modify equation captions to accommodate document requirements

- Avoid common formatting and stylistic mistakes

- Use various tips and tricks to improve your equations

Most technical documents contain multiple formulas, so writing teams must either create new equations from scratch or alter existing formulas. In this section, we describe the two most efficient ways to create equations and an equally efficient method for editing them.

Starting with Microsoft Word 2007, Word has a built-in math editing and display capability that combines ease of use with elegant mathematical typography. This chapter describes methods for entering and editing simple mathematical equations and expressions, and also covers more advanced aspects of the facility.

How to create equations in Word 2013

There are two methods for creating equations:

- Copy an existing equation (recommended for most cases).

- Create a new equation.

To copy an existing equation, see the "How to place equations" section in Chapter 1, "Using templates in Word 2013."

An equation consists of the equation (formula) itself and the equation number associated with it (unless it is an inline equation). Inline equations can be entered by using MathType or the equation editor. This chapter covers numbered equations. Generally, publishers expect the equation itself to be centered, and the equation number right-aligned and enclosed in parentheses on the same line, like this:

$$E = mc^2 \hspace{8em} (1)$$

Create an equation with the equation editor

In the past, the default equation editor that shipped with early versions of Word had a negative reputation, for its inconsistent functionality and less-than-attractive output. In striking contrast, the equation editor built in to Word 2013 is a powerful and flexible tool. It's more than likely that, with just a little bit of practice, you'll find that the Word 2013 equation editor will successfully handle all of the equations in your documents. More importantly, if you collaborate on a team, you will not have to worry about whether the other team members have a compatible version of MathType.

Get started

Mathematical typography rules are used in rendering text when the text appears in math zones. The quickest way to enter a math zone is to use the keyboard shortcut **Alt + =** to display a rectangle enclosing the words *Type equation here* or the equivalent in the user locale language. You can type any mathematical expression, even just a simple variable like *x*. If the expression's math zone is the only text on the line(s), it will be displayed in *display mode*; otherwise, it is displayed in the somewhat compressed *inline mode* (TeX's $$ vs $).

When you type enough information for an expression to become unambiguous, the expression automatically transforms into the proper format right in front of your eyes! This process is called *formula autobuildup*. For example, type **a^2+b^2=c^2<space>** and you'll see the Pythagorean Theorem

$$a^2 + b^2 = c^2 \hspace{8em} (2)$$

In this example, the plus (+) and equal (=) terminate the superscript expressions a^2 and b^2, respectively, causing them to be converted to their built-up forms shown in the two graphics (a^2 and b^2). Since no operator (or enter) follows the c^2 in the equation, you need to press the **spacebar** to build it up. The superscript notation a^2 is an example of the linear format documented in *Unicode Technical Note #28, Unicode Nearly Plain-Text Encoding of Mathematics*, and discussed later in this chapter. Symbols not on the keyboard can be typed in using their standard TeX names.

Insert an equation or insert a symbol

You can also insert a math zone using the **Equation** button from the **Insert** tab on the ribbon.

The Equation drop-down list has a list of well-known equations that you can insert into a math zone.

Using the Equation button to insert a math zone is discoverable, that is, you're likely to find it by browsing the Word ribbons. For example, if you point to the **Equation** button (π) a description of the functionality is displayed along with the keyboard shortcut **Alt + =**. Clicking π (or typing **Alt + =**) inserts a math zone. Clicking the word **Equation** displays a drop-down list of well-known equations you can insert. You can also add new equations to this list for your convenience.

Next to the **Equation** button (π) is the **Symbol** (Ω) button. Clicking the **Symbol** button displays a dialog box with symbols you can insert. More interestingly, click the **More symbols** option to display the **Symbol** dialog box for the current font. To see the characters in the *Cambria Math* font, for example, change the font *to Cambria Math* and admire the large number of math symbols available. Here's a sampling:

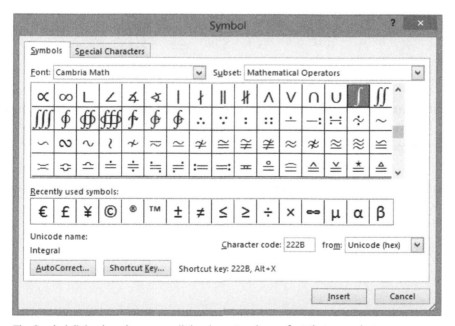

The Symbol dialog box shows you all the characters in any font that you select.

Use the math tab

When the text selection is inside a math zone, the **Equation Tools** (math) tab appears on the ribbon.

This math tab offers many mathematical objects and symbols that can be inserted into a math zone. It aids in making such objects and symbols discoverable. If you point to the symbols, tool tips are displayed revealing control words you can type to enter the symbols from the keyboard.

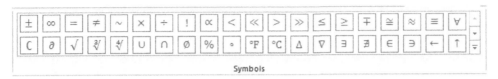

Symbols

For example, typing **\alpha** enters a math-italic α. You can change or add to these control words as described in the section on math autocorrect.

Incorporate math structures

The right side of the math ribbon contains the math **Structures** gallery.

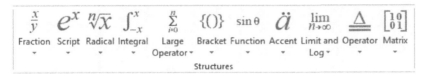

Structures

You can click the buttons in the structures gallery to get menus of math structures. For example, if you click the $\frac{x}{y}$ button, you'll see a menu of fraction templates and common fractions that you can insert into your math zone.

> **Note** As you may notice in the above paragraph, the built-up fraction in line adds extra vertical space. To avoid this, use a linear fraction as in x / y.

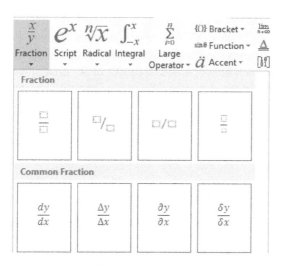

In the next subsection, methods are provided for entering math text more quickly with the keyboard. In addition, you can use the ribbon itself with the keyboard: type **Alt → J** to get to the ribbon followed by highlighted letters for the various options. For example, **Alt → J → E → F** displays the fraction structures menu. You can navigate the menu by using the arrow keys and insert a structure into the document by pressing the **Enter** key.

Enter algebraic expressions

Given Unicode's strong support for mathematics, how much better can a plain-text encoding of mathematical expressions look using Unicode? The most well-known ASCII encoding of such expressions is TeX, so we'll use it for comparison. Notwithstanding the phenomenal success of TeX in the science and engineering communities, a casual glance at its representations of mathematical expressions reveals that these expressions do not look very much like the expressions they represent. Unicode allows you to represent mathematical expressions in what we call the *linear format*. Using this format in Word is very powerful because you can easily enter and edit mathematical text in built-up form.

This section introduces the linear format with fractions, subscripts, superscripts, square roots, and mathematical functions and concludes with a subsection on how the ASCII space character **U+0020** is used to build up one construct at a time. The ASCII space character is a key command that makes the linear format ideal for inputting mathematical formulae. For a more detailed discussion, see the *linear format paper* at *http://www.unicode.org/notes/tn28/UTN28-PlainTextMath-v3.pdf*.

One way to specify a fraction linearly is LaTeX's **\frac{numerator}{denominator}**. The braces { } are not printed when the fraction is built up. These simple rules immediately produce *plain text* that is unambiguous, but looks quite different from the corresponding mathematical notation, thereby making it more difficult to read. Instead, we define a simple operand to consist of all consecutive letters and decimal digits; that is, a span of alphanumeric characters. As such, a simple numerator or denominator is terminated by most nonalphanumeric characters, including, for example, mathematical operators, and the space. The fraction operator is given by the usual slash (/) on your keyboard. So the simple built-up fraction

$$\frac{abc}{d}$$

appears in linear format as **abc/d**. To force a display of a normal-size linear fraction, you can use a backslash followed by a slash (\/).

For more complicated operands—such as those that include operators—parentheses ( ), brackets [ ], or braces { } can be used to enclose the desired character combinations. If parentheses are used and the outermost parentheses are preceded and followed by operators, those parentheses are not displayed in built-up form. So the plain text **(a + c)/d** displays as

$$\frac{a+c}{d}$$

In practice, this approach leads to plain text that is easier to read than, for example, LaTeX's **\frac{a + c}{d}**, because in many cases, parentheses are not needed, while TeX requires braces { }. To force the display of the outermost parentheses, you can enclose them, in turn, within parentheses, which then become the outermost parentheses. For example, **((a + c))/d** displays as

$$\frac{(a+c)}{d}$$

A really neat feature of this notation is that the plain text is, in fact, often a legitimate mathematical notation in its own right, so it's relatively easy to read.

Subscripts and superscripts are a bit trickier, but they're still quite readable. Specifically, you introduce a subscript by a subscript operator, which is displayed as the ASCII underscore _ as in TeX. A simple subscript operand consists of the string of one or more alphanumeric characters. For example, a pair of subscripts, such as $\delta_{\mu\nu}$ is written as **δ_μν** Similarly, superscripts are introduced by a superscript operator, which we display as a caret (^) as in TeX. So **a^b** means a^b.

As for fractions, compound subscripts and superscripts include expressions within parentheses, square brackets, and curly braces. So $\delta_{\mu+\nu}$ is entered as **δ_(μ + ν)**. Another kind of compound subscript is a subscripted subscript, which works using right-to-left associativity; for example, **a_b_c** stands for a_{b_c}. Similarly **a^b^c** stands for a^{b^c}. Parentheses are needed for constructs such as a subscripted superscript like a^{b_c}, which is given by **a^(b_c)**, since **a^b_c** displays as a_c^b (as does **a_c^b**).

While on the subject of subscripts and superscripts, let's discuss summation and integral, which often have upper and lower limits. You can enter summation and integral by using the structures on the math ribbon, but it's easier to just type them in. In TeX and the Microsoft Office linear format, summation and integral are entered in the same way as superscripts and subscripts, respectively. For example, to enter

$$\int_0^\infty e^{-x^2}\,dx = \frac{\sqrt{\pi}}{2}$$

type **\int_0^\infty e^-x^2 dx** $\boxed{\rightarrow}$ **=\sqrt(\pi)/2**, where $\boxed{\rightarrow}$ is the right arrow key. As soon as you type the underscore (_), **\int** is autocorrected into the integral sign $\int$. There are some *spaces* in this linear-format text that do conversions, too. The first space autocorrects **\infty** to ∞, and the second builds up the integral and leaves the insertion point inside the integrand. Typing **e^-x^2 <space> <space>** builds up to e^{-x^2}. The $\boxed{\rightarrow}$ moves the insertion point outside of the integrand. Word really wants to know what's in the integrand (or summand for a summation, and so forth) to allow for better typography. Knowing the integrand is useful in case you want to compute the value of the integral using the math plug-in. The left parenthesis converts the **\sqrt** into $\sqrt{}$ and the slash (**/**) builds up the $\sqrt{\pi}$.

Similarly, to enter

$$\sum_{i=1}^n n = \frac{n(n+1)}{2}$$

type **\sum_(i=1)^n n** $\boxed{\rightarrow}$ **=n(n+1)/2<space>**. Hence such *n*-ary expressions are entered in almost the same way as subscripts and superscripts.

These formulas are displayed in display mode; that is, by themselves on a line. In display mode, summation limits traditionally appear above and below the summation sign, whereas inline, they become subscripts and superscripts as in $\sum_{i=1}^n n = \frac{n(n+1)}{2}$. Also note that the letters in the inline fraction are the same size as the subscripts and superscripts, which makes the formula fit into the line more easily. Displayed integral limits are usually subscripts and superscripts, but you can overrule this choice by using the **Equations Options** menu described in the "Use and modify math autocorrect" section later in this chapter.

Note that entering equations using the keyboard doesn't require the mouse and is generally faster than using the mouse once you know the names of the variables.

Modify math spacing

Spacing in mathematical expressions involves well-defined rules. For example, in the expression **a+b=c**, a good math display engine automatically inserts 4/18 em space on each side of the binary operator plus (+), and 5/18 em space on each side of the relational operator equal (=). Thus, typing **a+b=c** in a math zone displays as $a + b = c$. Proper spacing between two characters depends on the properties of each character. Section 3.15 of the linear format paper summarizes the rules for the most common situations. This paper can be found at *http://www.unicode.org/notes/tn28/UTN28-PlainTextMath-v3.pdf*.

Users often realize that there should be extra spacing around operators, but generally they don't know how much, nor do they realize that a good display engine inserts the correct amount automatically. So the users type in spaces thereby compromising the quality of the typography. This really upsets authors of fine math display engines like TeX and the LineServices engine used by Word and RichEdit. The authors of these engines prefer to ignore such user spacing altogether in order to reduce the user's chances of creating ugly typography that reflects badly on the layout program. In fact, in TeX the ASCII space **U+0020** is used only to terminate control words like **\alpha**. All other spaces are ignored in math zones.

In Word 2013, spaces are used to terminate control words and to build up expressions, but it seems unfriendly to categorically ignore all other spaces. In some scenarios, the space can even be used to control which kind of behavior a particular character may have. For example, the single number **10,100** is entered with no space following the comma, but the sequence **10, 100** has a space after the comma and means two numbers instead of one.

Office math has a nice compromise to handle the knee-jerk tendency of some users to tarnish the typography by sticking unnecessary spaces around binary and relational operators. Basically, when a user types something like **a<space>+<space>b**, the formula autobuildup program checks to see if the layout engine would automatically insert space where the user has typed space. If so, the user's space is deleted. The user can choose to go back and insert more space anyway, but the typical case looks essentially the same as the user expected and the results look great instead of embarrassing. Of course, if the user navigates across the expression with left/right arrow keys, he can easily see that such spaces were deleted.

The moral of all this is that you shouldn't type spaces into a math zone unless you're building something up, choosing a different behavior for a character like a comma, or because you really do need more space than what is automatically provided by the math engine. It's a lesson one needs to learn, much as people who were used to typewriters had to learn not to type the return key at the end of every line.

Make selections in math zones

We've tacitly assumed you know what the selection object is in a Word document. This subsection describes the selection object a little more formally and describes how it behaves in math zones. The simplest form of the selection is the insertion point identified by a blinking cursor, which is the location in which characters appear when you type. Such a selection is degenerate because it doesn't select any text. If you drag the mouse over a character or type **Shift + →**, the selection becomes nondegenerate, and selects the character. The blinking cursor is gone and the selected character is highlighted. Selected text can be copied, deleted, and formatted. For example, typing **Ctrl + B** or clicking the **B** button on the **Home** tab of the ribbon toggles the Bold property on and off for the selected text.

Selection of text in a math zone follows some special rules concerning built-up math objects, such as fractions and superscripts. First, some background on how these objects are stored will help to clarify the rules. In memory, math objects start with a special 16-bit character and end with a different 16-bit character. An argument of an object ends with a special separator character when followed by another argument, and it ends with the end-of-object character if the argument is the last one of the object.

Selection of text in a math zone works the same way as it does in normal text as long as one of the three math-object delimiter characters isn't selected. As soon as one of the characters is selected, the whole object is automatically selected. For example, if you type **Shift + →** at the end of the numerator of a fraction, you attempt to select the numerator's delimiter, which causes the whole fraction to be selected. Similarly, if you type **Shift + →** at the start of a math object or **Shift + ←** at the end of a math object, the whole object is selected. The math object is also selected if you press **Delete** at the start of the object or **Backspace** at the end the object. A second **Delete** or **Backspace** then deletes the object. This behavior exists so that you don't delete things by mistake. If you do so anyway, you can always undo your deletion by typing **Ctrl + Z**.

You can select from outside a math zone partway into a math zone unless the math zone consists of a single math object. So if normal text precedes the equation $E = mc^2$, you can select that text along with, for example, E. As such, the math zone isn't treated as a single math object because math zones are identified by a character format effect like bold rather than by start and end delimiter characters. Nevertheless, it's desirable to make it seem as though math zones are delimited by characters so that you can easily insert something immediately before and after a math zone, and at the beginning and end of a math zone.

To illustrate how this works, suppose the insertion point (IP) is at the start of a line immediately following a displayed equation. Typing the left arrow key moves the IP before the ASCII CR (**U+000D**) that terminates the displayed equation, but the nice acetate rectangle that surrounds an equation when the IP is inside the equation does not appear. Even though the IP immediately follows the math zone, it's not in the math zone. At this point, if you type a character, it won't be in the math zone, and the displayed equation will be converted to an inline equation with correspondingly compressed typography.

Pressing the left arrow key another time moves the IP into the math zone and the acetate rectangle appears. This left arrow key didn't bypass any characters; it just changed the selection IP to have the math zone character formatting property. Consequently, if you now type a character it will be inside the displayed equation and will be formatted according to math-zone rules. In summary, to move the IP from outside a math zone to inside the zone or vice versa, press the appropriate arrow key. You'll find that no character is bypassed, and only the selection's math-zone property is changed; therefore, it feels as though math zones have start and end delimiters even though they don't.

To create equations with the Word 2013 equation editor

Equation

1. Create a new line for the equation, and then insert a tab on the line (**Ctrl+Tab**).

2. On the **Insert** tab, click the drop-down list arrow half of the **Equation** button.

3. Click one of the generic equations (for example, Fourier Series).

4. Insert a tab (**Ctrl+Tab**) on the right side of the equation, outside of the equation box.

> **Note** If the ruler is not visible below the ribbon, on the **View** tab, in the **Show** group, click **Ruler**.

5. Insert a center tab stop (⊥) in the middle of the ruler (at about the 3.25" mark for letter-sized paper) for the equation, and a right (⅃) tab stop at the right margin for the page number.

> **Note** To insert a tab stop, click the tab stop selector ⌐ (under the ribbon, to the left of the ruler) until it changes into the type that you wish to place. Next, click the bottom border of the ruler (and drag left or right, as needed) to place the tab stop.

$$f(x) = a_0 + \sum_{n=1}^{\infty} \left(a_n \cos \frac{n\pi x}{L} + b_n \sin \frac{n\pi x}{L} \right)$$

1¶

> A left tab stop resembles a short "L". Tab stops can be placed anywhere on the ruler. A dotted line will appear below the tab stop during placement, to help with alignment.

Alternatively, you can specify tab stops with exact measurements. Simply right-click the line to which you would like to add a tab stop, click **Paragraph**, and then click **Tabs** to access the dialog box.

This method is more exact, but less intuitive. You can also access the **Paragraph** dialog box through the **Home** tab on the ribbon. Place the cursor on the line in question and click the dialog box launcher (⌐) in the paragraph group.

Tab stops can be inserted through the Tabs dialog box with greater precision.

6. On the **Home** tab of the ribbon, click the button to the lower right of the **Styles** group (⏷), and then click **Create a Style**.

7. Name the style **Equation**, and click **OK**.

Insert Caption

8. Place the cursor at the right side of the equation line, and on the **References** tab, click the **Insert Caption** button.

9. In the **Label** drop-down list, choose **Equation**.

10. Make sure **Exclude label from caption** is selected.

11. Click **OK**.

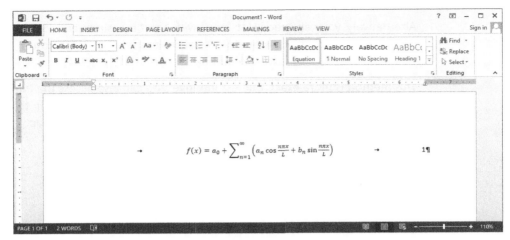

Your equation should appear centered, with the number aligned to the right margin.

12. Select the number, and on the **Insert** tab, click the **Bookmark** button.

Bookmarks work well with fields, and you can use them to directly quote text, even if the source material changes.

13. Type a name for the equation, such as **eqFourierSeries**, and click **Add**. If you will use Bookmarks for other purposes, it is advisable to begin every equation name with *eq*.

14. Insert parentheses around the number.

15. Make sure the cursor is on the equation line, and in the **Style** gallery, click the **Equation** style.

Create advanced equations in Word 2013

You can use the process described in the previous procedure to create equations for which the numbering will automatically update when copied and moved throughout the document. You can modify these equations with a point-and-click approach to easily create equations of virtually limitless complexity by using the buttons on the **Equation** tab of the ribbon. However, you should also be aware that the Word 2013 equation editor offers an alternative input method and other advanced functionality that can greatly increase your productivity.

The primary input method with which you should become acquainted is the *linear format*, which is automatically converted through the *formula buildup* function described in the "Use and modify math autocorrect" section later in this chapter. You can use this linear format to create fractions, subscripts, superscripts, square roots, and other mathematical functions. In addition to the procedures explained later in the chapter, many shortcut codes have been built into the equation editor, which you can use to quickly insert operators, symbols, logic and grouping characters, and more. These shortcut codes are detailed at length in the "Tips and tricks" section later in this chapter.

To create fractions

1. Press **Alt + =** to create an equation field.

2. Type the numerator. (For more complicated numerators involving mathematical operations, enclose with parentheses or brackets.)

3. Type a forward slash, or solidus (**/**).

4. Type the denominator. (For more complicated denominators involving mathematical operations, enclose with parentheses or brackets.)

5. Press the **Spacebar** to convert the fraction through formula buildup.

> **Note** To force the display of parentheses in fractions, enclose them within an additional set of parentheses.

To create superscripts

1. Press **Alt + =** to create an equation field.

2. Type the base text, enclosing with parentheses, if needed.

3. Type a caret symbol (**^**).

4. Type the superscript text. (For more complicated superscripts involving mathematical operations, enclose with parentheses or brackets.)

5. Press the **Spacebar** to convert the superscript through formula buildup.

To create subscripts

1. Press **Alt + =** to create an equation field.

2. Type the base text, enclosing with parentheses, if needed.

3. Type an underscore (_).

4. Type the subscript text. For more complicated subscripts involving mathematical operations, enclose with parentheses or brackets.

5. Press the **Spacebar** to convert the subscript through formula buildup.

> **Note** For compound superscripts and subscripts, simply include the requisite number of carets or underscores. Superscripts and subscripts can even be used together in this way. For example, to create a_{b_c}, simply type **a_b_c**, and press the Spacebar two times to activate formula buildup. To create $a_b{}^c$, simply type **a_(b^c),** and press the Spacebar.

To create full equations

1. Press **Alt + =** to create an equation field.

2. Type the right side of the equation (for example: **\int_0^\infty e^-x^2 dx**).

3. Press the right arrow key, and then type an **equal** sign (=).

4. Type the left side of the equation, for example: **\sqrt(\pi)/2**).

$$\int_0^\infty e^{-x^2}\, dx = \frac{\sqrt{\pi}}{2}$$

> **Note** For nearly all cases, Word 2013 will correctly handle the spacing of equation elements automatically. When you type something such as **a<space>+<space>b**, Word will ignore the spaces and align the expression automatically. If you determine that the spacing still requires adjustment, you can go back and insert extra spaces manually. Generally, you should refrain from inserting spaces unless the appearance is unsatisfactory.

Create and modify matrices

The math ribbon has a few examples of matrices, but you might want more options from to which to choose and also be able to enter them substantially faster, in which case you can use the linear format. For example, a 2x2 matrix is entered by typing **\matrix(...&...@...&...)**, where the ellipses are the contents of the matrix elements. As in TeX, ampersands (&) separate matrix elements. Rows are separated by at signs (@).

You don't have to enter anything in the matrix elements if you're willing to enter them explicitly later. For example, to enter a 4x4 empty matrix, you can type **\matrix(&&&@@@)**. This is missing the ampersands (&) for the second through fourth rows; however, the build-up machinery automatically generates a rectangular matrix with each row containing the same number of elements as the row with the maximum number of elements. So in the case of the 4x4 **\matrix(&&&@@@)**, the first row has four elements and, therefore, each of the three subsequent rows has four elements as well:

$$\begin{matrix} \square & \square & \square & \square \\ \square & \square & \square & \square \\ \square & \square & \square & \square \\ \square & \square & \square & \square \end{matrix}$$

Here the $\square$ character stands for an empty argument placeholder. As soon as you type something on it, it's replaced by what you type. The matrices don't have to be square. A six-element, single row empty matrix is entered by typing **\matrix(&&&&&)**, and a five element, single column empty matrix is entered by typing **\matrix(@@@@)**.

Often you want parentheses surrounding the matrices. You can enter them explicitly as in (**\matrix(&&@@)**), or in Office 2013 you can use the TeX control word **\pmatrix(&&@@)**, which is slightly faster to enter:

The maximum number of elements is 254, so you can enter a 15x15 matrix and a 127x2 matrix without error. If anyone needs larger matrices, we'd like to hear about it. We don't want to allow arbitrarily large matrices because unrealistic test scenarios might grind the machine to a virtual halt.

To create matrices

1. Press **Alt + =** to create an equation field.

2. Type (**\matrix (a1&a2&a3@b1&b2&b3@c1&c2&c3)**), where the ampersand (&) separates column elements and the at sign (@) separates rows.

3. Press the **Spacebar** to convert the parentheses through formula buildup.

$$\begin{pmatrix} a1 & a2 & a3 \\ b1 & b2 & b3 \\ c1 & c2 & c3 \end{pmatrix}$$

> **Note** You can also quickly specify blank matrices with the formula **(\matrix (@@&&))**, which will create a blank 3x3 matrix. Finally, you can use square brackets and curly braces, instead of parenthesis, by replacing them like so: **[\matrix (@@&&)]** or **{\matrix (@@&&)}**.

Create accents

Accents are quite common in mathematical text. For example, in physics you use one-dot to four-dot accents to designate the first through fourth time derivatives, respectively. Primes are often used on integration variables. Transforms can be designated by tildes and averages by overlines. Although accents are usually applied to a single base character, they can, in principle, be applied to any mathematical expression. This differs considerably from natural language accents, which generally apply to a single character. Accordingly, no attempt to handle math accents using fully composed characters was made in Unicode even though most accented characters for natural language have managed to sneak into Unicode as fully composed characters. Instead, for math accents, you need a special accent object that sizes the accent to fit the base.

Because Unicode-combining marks follow the associated base characters, the linear format accent operators do so as well. For example, for ä, one would type **a\ddot** followed by an operator or, if no operator is needed, by two spaces. You can also enter one of the math accent structures on the math ribbon, and then fill in the base and accent. The linear format approach is significantly faster, but not as easily discovered.

To create accents

1. Press **Alt + =** to create an equation field.

2. Type any character.

3. Type **\dot**, **\ddot**, **\tilde**, **\hat**, or any of the shortcuts listed in the "Enter TeX or LaTeX directly" subsections.

4. Press the **Spacebar** bar two times to convert the accent through formula buildup.

> **Note** When adding accents to **i** and **j**, Word removes the dots, even when the base has more than one character. You can force the dots to appear, by entering **i\dot** or **j\dot**. You can also get dotless versions by using **\imath** and **\jmath**.

How to use MathType to create and edit equations

If you find that the built-in equation editor is not your cup of tea, or you already have a preferred external editor, you will find that the instructions in this chapter are perfectly compatible with such tools. For instructive purposes, we have chosen MathType as an example because many journal publishers prefer that equations be formatted in MathType. If you're looking for an external equation editor, we recommend that you give MathType a try.

Excellent resources for learning the intricacies of MathType are available both with MathType and on the web. After you have created a basic equation, follow the instructions in the following procedure to integrate the equation into your template.

To create an equation with MathType

1. Create a new line for the equation.

Σ Inline   2. On the **MathType** tab, click the **Inline** button.

3. Create an equation in the MathType editor, and then click the **Close** button, or click **File ⇒ Close and Return to DocumentName.docx** (where **DocumentName** is the name of your current document).

4. Click **Yes** in the dialog box.

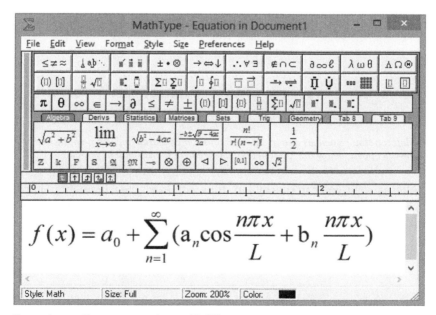

To create equations, you can also use MathType.

Although MathType does offer functionality to number and cross-reference equations, using it can severely limit the interoperability of your documents. Therefore, it is highly recommended that you use the procedure for numbering and referencing equations with the Word 2013 equation editor, which are duplicated here, for convenience:

To add the caption and format the equation

1. Insert a tab (**Ctrl+Tab**) on both sides of the equation.

> **Note** If the ruler is not visible below the ribbon, on the **View** tab, in the **Show** group, click **Ruler**.

2. Insert a center tab stop (⊥) in the middle of the ruler (about the 3.25" mark for letter-sized paper) for the equation and a right (⊿) tab stop at the right margin for the page number.

> **Note** To insert a tab stop, click the tab stop selector ⌐ (under the ribbon, to the left of the ruler) until it changes into the type that you want to place. Next, click the bottom border of the ruler (and drag left or right, as needed) to place the tab stop.
>
>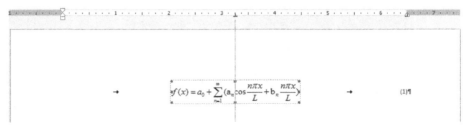
>
> *A left tab stop resembles a short "L". Tab stops can be placed anywhere on the ruler. A dotted line will appear below the tab stop during placement to help with alignment.*
>
> Alternatively, you can specify tab stops with exact measurements. Simply right-click the line to which you would like to add a tab stop, click **Paragraph**, and then click **Tabs** to access the dialog box.

This method is more exact, but less intuitive. You can also access the **Paragraph** dialog box through the **Home** tab on the ribbon. Place the cursor on the line in question and click the dialog box launcher in the paragraph group (⌐).

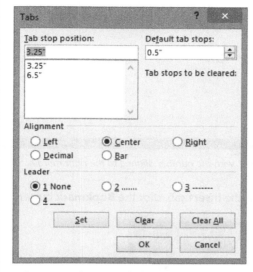

Tab stops can be inserted through the Tabs dialog box with greater precision.

3. On the **Home** tab of the ribbon, click the **More** button (⩧) to the lower right of the **Styles** group, and then click **Create a Style**.

4. Name the style **Equation**, and click **OK**.

Insert Caption

5. Place the cursor at the right side of the equation line, and on the **Reference** tab, click the **Insert Caption** button.

6. In the **Label** list, choose **Equation**.

7. Make sure **Exclude label from caption** is selected.

8. Click **OK**.

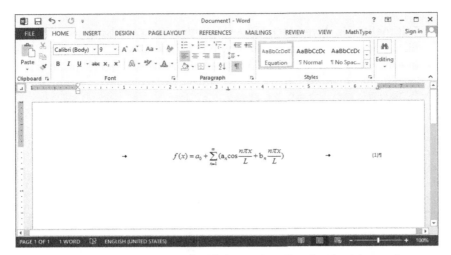

Your equation should appear centered, with the number aligned to the right margin.

9. Select the number, and then on the **Insert** tab, click the **Bookmark** button.

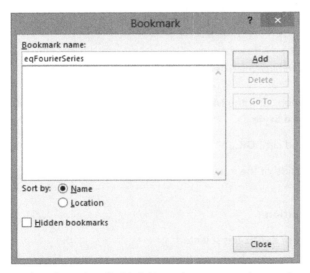

Bookmarks work well with fields, and you can use them to directly quote text, regardless if the source material changes.

10. Type a name for the equation, such as **eqFourierSeries**, and click **Add**. If you will use Bookmarks for other purposes, it is advisable to begin every equation name with *eq*.

11. Insert parentheses around the number.

12. Make sure the cursor is on the equation line, and in the **Style** gallery, click the **Equation** style.

How to cross-reference equations

As you are probably know by now, cross-references in Word 2013 are commonly generated by creating references to the caption labels. This method works because the label is the first text on the line, followed immediately by the number. In the case of properly formatted equations, the number appears near the end of the line, preceded by the equation and formatting characters. As a result, any cross-references to **Only label and number** will inadvertently include this unwanted text, as well.

In the previous section, you learned the first half of the procedure for avoiding this complication: using bookmarks to link directly to the equation number. In this section, you will learn the simple procedure for creating references to these bookmarks. As you might imagine, it's almost identical to the procedure for other elements, and it works just as flawlessly.

> **Note** It is also possible to use a **Style Separator**, which is available via the **Customize the ribbon** and **Customize the Quick Access Toolbar** dialog boxes.
>
> First, place a **Style Separator** between the equation and the number, and then insert a cross-reference to the number. Notice that the cross-reference dialog box includes only the number. Unfortunately, this can make choosing the correct number a challenge; therefore, you should use the bookmark method, instead.

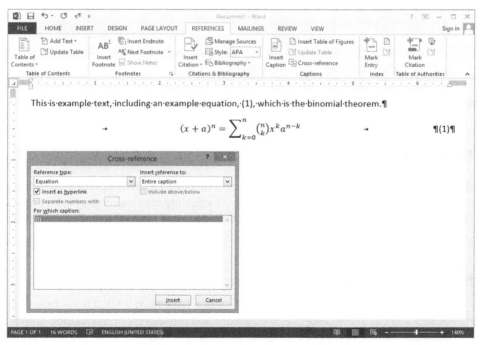

Although Style Separators are a viable alternative to bookmarks, the cross-reference dialog box will not include identifying information about the equations—just the numbers.

To cross-reference an equation

Cross-
reference

1. Click **Insert** ⇒ **Cross-Reference**.

2. Under **Reference Type,** click **Bookmark**.

3. Clear **Insert as Hyperlink**, unless you have a strong reason to have a hyperlink in your document.

4. Under **Insert Reference To,** click **Bookmark Text**.

5. Pick the desired bookmark from the list, and then click **Insert**.

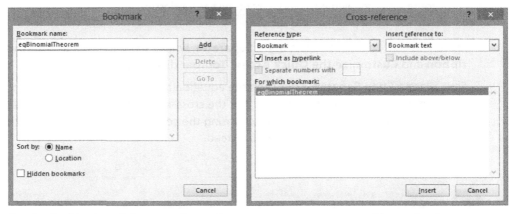

By using bookmarks and the cross-reference feature, you can create an extensible template for your equations, which will adjust the numbering automatically.

To update the equation, press **Ctrl+A** and then **F9,** and be sure to save your document as well.

How to alter equations

The variety of alterations your team might make to your equations depends upon the requirements of your audience; however, two primary variations most frequently occur: switching from single to double columns in the manuscript, and switching from single numbering to dual numbering (for example, changing from 1 to 1.1).

Switch from single to dual columns

Manually switching from a single column to a double column (and back) is not a trivial task if you have many equations because the centering of equations and the alignment of equation numbers does not adjust automatically. In order to switch automatically, change the settings for the equation style.

To switch to double columns

Columns

1. On the **Page Layout** tab, click **Columns** ⇒ **More Columns**.

2. In the dialog box that appears, choose the column settings for your template.

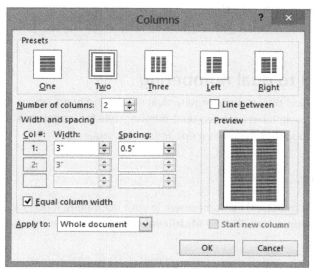

In the Columns dialog box, you can specify details such as the individual column width, in addition to the spacing between columns. You can use section breaks to switch between layouts within a single document.

3. Place the cursor on the line of one of the equations.

4. Move the center tab stop (⊥) to the center of the ruler in the column.

5. Move the right-justified tab (⅃) to the right margin of the column.

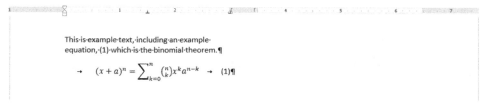

This·is·example·text,·including·an·example·
equation,·(1)·which·is·the·binomial·theorem.¶

$$(x + a)^n = \sum_{k=0}^{n} \binom{n}{k} x^k a^{n-k} \quad (1)¶$$

You can use tab stops to update the alignment of your equations for multicolumn formats.

To update the equation style

1. Highlight the new equation.

2. In the **Style** gallery, right-click the **Equation** style.

3. Click **Update Equation to match selection**.

4. Click **OK**.

Switch from standard to dual numbering

Long manuscripts such as books and dissertations require dual numbering of equations (in addition to figures and tables). In order to switch between the dual-number style for longer manuscripts and a single-number journal style throughout the manuscript, follow this sequence.

To switch to dual numbering

1. Make sure you are using a multilevel list somewhere in your document. If not, locate the nearest heading, and on the **Home** tab, click the **Multilevel List** button. Then select a list that uses heading styles.

2. Create a new line.

3. Click **References** ⇒ **Insert Caption**.

4. Select the **eq** label.

5. Click the **Numbering** button.

6. Select your preferences for the appearance of the caption (such as single or dual number, and dash or period between the numbers).

7. Click **OK** in all dialog boxes.

8. Delete the new caption and the line.

9. Press **Ctrl+A** → **F9** to update the cross-references.

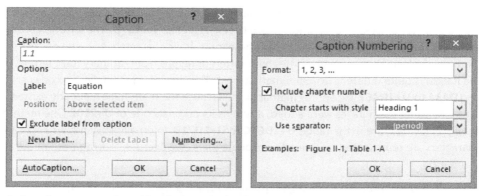

By inserting a new caption with a dual-numbering format, Word 2013 will automatically update the numbering style for all of your document's captions.

Tips and tricks

If you have a lot of math in your manuscripts, your team should probably invest time in learning MathType and Word keyboard shortcuts. The following section provides a list of frequently used shortcuts and features from both programs.

Use mathematical bold, italic, and sans serif

Mathematical text styles play an important role in distinguishing variables from one another. For example, the math-italic H is a different variable from the math-script $\mathcal{H}$, and both might appear in the same equation with distinct meanings. Mathematical variables represented by Latin and lower-case Greek letters are usually displayed in italic. Vectors are often displayed in upright boldface. Word allows the user to control and change these choices with the italic and bold formatting buttons on the Home tab of the ribbon or with the italic and bold keyboard shortcuts (**Ctrl + I** and **Ctrl + B**). A basic principal is that in a math zone, letters are the only characters that are affected by these attributes. Operators like plus (**+**) and equal (**=**) and delimiters like brackets (**[ ]**) are not changed by the states of the italic and bold buttons. Such characters are always rendered as upright, normal-weight characters in a math zone. The Unicode *Mathematical Alphanumeric Symbols* are defined in the **U+1D400** to **U+1D7FF** block except for a few characters that were defined in the *Letterlike Symbols* block before the complete set was added.

We'll start with italic letters. If the italic button is on, as it normally is in a math zone, and you type a Latin letter (A–Z or a–z) or lowercase Greek letter like **\beta** (β), the letter is converted to the corresponding Unicode math-italic letter. These math-italic characters have the correct spacing for mathematical variables and sometimes have different glyphs from ordinary italic letters. In particular, the italic *a* is quite different from the math italic a. The Unicode math italic A-z codes are in the range **U+1D434** to **U+1D467**, except for math italic h. Because the math italic h already existed in Unicode when the other math italics were added, it retains its original code of **U+210E**. The math-italic lowercase Greek letters are in the range **U+1D6FC** to **U+1D71B**. Internally in Windows applications, these characters are represented by Unicode surrogate pairs (see Sec. 3.8, "Surrogates," of the Unicode Standard).

You can see the code for a character by typing **Alt + X** immediately after the character. This keyboard shortcut replaces the character by its code. Typing **Ctrl + Z** undoes this transformation or you can type **Alt + X** again, because **Alt + X** toggles between code and character. For example, if you type **Alt + X** after a math italic b (b) the b will be replaced by its code **1D44F**. Typing **Alt + X** again, replaces the **1D44F** by the math italic b.

If you want to convert math-italic characters to upright (nonitalic) characters, select the character, and then click the italic button to the off state or type **Ctrl + I**, which toggles the italic state to off. Clicking it back to the on state (or typing another **Ctrl + I**) converts the characters back to math italic. You can also get upright characters by enclosing them in double quotes. For example, **a_"coh"** builds up to a_{coh}, where coh might be an abbreviation for *coherent*. Such an abbreviation doesn't represent the product of the letters c, o, and h, and hence should be displayed with upright letters rather than math italic.

The **Bold** button and **Ctrl + B** work similarly to the **Italic** button and **Ctrl + I**, respectively, in toggling the math bold attribute for Latin and Greek letters. For regular roman-style characters you can use these buttons and keyboard shortcuts to switch between upright, italic, bold, and bold italic. You can use the **Bold** button and keyboard shortcut to switch between Fraktur and bold Fraktur and between Script and bold Script. Examples of such characters are $\mathfrak{G}$, $\mathfrak{G}$, $\mathcal{G}$, $\mathcal{G}$.

Although the use of italic and bold in math zones differs from that in normal text, it feels quite natural and it facilitates editing these properties of mathematical variables.

Most mathematical documents and books use fonts with *serifs*, such as Times Roman; however, mathematical expressions can also be displayed with *sans-serif* letters. In fact, sans-serif letters are used sufficiently often in mathematical typography that six sets of them are included in the *Unicode Mathematical Alphanumeric Symbols*. Further, rationale for these Unicode symbols is given in Section 2.2 of *Unicode Technical Report #25, "Unicode Support for Mathematics."*

Using sans-serif variables in Microsoft Office math zones isn't as simple as toggling italic on and off by using the italic tool or the **Ctrl + I** keyboard shortcut. The sans-serif letters A, **A**, *A*, and **A** have the codes **1D5A0**, **1D5D4**, **1D608**, and **1D63C**, respectively (see *Mathematical Alphanumeric Symbols*). You can enter them by their codes either directly into a document by using **Alt + X**, or you can add them to your math autocorrect file also by using **Alt + X**.

Create equation arrays

To align equations relative to each other, you can use an equation array, such as

$$\begin{aligned} 10x + 3y &= 2 \\ 3x + 13y &= 4 \end{aligned}$$

This has the linear format **\eqarray (10&x+&3&y=2@3&x+&13&y=4)**. Here the meaning of the ampersands alternate between *align* and *spacer*, with an implied spacer at the start of the line. Each odd **&** is an alignment point and each even **&** marks a place where space is added if necessary. This convention is used in AmSTeX, the American Mathematical Society's version of TeX.

The following is a linear format for a more complicated example:

■(Z-3&x_1-&5&x_2-&6&x_3&&&=&0 @

2&x_1+&&x_2+&&x_3+x_4&&&=&4 @

&x_1+&2&x_2+&&x_3+&x_5&&=&4 @

&x_1+&&x_2+&2&x_3+&&x_6&=&4 @

&x_1+&&x_2+&&x_3+&&&x_7=&3)

which builds up to

$$\begin{aligned}
Z - 3x_1 - 5x_2 - 6x_3 &&&&&= 0 \\
2x_1 + x_2 + x_3 + x_4 &&&&&= 4 \\
x_1 + 2x_2 + x_3 + &x_5 &&&= 4 \\
x_1 + x_2 + 2x_3 + && x_6 &&= 4 \\
x_1 + x_2 + x_3 + &&& x_7 &= 3
\end{aligned}$$

Modify equation alignment and breaking

The equation array gives substantial power in displaying mathematical text with precise alignment and line breaking, but it does require a fair amount of effort from the user and doesn't automatically rewrap if the page width gets too small. Long equations often do not fit on a single line and methods are needed to break them up for display on multiple lines. Word offers two approaches: automatic and manual line breaking. A related feature is alignment of multiple equations, such as aligning the equal signs of a group of equations. This section describes all three subjects.

Automatic line breaking occurs when an equation doesn't fit on a single line and user-defined breaks do not exist. This kind of line breaking is essential for viewing in rendering environments like webpages that can be resized and don't generally require the panning and scrolling used by fixed-width displays such as for pdfs.

The algorithm used for automatic breaking is similar to that for optimal line breaks in a paragraph: various possible line breaks are assigned penalty values and the line breaks with the minimum total penalty are chosen. Binary and relational operators outside of built-up functions have the lowest penalties, whereas these operators inside built-up functions like parenthesized expressions have higher penalties. In addition, the distance from the maximum break point is an important factor in the breaking formula. Each line break starts a new line at a document-specified indentation. Such breaking is effective, but it might not be the most aesthetically satisfying.

Users who want more pleasing line breaking can right-click a binary or relational operator and choose the **Insert Manual Break** option. Three document-level possibilities exist: **break before, break after,** and **duplicate**. In the United States, mathematical typography is almost always *break before*—that is, the operator chosen starts the new line. But some locales prefer another option. In particular, the duplicate option (display operator at the end of the broken line and at the start of the new line) is popular in Russian mathematical typography.

After such a line break is selected, the user can press the **Tab** key to tab into the position of a binary or relational operator on the line above. Each successive **Tab** key aligns to the next binary/relational operator on the first line. Such operators can be inside parenthesized expressions, even if the expression ends up spanning several lines. The parentheses (or other brackets) are sized to fit the total expression within, in spite of the line breaks.

For example, in the equation

$$\pi_2(x, p_i) = x_2 \left(1 - \frac{2^1}{3} - \frac{2^1}{5} + \frac{2^2}{3 \cdot 5} - \frac{2^1}{7} + \frac{2^2}{3 \cdot 7} + \frac{2^2}{5 \cdot 7} - \frac{2^3}{3 \cdot 5 \cdot 7} - \frac{2^1}{11} \right.$$
$$+ \frac{2^2}{3 \cdot 11} + \frac{2^2}{5 \cdot 11} - \frac{2^3}{3 \cdot 5 \cdot 11} + \frac{2^2}{7 \cdot 11} - \frac{2^3}{3 \cdot 7 \cdot 11}$$
$$\left. - \frac{2^3}{5 \cdot 7 \cdot 11} + \frac{2^4}{3 \cdot 5 \cdot 7 \cdot 11} - \cdots \pm \frac{2^i}{p_1 p_2 \cdots p_i} \right)$$

the second line begins with a plus (+) that has been assigned a manual break. To move this plus (+) underneath the first minus on the first line, two tabs were typed after the manual break was assigned. The first tab moved the leading plus (+) under the equal (=) and the second under the minus (-). The leading minus in the third line has the same treatment. Naturally, if the window width is made too small, additional automatic breaks can occur that don't look as nice.

A common scenario is grouping several related equations aligned at particular equal signs or other relational operators. To do this, separate the equations not by the usual **Enter** key, but by **Shift + Enter**, which is a special soft break that does not terminate the paragraph. Next, select the desired operators to be aligned with one another by choosing the **Align at this Character** option for each. The operators will line up precisely, or you can select the equations, right-click, and choose the **Align at =** option.

In this way, you can line up *Maxwell's equations* nicely as

$$\nabla \cdot \mathbf{B} = 0$$
$$\nabla \cdot \mathbf{D} = \rho_{\text{free}}$$
$$\nabla \times \mathbf{E} = -\frac{\partial \mathbf{B}}{\partial t}$$
$$\nabla \times \mathbf{H} = \mathbf{J}_{\text{free}} + \frac{\partial \mathbf{D}}{\partial t}$$

Include typographical niceties

To get even better typography, Word offers facilities for *tweaking* the spacing in equations.

Consider the equation

$$\frac{1}{2\pi} \int_0^{2\pi} \frac{d\theta}{a + b \sin \theta} = \frac{1}{\sqrt{a^2 - b^2}}$$

In this equation, there is a little too much room between the upper limit 2π and the integrand. You can pull the integrand to the left under the π by *smashing* the width of the π. Inside the upper limit, type **\hsmash \pi**, and the π is displayed, but has no horizontal width, as in

$$\frac{1}{2\pi} \int_0^{2\pi} \frac{d\theta}{a + b \sin \theta} = \frac{1}{\sqrt{a^2 - b^2}}$$

Another example is

$$\sqrt{x} + \sqrt{y}$$

The $\sqrt{y}$ is taller than $\sqrt{x}$ because the y has a descender. It would look better if we "smashed" the y descender by typing **\sqrt\dsmash y**.

By doing so, both square roots have the same size, as in

$$\sqrt{x} + \sqrt{y}$$

These smashes are examples of the *phantom* object. This object can display its argument as in the smashes, or it can hide the argument while occupying space with one or more dimensions of the argument. With phantom objects, you can create spacing based on the exact size of an expression, which is not generally possible using simple spaces.

For example, the equation array

$$10x + 3y = 2$$
$$3x + 13y = 4$$

can be entered as two separate equations with horizontal phantoms for the two 1s as in **10x+\phantom 1 3y=2** followed by **\phantom 1 3x+13y=4**. To reproduce exactly the same vertical spacing, separate the equations by using **Shift + Enter**, rather than just **Enter**. This keeps the equations in the same field, eliminating the standard text paragraph space before and after.

Create prescripts

Special parenthesized syntax can be used to form *prescripts*—that is, subscripts and superscripts that precede their base. Variables can have both prescripts and postscripts (ordinary subscripts and super-scripts). The **Script** button on the **Equation Tools** tab reveals some potential combinations, including a prescript template.

In general, you can use the TeX-like syntax to create prescripts. To do so, just type a subscript and/or a superscript not preceded by a base and then follow it with a character to be used as the base.

For example, **_c^b a** creates the prescripted variable $_c^b a$.

> **Note** If a variable precedes the prescript, you also need to precede the prescript with a space.

A common use of prescripts is for the confluent hypergeometric functions, such as $_1F_2$. This can be input as **_1 F_2** or as **(_1^)F_2**.

Additional steps are required to make $_1F_2$ appear correctly. The prescript object has a superscript and a subscript, while the post subscript object has only a subscript. This leads to two complications.

First, if you put nothing in the superscript, it displays as ▯, although that character will not print. To eliminate it, you can enter a zero-width space (**U+200B**), which you can type as **\zwsp**. This changes $_1^{\square}F$ into $_1F$.

Second, because the prescript object allows vertical space for the superscript, even with the **\zwsp**, the presubscript is just a little lower than the postsubscript. To lower the postsubscript, add a **\zwsp**, as in

    _1^\zwsp F_1^\zwsp

The following are large versions of both cases, which reveal that the 2 on the left is just slightly higher than the 2 on the right:

$$_1F_2 \quad _1F_2$$

Use math context menus

A convenient method for editing mathematical text in the equation editor is through the use of *math context menus*. These menus are displayed when you right-click an equation in Word 2013. In addition to the usual Font and Paragraph options, you will see options relevant to the math object that is clicked. For example, if you point the mouse at a stacked fraction, the context menu includes entries to change to a skewed or linear fraction and to remove the fraction bar. If you point the mouse at an accented character, you'll see an option to remove the accent.

Of course, you can make these changes by returning to the linear format, making the appropriate edits, and returning to the professional format. This approach is a general method for making low-level changes; however, you can often save time by using the appropriate context menu options.

Table 6-1 summarizes the math context menus that could appear when using Word 2013.

Table 6-1 Word 2013 math context menu options

Object	Context menu options
Accent	Remove accent
Bar	Switch between overbar and underbar Remove bar
Box	Increase/decrease argument size
BorderBox	Hide/show (top/left/bottom/right) border Add/remove (horizontal/vertical/top-left-diagonal/ bottom-left-diagonal) strike
Brackets (delimiters)	Insert/delete argument before/after Stretch delimiters, match delimiters Hide/show left/right delimiter
Equation array	Insert row before/after Delete row Align array at top row, center, or bottom row
Fraction	Change to skewed/linear/stacked Remove/replace fraction bar
LeftSubSup	Make into subsup Increase/decrease argument size
Limit	Switch between upper and lower limit Remove limit Change limit size
Math zone	Build down/up—that is, Linear or Professional
Matrix	Insert row/column before/after Delete row/column Show/hide empty-argument placeholders Set row/column spacing Align matrix at top row, center, or bottom row Align column left/center/right

Object	Context menu options
n-ary	Change limit location Hide/show upper/lower empty limit place holder Grow with content
Radical	Remove radical Hide/show empty degree place holder
Group character	Display group (horizontal stretch) character above/below Remove group character
Subscript/superscript	Delete script Increase/decrease script size
SubSup	Align subscript and superscript Make into left subsup Increase/decrease script size

In addition, if the Microsoft Math graphing calculator add-in is installed, right-clicking on a formula gives you context menu options that Microsoft Mathematics 4.0 is able to perform on the formula. Select an option and a window appears with the results and offers the possibility to insert them into your document.

Use the Math Input Panel

Windows 7 introduced a math handwriting recognition program called the *Math Input Panel*. With this applet, you can enter mathematical text by using a pen or a mouse. It recognizes what you enter and displays the result by using RichEdit and looks as it does in Word. You copy the results to Word, Mathematica, or any other application that reads *Presentation MathML*. For example, here's an image showing a handwritten entry of the Pythagorean Theorem:

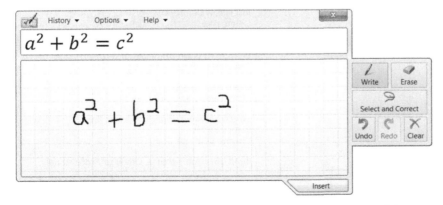

Clicking the **Insert** tab, switching back to Word (**Alt + Tab** is a useful way to switch back), and typing **Ctrl + V** to insert, we have

$$a^2 + b^2 = c^2$$

To find the Math Input Panel in Windows 8, press the **Windows** key and then type the word **math**. You'll see an icon for it. If you like, right-click the icon, and choose the option to pin it to your **Start Screen**.

Use the math graphing calculator

The Microsoft Mathematics *Add-in* for Word and Microsoft OneNote makes it easy to simplify, solve, calculate, and graph your equations in 2-D or 3-D. With the add-in installed, your technical paper becomes alive. For example, your paper may have graphs of the formula, but a reader might want graphs for a different set of parameters. The reader can simply right-click a formula and a context menu appears that includes options that Microsoft Mathematics is able to perform on the formula. Select an option and a window appears with the results and offers the possibility to insert them into your Word document.

For example, right-click the formula

$$z = e^{-\left(x^2 + y^2\right)}$$

and select the **Graph 3D** option. This displays a figure.

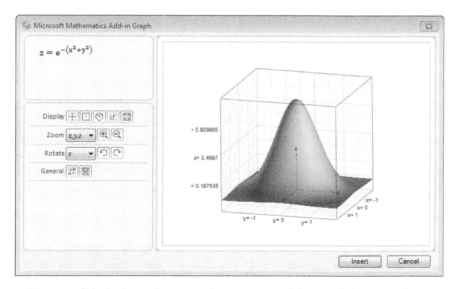

You can click the Insert button to insert a copy of the graph into your document. You can also choose other options, such as to solve for x or y.

Interoperate with other programs

As described in the previous two sections, Word can exchange math text with other programs. Typically this is done by using the *Presentation MathML format* as with the Math Input Panel. When copying a math zone as plain text, MathML is used if the corresponding **Math Options** setting is selected:

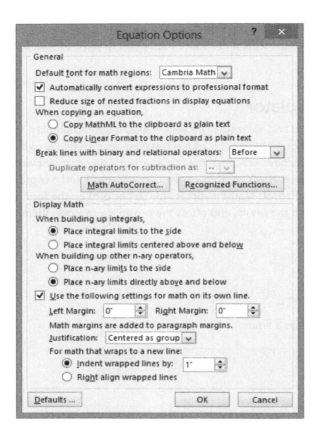

Copying text to and from Microsoft PowerPoint, OneNote, and Excel use HTML with special comments that represent math zones by using the Office MathML (OMML) format. This format differs from MathML, but all of these applications can read and write MathML as well. The HTML includes .png images of the math zones as fallbacks for programs that do not understand OMML. The OMML is included as part of the .png image so that math content can be preserved when a document is edited by an earlier version of Word or another program that doesn't understand OMML.

You might wonder why Word uses OMML for mathematics rather than MathML in its main file format (.docx). OMML is a pretty close representation of the internal math objects, which were created after extensive study of mathematical typography, rather than by study of MathML. It's natural to have a file format that mirrors the internal formats. In addition, it was necessary to be able to put any inline text and objects inside math zones. MathML doesn't handle embedding of other XML namespaces, at least in a way that's exposed to an XML parser. Also, OMML is a little closer to the math content than Presentation MathML. For example, OMML has an *n-ary* object that's used for summations, integrals, and the like. MathML uses subscript, superscript, over, under, subsup, or over-under constructs with a base that's an *n-ary* operator. So to know that an *n-ary* expression is involved, additional parsing is needed. Nevertheless, Word does a good job of reading and writing Presentation MathML.

Use and modify math autocorrect

For many years, Word has had the very useful feature known as autocorrect. When the selection is in a math zone, the *language* is math and the math autocorrect dictionary is used.

When you type enough for an expression to be unambiguous, it builds up right in front of your eyes! This process is called *formula autobuildup*. For example, type **a^2+b^2=c^2<space>** and you see the Pythagorean Theorem

$$a^2+b^2=c^2 \qquad\qquad (1)$$

Here the plus (+) and equal (=) terminate the superscript expressions **a^2** and **b^2**, respectively, causing them to be converted to their built-up forms **a^2** and **b^2**. Because no operator (or enter) follows the **c^2** in the equation, you need to type a space to build it up.

To work with the Word 2013 math dictionary

1. With the insertion point in the math zone, in the **Tools** group on the **Equation Tools Design** tool tab, click the **Tools** dialog box launcher.

   The Tools group will allow you to quickly create new equations from existing templates, change the appearance of equation text, and access the Equations Options dialog box.

2. Click the **Math AutoCorrect** button.

3. Add new string pairs or change existing string pairs as desired.

Generally, the default choices are those used in LaTeX; however, if you type Greek letters a lot, you might prefer to use shorter strings, such as **\a** for α, **\b** for β.

> **Note** If you know the Unicode hex value for a character, you can type it and press **Alt + X** to convert it into the character anywhere in your document. For example, type **3b1 Alt + X** to insert **α**; its Unicode hex value is **U+03B1**.

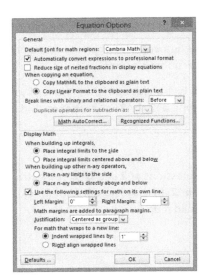
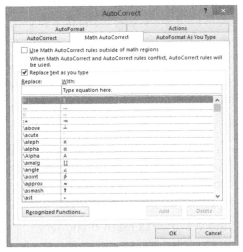

With the Equation Options dialog box, you can customize the behavior of the Word 2013 equation editor; with the AutoCorrect dialog box, you can add, edit, and delete your own shortcut codes.

You can also give names to expressions and equations written in the linear format. For example, **\quadratic** has the quadratic formula replacement string **x=(-b±√(b^2-4ac))/2a**. Typing **\quadratic<space><space>** in a math zone displays

$$x = \frac{-b \pm \sqrt{b^2 - 4ac}}{2a}$$

Similarly, you can type **\binomial** to insert the Binomial Theorem

$$(a+b)^n = \sum_{k=0}^{n} \binom{n}{k} a^k b^{n-k}$$

Insert an equation shortcut

Press **Alt + =** to quickly insert an equation. When creating many equations at once, or using an equation to quickly insert a symbol, this shortcut can be very useful.

Keyboard shortcuts in MathType

MathType has many keyboard shortcuts that can help you save time.

Function	Shortcut	Function	Shortcut
Superscript	Ctrl+H	Fraction	Ctrl+F
Subscript	Ctrl+L	Slash fraction	Ctrl+/

Function	Shortcut	Function	Shortcut
Joint super/subscript	Ctrl+J	Parentheses	Ctrl+(or Ctrl+9
Underscript	Ctrl+T, U	Brackets	Ctrl+[
Matrix template	Ctrl+T, M	Braces	Ctrl+{
nth root	Ctrl+T, N	Overbar	Ctrl+Shift+Hyphen
Product	Ctrl+T, P	Vector arrow	Ctrl+Alt+Hyphen
Summation	Ctrl+T, S	Tilde	Ctrl+~
Absolute value	Ctrl+Shift+T, |	Single prime	Ctrl+Alt+'
Root	Ctrl+R	Double prime	Ctrl+Alt+"
Integral	Ctrl+I	Single dot	Ctrl+Alt+.

Inserting space into equations

Space size	Shortcut
Zero space	Shift+Space
1-point space	Ctrl+Alt+Space
Thin space (one-sixth em)	Ctrl+Space
Thick space (one-third em)	Ctrl+Shift+Space

Inserting symbols

Space size	Shortcut
Arrow	Ctrl+K, A
Partial derivative	Ctrl+K, D
Infinity	Ctrl+K, I
Element of	Ctrl+K, E
Times	Ctrl+K, T
Not an element of	Ctrl+K, Shift+I
Contained in	Ctrl+K, C
Not contained in	Ctrl+K, Shift+C
Less than or equal to	Ctrl+K, <
Greater than or equal to	Ctrl+K, >

Convert equations from MathType to TeX/LaTeX

Some readers might need to maintain compatibility between their Word documents and LaTeX documents because, for example, they have a subset of collaborators who use only LaTeX. MathType offers a convenient tool for converting Word equations to LaTeX. To convert an equation from MathType to TeX or LaTeX, pick your preferences by clicking the **MathType** window, **Preferences** ⇒ **Transla-tors** ⇒ **Translation to other Language (text)**. After setting your preferences, copy your equation from the MathType window into a TeX/LaTeX window by using the standard **Ctrl-C/Ctrl-V** (copy/paste) commands.

Enter TeX or LaTeX directly

Starting with Word 2007 and recent versions of MathType, it's now possible to type TeX or LaTeX commands directly into equation editors. This long-awaited feature ameliorates the complaints of many LaTeX users who feel that it's important for them to enter math without using the mouse. In addition, incorporating TeX/LaTeX features will produce, generally speaking, the most professional-looking output.

Presenting the entire array of the TeX/LaTeX language is beyond the scope of this book; however, if you're a novice, you can rely on the shortcuts described in the following sections to get started and supplement them with an occasional point-and-click of the mouse. If you use a lot of math, you will eventually memorize all the commands that you use frequently. As you increase your expertise with TeX, you might even arrive at a point in which you discover commands and possibilities that are not well documented.

Greek letters

When the text selection is inside a math zone, the Equation Tools (math) tab appears. The math rib-bon offers many mathematical objects and symbols that can be inserted into a math zone. If you browse over the symbols, tooltips are displayed, revealing control words you can type to enter the symbols from the keyboard. For example, typing **\alpha** enters a math-italic α. You can change or add to these control words as described in the section on math autocorrect.

Symbol	Command	Symbol	Command	Symbol	Command
α	\alpha	Σ	\Sigma	ψ	\psi
β	\beta	Λ	\Lambda	υ	\upsilon
δ	\delta	Θ	\Theta	Δ	\Delta
γ	\gamma	Ω	\Omega	Γ	\Gamma
ϵ	\epsilon	Υ	\Upsilon	Π	\Pi
ω	\omega	π	\pi	Φ	\Phi
λ	\lambda	σ	\sigma	Ξ	\Xi
ρ	\rho	μ	\mu	Ψ	\Psi
τ	\tau	ϕ	\phi	φ	\varphi
ξ	\xi	η	\eta	ζ	\zeta
χ	\chi	κ	\kappa		
ω	\omega	θ	\theta		

Function names

When a consecutive string of English alphabetic characters is typed followed by a space or bracket of some kind, the resulting math italic string is converted to the corresponding upright (ASCII) letter string and compared to entries in a mathematical function dictionary by using the math autocorrect dialog box. If the string is found, the upright version of the string is used as the name of a function object. The dictionary includes trigonometric functions like sin, cos, tan, along with many other famous math function names. Users can modify this dictionary; for example, if you type **sin x** in a math zone, you see $\sin x$. Note that a thin space automatically appears between the sin and the x. Also if you type a **sin x**, you see a properly spaced $a \sin x$. No explicit spaces exist in the text; the math layout program takes care of the spacing.

Mathematical functions							
arccos	cos	csc	exp	ker	lim sup	min	sinh
arcsin	cosh	deg	gcd	lg	ln	Pr	sup
arctan	cot	det	hom	lim	log	sec	tan
arg	coth	dim	inf	lim	max	sin	tanh

Note If you follow a math function name by a subscript or superscript, that script becomes part of the function name. This is handy for typing in expressions like $\sin^{-1} x$.

Miscellaneous symbols

Symbol	Command	Symbol	Command
$\sqrt{x}$	\sqrt(x)	$\forall$	\forall
♠	\spadesuit	∂	\partial
∞	\infty	♮	\natural
▲	\blacktriangle	$\exists$	\exists
▼	\blacktriangledown	$\aleph$	\aleph
∇	\nabla	$\parallel$	\parallel

Arrows

Symbol	Command	Symbol	Command
←	\leftarrow	↔	\leftrightarrow
↑	\uparrow	↕	\updownarrow
→	\rightarrow	⇔	\Leftrightarrow
↗	\nearrow	⇒	\Rightarrow
↘	\searrow	⇓	\Downarrow
↓	\downarrow	⇑	\Uparrow

Binary and operational symbols

You've already seen many basic keyboard shortcuts and hopefully you're familiar with **Alt+=** to insert a math zone. You can also use this keyboard shortcut when normal text is selected to insert that text into a new math zone. This is particularly handy when you paste in text from a source that does mark math text as mathematical. This section describes other shortcuts that are handy for entering mathematical operators.

Sometimes you need to enter a negated operator such as ≠. If you're a C/C++ programmer, you might think that **!=** should map to ≠, because that's what != means in those languages (and some others). But since **!** means factorial in math, this choice isn't ideal for inputting ≠ into mathematical text. You can type in **\ne** to get ≠, but there's the simpler combination: **/=**. In the *linear format* used in Microsoft Office math, **/** is used for "stacked" fractions. But having **/=** build up to a fraction with an empty denominator followed by an equal sign isn't very useful. Also if you really want such a fraction, you can get it by typing **/<space>**.

Accordingly in Office math entry, **/=** builds up to ≠. This approach can be used to input many other negated operators, as listed in the following table.

Symbol	Command	Symbol	Command
×	\times	÷	\div
⊕	\oplus	⊗	\otimes
<	<	≮	/<
>	>	≯	\>
≤	\leq, \le	≠	/=

Symbol	Command	Symbol	Command
$\geq$	\geq, \ge	$\prod$	\prod
$\ll$	\ll	$\bullet$	\bullet
$\gg$	\gg	$*$	\ast
$\sim$	~	$\nsim$	/\sim
$\simeq$	\simeq	$\nsimeq$	/\simeq
$\cong$	\cong	$\ncong$	/\cong
$\approx$	\approx	$\napprox$	/\approx
$\asymp$	\asymp	$\neq$	/\asymp
$\equiv$	\equiv	$\nequiv$	/\equiv
$\exists$	\exists	$\nexists$	/\exists
$\in$	\in	$\notin$	/\in, \notin
$\ni$	\ni	$\therefore$	\therefore
$\cap$	\bigcap	$\supset$	\superset
$\subset$	\subset	$\supseteq$	\superseteq
$\mid$	\mid	$\perp$	\perp
$\subseteq$	\subseteq	$\subseteq$	\subsetneq
$\pm$	\pm, +-	$\mp$	\mp, -+
$\sum_{n=1}^{\infty} a_n$	\sum^\infty_(n=1) a_n	$\int_0^\infty x\,dx$	\int^\infty_0 <space> x <right arrow> dx
$\lim_{x \to 0} x$	lim_(x->0)<space>x	$\log_x n$	log_x<space>n

Note If you don't like an automatic translation when entering math, you can undo the translation with **Ctrl+Z.**

All of these operators are in the U+2200 Unicode block (*Mathematical Operators*) except for the ASCII characters <, =, and >. TeX has a similar approach that uses the control word **\not** followed by the name of the operator. For example, in TeX, **\not\exists** produces ∄.

There are other shortcuts (actually autocorrections) such as **+-** giving $\pm$. The **^** and **_** operators are not combined with other operators because a user might want to superscript or subscript an operator. Even the case **+-** giving $\pm$ could be ambiguous, because one might want to write $a + -b$. The user can enter this by typing **A + - <undo> B**, where **<undo>** is **Ctrl + Z**. An interesting example is <-, which has a mathematical meaning as illustrated by the relation $a < -b$. Accordingly, the sequence **<-** isn't used to produce ←. In contrast, **->** has no mathematical meaning and therefore produces → unambiguously. Fortuitously → is much more common in mathematics than ←, because → is used in limit expressions. The simple operator combinations included in the math autocorrect file that ships with Office are given in the following table.

Input₁	Operator	Input₂	Input₁	Operator	Input₂
+-	$\pm$	\pm	<<	$\ll$	\ll
-+	$\mp$	\mp	<=	$\leq$	\le
->	$\rightarrow$	\to	>=	$\geq$	\ge
~=	$\cong$	\cong	>>	$\gg$	\gg

You can add new ones to your math autocorrect file.

Accent marks

Mark	Shortcut Code	Mark	Shortcut Code
$\dot{a}$	a\dot<space><space>	$\tilde{a}$	a\tilde<space><space>
$\ddot{a}$	a\ddot<space><space>	$\widetilde{(a+b)}$	(a+b)\tilde<space><space>
$\ddot{a}$	a\ddot<space><space>	$\hat{a}$	a\hat<space><space>
$\bar{a}$	a\bar<space><space>	$\check{a}$	a\check<space><space>
$\bar{a}$	a\Bar<space><space>	$\vec{a}$	a\vec<space><space>

> **Note** Occasionally, formatting is not successful when you update your document. If this happens, try turning on the **Formatting** view in Word by clicking the paragraph symbol (¶). This view uncovers hidden formatting commands in Word. From this view, confirm that you have selected all appropriate formatting elements, including those just before and just after the element you copied.

Common formatting mistakes for equations

Sloppy centering and justification

Positioning the equation and number with strings of tab or space characters does not work well for camera-ready manuscripts. It will generally cause the alignment of each element to be off by a few millimeters, resulting in the entire document looking sloppy. Additionally, it will make any adjustments or modifications more difficult because changing the numbering scheme, page layout, or the equations themselves will force you to go through the document and reset the alignment by hand. Remember to *always use styles and tab stops to set alignment and positioning*.

Inconsistent variable sizes

The font size of variables should be proportional to the size of text, and the font size of variables in equations should be the same as the font size of the variables in the text. When using the Word 2013 equation editor, simply make sure that the font size of your **Equation** style matches that of your body text.

Using different fonts in equations and in text

Novices are notorious for ignoring font conventions for variables when they use Word. It is not uncommon to see "W" in the equation, "W" in another part of the text, and "**W**" in a figure caption, all referring to the same variable. Although the font selection is inconsequential in undergraduate homework, it's important in rigorous technical and scientific writing. For instance, the distinction between a matrix, a vector variable, and a scalar variable is maintained through proper font selection. Users of Word 2013 must apply a conscious effort to maintain a consistent style.

Here is an example of poor formatting:

$$E = mc^2$$

(1.1)

where m is mass.

Common stylistic mistakes for equations

Incorrect cross-referencing

In the middle of the sentence, the equation numbers should be placed in parentheses and referenced without the word *equation*.

The proper style for cross-referencing equations is

 ... substitution of (3) into (2) yields (4)...

Examples of improper style

 ...substitution of equation 3 into equation 2 yields equation 4...

 ...substitution of 3 into 2 yields 4...

 ...substitution of [3] into [2] yields [4]...

In the beginning of the sentence, the proper style is

 Equation 3 shows...

Forgetting to define variables

All new variables that appear in the equation should be defined in the text, immediately following the equation.

Using subscripts and superscripts incorrectly

Large variations exist between disciplines for subscript and superscript font conventions. Be sure to check the conventions for your field.

Using confusing bookmark names

A bookmark named "eq14" will not work well, because the equation is not likely to be equation number 14 an hour later. A bookmark named "newt" will not work well either because it's too short and will mix with other bookmarks (including non-equation bookmarks). A bookmark "eq:NewtonsFirstLaw" will work well. It has "eq:"—an equation identifier, and a clear description of what it is. Spaces are not allowed in bookmarks; capitalization of individual words is a convenient alternative.

Bookmarking the parentheses next to the equation number

Most of the time, highlighting parentheses with the equation number while creating a bookmark makes it more convenient to cross-reference the equation in the text. However, some publishers expect equations to be referenced in the text as "Equation 5 shows..." instead of "(5) shows...", so including parentheses around "5" in the original bookmark will make typesetting more difficult. Therefore, parentheses should be kept as regular text both in the equation line and in the cross-referencing text.

Ambiguous display of units and use of incorrect units

Although the standards for indicating units are delineated quite clearly for each scientific discipline, many writers routinely ignore these standards. Conference committees are usually forgiving, and important publications are often typeset by professionals who take care of errors automatically. On the other hand, you can follow the conventions of your field with almost no additional effort. Most technical publishers require the use of either SI (metric) units or, when necessary, dual units, including SI as well as other systems. Units representing ranges should be separated by the word "to," as opposed to ellipsis ("...") or dash ("-"). The following table provides examples.

Incorrect version	Correct version
... in the range of 200 to 400 lfm...	... in the range of 1 m/s to 2 m/s (200 lfm to 400 lfm)
... the air velocity is 1-2 m/s ...	... the air velocity is 1 m/s to 2 m/s ...
... the air velocity is 1...2 m per second ...	... the air velocity is 1 m/s to 2 m/s ...

Recap

After completing this chapter, you should be able to properly and effectively create equations and implement them into your Word 2013 templates. You should be able to use the bookmark method of cross-referencing, which is one of the only methods available to be able to use captions and auto-numbering on the same line as the equation, and by far the most efficient. Finally, you should be well-versed in the most common novice mistakes, and well-prepared to identify and correct them, should they make their way into your documents.

By now, you should be able to

- Create equation templates

- Create templates with the Word 2013 equation editor

- Create templates with MathType

- Use a whole series of LaTeX commands to quickly create math symbols

- Use keyboard shortcuts to increase your productivity

- Cross-reference equation templates

- Modify equation styles for dual-column and dual-number templates

- Avoid common formatting and stylistic mistakes

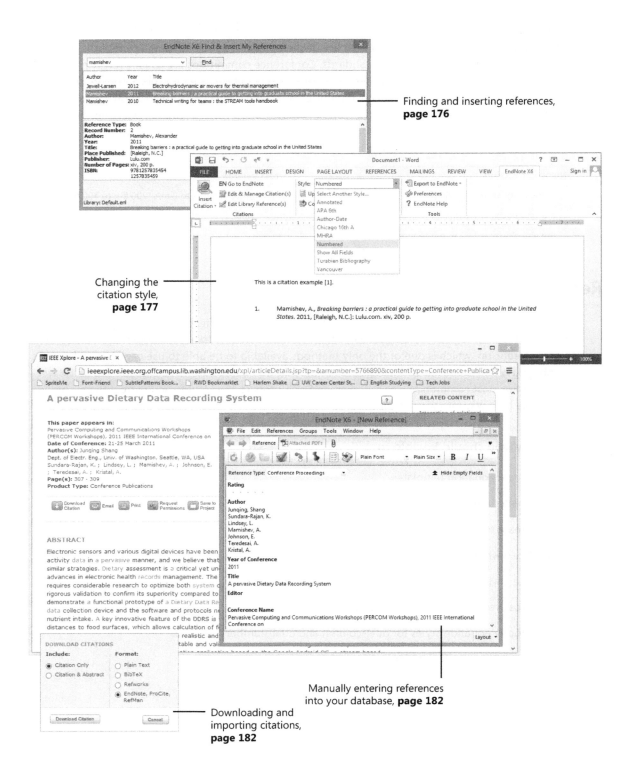

Finding and inserting references,
page 176

Changing the
citation style,
page 177

Manually entering references
into your database, **page 182**

Downloading and
importing citations,
page 182

CHAPTER 7

How to work with citations

In this chapter, you will learn how to

- Add, modify, and remove database citations

- Insert citations into your paper

- Construct a bibliography

- Export and share your database

- Copy citations from one database to another

This chapter covers using bibliographic databases, including how to share databases with others as you collaborate on a project.

A key difference between references and all the other non-textual elements of a document (for example, headings, figures, and tables) is that managing references requires a steeper learning curve. With other elements, you can download a template, and after brief instructions on how to "reuse the templates," you are ready to go.

Incorporating references, however, requires a separate software package and substantial learning time. If the number of references you are dealing with is small, you can forgo additional software and simply process them manually. For example, if you are a plant floor manager and you need to reference a couple of manuals and a newspaper article, just type them in using plain text or footnotes. If, on the other hand, you are a member of a research organization and you need to write a journal, a PhD thesis, a large federal agency proposal, or a book, then the time you invest in learning reference management techniques will be returned to you and your colleagues many times over.

How to choose a citation management suite

There are quite a few popular citation management suites from which you can choose, including EndNote, Reference Manager, Mendeley, Papers, RefWorks, ProCite, and more. All of these database software suites have different pros and cons, but for the purposes of writing research documents and managing a large number of references, we have found that the software most compatible with the methods described in this book is EndNote, by Thompson Reuters. The latest version as of this writing is X6. You are, of course, free to choose whichever management software you would like, and the principles of citation management taught here generally apply across the board. However, it is likely that you will run into the fewest snags during the course of writing should you choose EndNote.

Why use a bibliographic database?

There are several reasons for using a bibliographic database.

First is the need for automatic numbering of your literature citations and automatic ordering of the citations at the end of the document. Many journals require that your citations be numbered consecutively in the order in which they appear in the document. In this case, the text would look like this:

> "Although bird worms were proven to be affected by zero gravity [22], it has been demonstrated that alien forms are not susceptible to these conditions [23]."

Second is the need for automatic formatting of the citations list. The expected format is different for each journal. For example, some journals require that the citations appear alphabetically and are referenced by the name of the first author and the year they were published. The previous example would then look like:

> "Although bird worms were proven to be affected by zero gravity [Dinkley 2003], it has been demonstrated that alien forms are not susceptible to these conditions [Lawrence 2004]."

Third is the opportunity to keep your references organized by your own categories. You might want to be able to generate a quick list of all papers published in your research group in the last five years, or a list of all papers that make new contributions to the body of knowledge on environmental impact of a certain technology, or a list of all papers by a competing group. Some of these lists will be an ongoing effort, to which several people on your team should contribute. For example, if you want your group to write a review article on research in your field, you could ask every group member to add or mark papers in the database that they believe to be relevant to the project.

Fourth is the ability to share references. For example, say a graduate student just finished a dissertation, which consists of a 250-page manuscript with 350 references. The next graduate student is continuing the work, starting from scratch. Standing on shoulders of giants does not mean doing things from scratch.

Managing hundreds or even thousands of references manually in light of all the above issues is an extremely daunting task that can quickly turn into busy work of no practical value. The following section presents additional justifications for using bibliographic databases and the basics of using EndNote for citation management.

Choice of software

If you adopt Microsoft Word as your flagship writing software, you can use the built-in Citations & Bibliography features. However, capabilities of this option are so limited that we do not recommend it for collaborative work, particularly because it's difficult to share the database among team members because it resides on a single computer.

At the time of writing this book, we found three main software packages most suitable for collaboration: EndNote, Reference Manager, and ProCite. EndNote is considered the most popular and easiest to use, and we recommend it as your first choice. Reference Manager comes in at a close second; it has sophisticated network features, allowing multiple users to access numerous databases at the same time. The problem is that Reference Manager isn't compatible with individual EndNote users, who could be scattered across various locations and do not necessarily belong to your organization. Importing or exporting between EndNote and Reference Manager is not prohibitively difficult, but it's a cumbersome extra step, so be sure to select your software carefully. If you have a powerful IT department and highly streamlined computer support, the network advantages of Reference Manager might outweigh the fact that it's less popular than EndNote. The third option, ProCite, is a close relative to the other two; however, it does not offer clear advantages over either.

If you need to interface to LaTeX, you will also need BibTeX. EndNote, Reference Manager, and ProCite are bibliography management systems to be used with Microsoft Word, and BibTeX is the bibliography management system for LaTeX. Because the differences between the first three are mostly cosmetic, you might want to make your choice based on what your potential collaborators are already using, and then configure them in such a way that you maintain compatibility with LaTeX.

In short, if you are not sure what to pick, use EndNote. You will need to choose between the web-based and the desktop-based modes. The instructions on using EndNote later in this chapter correspond to the desktop version.

The following section explains how to use the built-in citation manager in Microsoft Word 2013.

How to use the built-in citation manager in Word 2013

If you are writing a research document by yourself, the built-in citation management tools included with Word 2013 will help you keep track of your citations and update them as you develop your document. The tools are built to be used on one machine, but, in the event that you need to share your references with someone else or transfer them to another computer, you can do so without much difficulty. The following section will walk you through setting up a basic set of references, constructing a citations section for your template, setting up a citation style, and creating citations within your document.

Set up the interface

The first step in setting up the interface is to confirm that your Word 2013 installation has a copy of the reference style that you want to use. The reference style will vary by journal, so be sure to check which style is required.

To choose a reference style

1. On the **References** tab, in the **Citations & Bibliography** group, click the **Style** ( ) drop-down menu.

2. Click your preferred reference style.

If you do not see your reference style, you can download styles from the BibWord download page at *http://bibword.codeplex.com*. For the purposes of these instructions, we will use the *IEEE – Reference Order* style template.

To install and use the IEEE – Reference Order style template

1. In your web browser, go to *http://bibword.codeplex.com*.

2. On the website's top menu, click **Downloads**.

3. Under **Recommended Download**, click the link to *styles.zip*.

4. Click the **I Agree** button, and download the file.

5. Open the .zip file and extract it to C:\Program Files\Microsoft Office\Office 15\Bibliography\ Style.

> **Note** Make sure that you extract just the .xsl files, and that they are not extracted to another directory within the "Style" directory. The files must be placed with the other .xsl files in order for Word 2013 to load them.
>
> Additionally, if you have the 64-bit version of Microsoft Office, the files should be extracted to C:\Program Files\Microsoft Office\Office 15\Bibliography\Style, not C:\Program Files (x86)\Microsoft Office\Office 15\Bibliography\Style.

6. Close and restart Word 2013.

7. Follow the steps in the procedure "To choose a reference style" to choose *IEEE – Reference Order* as your bibliography style.

To add entries to your bibliographic database

1. On the **References** tab, in the **Citations & Bibliography** group, click **Manage Sources** ( ).

2. In the window that appears, click **New**.

3. In the **Create Source** dialog box, select **Journal Article** from the **Type of Source** drop-down menu.

4. Fill in the other text boxes with sample information (when you click inside each box, the bottom of the window will show an example for the format and content of that box).

5. Click **OK**. The entry you created will appear in the **Current List**.

6. To add more entries, click **New**.

> **Note** You can manage which sources are included in the document's list by first selecting a source from **Master List** or **Current List,** and then clicking **Copy and Delete**. You can modify an existing source by clicking **Edit**.

7. Click **Close**.

Cite references

Inserting an in-line citation is simple.

To cite a reference

Insert
Citation ▾

1. On the **References** tab, click **Insert Citation**, and then click **Add New Citation.**

2. Locate and click the source you would like to cite.

> **Note** If you would like to change the formatting of this citation, you can do so manually, but be warned that it will reset when you update the document's fields with **Ctrl+A → F9**.
>
> To avoid resetting the format of your citation when you update field codes, you could modify the XSL template directly; however, this process is complex and beyond the scope of this book. A much easier and reliable method is to search for a more suitable template on the web. Do make sure to check the formatting requirements of your journal or publication because they are most likely to coincide with one of the standard templates provided by BibWord.

Share a database

To share your bibliographic database, all you have to do is copy the .xml file from your C:\Users\USERNAME\AppData\Roaming\Microsoft\Bibliography folder. This folder can be easily accessed through the Source Manager window.

To share your database

1. On the **References** tab, in the **Citations & Bibliography** group, click **Manage Sources** (![icon]).

2. Click **Browse**.

3. Right-click and drag *Sources.xml* onto your desktop.

You can now share that file with any user of Word 2013. All they have to do is copy the file to their C:\Users\USERNAME\AppData\Roaming\Microsoft\ Bibliography directory. To preserve their citation master list, they should rename the *Sources.xml* file before moving it.

In addition, bibliographic database entries can be combined into one XML file. It's as easy as opening a blank document and copying the sources right over.

To combine database entries into one file

1. Copy both XML database files to the Bibliography directory, as described in the previous procedure.

2. Open a new document.

3. On the **References** tab, in the **Citations & Bibliography** group, click **Manage Sources**.

4. Click **Browse**.

5. Select the XML database file you would like to copy.

6. Click **OK**.

7. Select the entries you would like to copy from the list on the left side. (Use **Ctrl+Click** to select multiple entries, or click the first entry and drag to the bottom of the list to select all of the entries. Additionally, you can select multiple entries in the list by holding down the **Shift** key and pressing the up and down arrows on the keyboard.)

8. Click **Copy** to add the entries to the blank **Current List**.

9. Click **Browse**.

10. Select the destination XML database.

11. Click **OK**.

12. Select all of the entries from the **Current List**.

13. Click **Copy**.

14. If Word issues you a warning, choose either to overwrite the files in question, or cancel and deselect the duplicate entries that you do not want to replace. You can manually select and deselect files by holding **Ctrl** while you select the desired files.

15. Click **Close**.

16. Close Word 2013 to ensure that your changes propagate to Sources.xml.

Construct a citations section

To create the citations section, you must decide whether you would like it to begin on a new page, or have it included among the rest of your content.

To create the citations section

1. On the **Page Layout** tab, in the **Page Setup** group, click **Breaks**, and choose either **Next Page** or **Continuous**, depending on your preferences.

2. On the **References** tab, in the **Citations & Bibliography** group, click **Bibliography** ⇒ **Insert Bibliography**.

Note By default, the bibliography will rely on the **Normal** style. If you have set your **Normal** style with special indentation, line spacing, and so forth, you will likely find that the format of the bibliography is broken. To fix this, you can simply select the entire bibliography and click **Home** ⇒ **Styles** ⇒ **Clear Formatting**.

Alternatively, you can create a special style, **Body**, for use with your document's main text, and reserve the **Normal** style for your document's truly vanilla text.

How to use EndNote

Although the built-in citation manager in Word is suitable for smaller projects, the lack of features and functionality is cumbrous for larger projects or for use within a collaborative setting. For extensive team writing, it's highly advisable to equip all team members with a dedicated software package specifically designed for citation management.

The two leading packages are *EndNote* and *Reference Manager*. Both programs seamlessly integrate into Word and provide very similar functionality with only a few differences.

For a team that has not yet selected a software package, further research may be necessary to decide on a software package that best provides the desired features and functionality.

The following steps outline only the core functionalities required to create and implement reference databases. You may need to refer to the software manual or consult an experienced user to learn how to use all of the relevant features of EndNote. This section begins with a quick overview of the key functionalities and tasks, and concludes with a comprehensive guide for setting up and using EndNote.

To cite a reference already in the EndNote database

1. Place the text cursor where you would like the reference to appear.

2. On the **EndNote X6** tab of the ribbon, click the **Insert Citation** button.

3. In the dialog box that appears, click the searchable text field and type several keywords that identify the reference that you want (for example, title, author(s), journal, or other relevant keywords).

4. Click the **Find** button.

5. After the program has compiled a list of relevant citations that match the keywords, click the reference you want, and then click **Insert**.

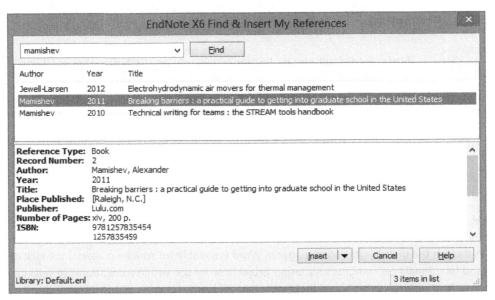

The EndNote X6 Find & Insert My References dialog box makes it easy to insert any reference in your EndNote X6 database into a Word document.

To change the style of the list of citations

1. On the **EndNote X6** tab, click the **Style** drop-down menu, and then choose the style you want.

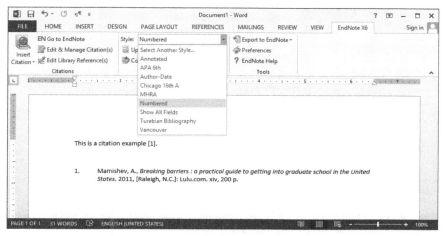

Generally, scientific publications use the "Numbered" citation style.

2. Click **Update Citations and Bibliography** ( ) to update the list of references.

Use online resources to cite a reference not in the database

1. Place the text cursor where you would like the reference to appear.

2. On the **EndNote X6** tab of the ribbon, click **Go To EndNote** (**EN**).

3. In the **EndNote X6** dialog box that appears, find the **Online Search** section located toward the left side of the screen, and then click the online database most likely to have your citation.

> **Note** There are two ways to use the online search function in the EndNote X6 interface. By default, the **Integrated Library & Online Search Mode** appears, which allows you to quickly switch between your library and online searches. This interface will automatically add the results of your search to your library. It is most useful if you have a specific reference in mind and can provide several key terms for the search.
>
> To search for a single term and choose from a list of results, perform your search in the **Online Search mode** ( ), accessible from the menu bar.

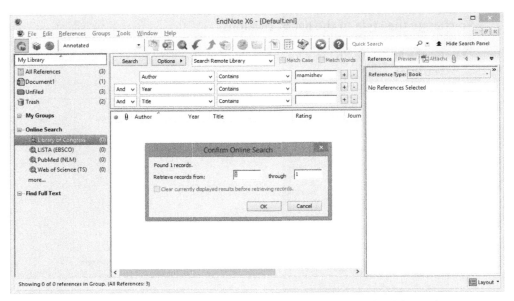

When you conduct an online search in the "Integrated" mode, EndNote X6 will add the results to your library. Be as specific as possible with your search terms.

4. In the search fields that appear in the main window of the EndNote X6 program, click either the **Author, Year, or Title** field, and type the information most relevant to the citation you want.

5. Click the **Search** button.

6. In the dialog box, click **OK**.

7. After the search results appear in the citation list below, find and click the citation you want.

8. Click the **Insert Citation** (🖺) button, found toward the top of the program, underneath the menu bar (**Alt+2**).

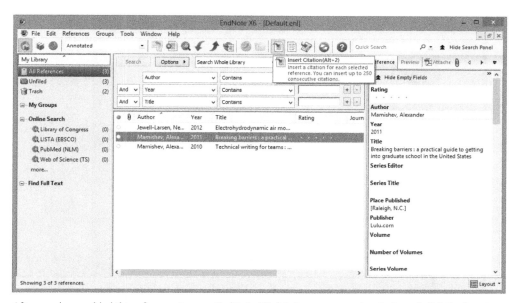

After you have added the reference to your EndNote X6 database, you can locate it, and click the Insert Citation button to place it at the location of the cursor in your document.

The reference to your entry will appear in the text, and the literature citation itself will be at the end of the document. The following section provides a more detailed discussion of bibliographic database management.

Set up the EndNote interface

Install the EndNote software. The website *www.endnote.com* offers a 30-day trial of Endnote X6, as well as multiple tutorials and webinars teaching the more advanced functions of EndNote. The following example will cover the very basics of getting started, as well as a discussion of the applications available for using EndNote in teams. You may need to supplement this info with additional instructions and tutorials.

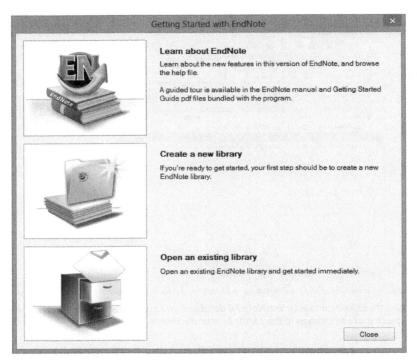

You are presented with a dialog box that allows you to quickly create a new reference database (also known as a "library") after installing and opening EndNote X6 for the first time.

After your software is installed, you can either select an existing database (for example, one created by your colleagues) or create a new one.

To create a new database, click the image next to **Create a new library**, and choose a location for the database files.

Note When you create a new file, EndNote will generate an .enl file and .data file folder. Both the file and the folder should be kept together to allow attached files to be opened from the associated references.

Your next step is to customize the database interface. Specifically, you should decide which database field entries to display (for example, author, title, year, journal), and which custom fields (if any) to create. This customization step may differ between teams. For example, some teams may want to include classification terms for each paper in their database, whereas other teams may need a custom field to convert to BibTeX, and others still may want to include associated web addresses. Each user and group will have their own preferences for the interface, which will evolve over time and after successive collaborative use.

Add references to EndNote

Now you are ready to add references into your database, which you can accomplish in several ways, as described in the following section:

- You can search for references online from within the EndNote program by clicking the **Online Search** ( ) button, and then selecting a database from the list on the left side. You will be directed to a classic search interface, in which you can search by author, title, keyword, and more. After completing the search, you can select references of interest to you, and then move them to your permanent database.

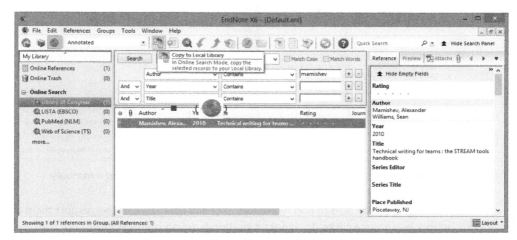

You can use the Online Search function to quickly search a long list of databases for a reference. Click the More button to access additional databases. Click the Copy to Local Library button to add the reference to your database.

- You can use a web browser to find citations online through services like Google Scholar, and then enter the information into EndNote manually. To enter citations, click the **New Reference** ( ) button, and then add the details in the window that appears. When you are finished, click **File** and then **Save** to add the reference to your database.

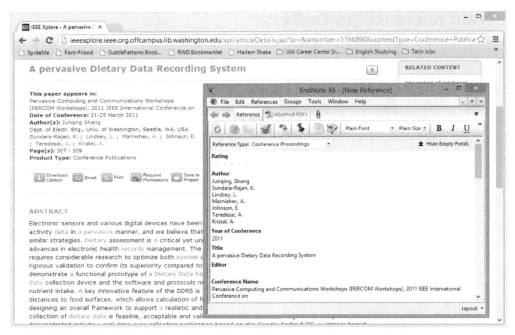

By using an online database, you can find reference information and insert it manually.

- You might also be able to find references in online libraries, and then export them to EndNote with a few mouse clicks. To export a citation from an online library, click the link on the reference page labeled **Download Citation** or **Export Citation,** and then simply open the downloaded file.

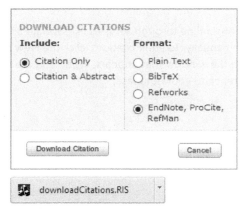

On the IEEE Xplore website, you can click the Download Citation button to download a file that will add the reference to your database automatically.

- You may obtain reference collections from your collaborators, and if they use Reference Manager, you can import their files into your EndNote database by clicking **File ⇒ Import**, and then choosing the reference collection.

- You can acquire references located in Word that have been previously entered into the document by your group members. A more detailed discussion of this method comes later.

- If all of the preceding methods are not applicable to your needs, you can manually enter citations into the database.

Cite references by using EndNote

After you have created the database, citing references is easy. If you use Word 2013 and have already installed EndNote, you will see a dedicated EndNote ribbon on your screen. After selecting the EndNote ribbon, select the Style for your references (for example, *IEEE* requires one style, and *Nature* requires a different style). It should be noted that, unfortunately, many of the provided styles are placeholders rather than real styles. In other words, their output is quite different from the actual publisher requirements and it will be necessary to modify the style files to produce an output that matches the exact specifications and requirements of the journal.

Click **Insert Citation → Find Citation**. An EndNote window will appear. Search for and select the citations that you would like to add, and then click **Insert**. Finally, click **Update Citations and Bibliography**.

These instructions provide you with a bird's-eye view of the main functions that you need; we also encourage you to review the free online tutorials available at *endnote.com*, partly because of the interactive multimedia delivery mode and partly because newer versions of the software may change some of the functions and the steps to use them. It's not likely, however, that any major changes will be made, because EndNote is a mature software package.

Share a database with other EndNote users

A research group that works closely in the same field might want to share the same database. Doing so will make the references entered by one person reusable by others in the future. In addition, the group member who entered that reference might choose to add comments, such as *"this is a very important paper for us, because it describes the methodology for the numerical modeling of thermal diffusion."* An even more sophisticated approach is to create a classification scheme for relevant papers.

Maintain compatibility with BibTeX

Early on, you will want to determine if you need to maintain compatibility with LaTeX. The software module in LaTeX that manages literature references is called BibTeX. In BibTeX, each reference has a field for unique identification. The most common way to identify a paper in the BibTeX database is to use the first author's name and the year of publication. After you dedicate one of the custom-defined columns in the database for this field, you will be able to conduct import-export actions between BibTeX and EndNote or Reference Manager.

One can also add custom fields in EndNote. To display user-defined columns, right-click the **RefID** tablet and select **Reference List Display**. Increase the number of columns viewed and select the columns that you want to be visible.

For example, consider the following paper:

C. P. Hsu, N. E. Jewell-Larsen, I. A. Krichtafovitch, S. W. Montgomery, J. T. Dibene II, and A. V. Mamishev, "Miniaturization of Electrostatic Fluid Accelerators," *Journal of Microelectro-mechanical Systems*, vol. 16, no. 4, pp. 809-815, Aug. 2007.

The entry in the column User Def 1 would be *Hsu07*, and if you expect to see more papers for the same author, you can add the first word of the title, so that the entry would look like this: *Hsu07Miniaturization*.

Another facet of compatibility is providing readily formatted database entries to others. Some academic authors choose to put readily formatted BibTeX and EndNote collections of references to their own work on their websites, thus inviting webpage visitors to cite their work. Although this practice could be considered slightly aggressive and self-serving, it is entirely within the ethical bounds of the academic community.

What about Reference Manager?

Another popular choice for managing references is Reference Manager. The current version at the time of this writing is version 12. Also published by Thomson Reuters, Reference Manager has many of the same features as EndNote; however, because of a slightly superior feature set, we recommend EndNote X6 over Reference Manager 12.

Another important consideration is multiuser functionality—EndNote limits you to a single-user database, whereas Reference Manager allows multiuser access via a network or the Internet. Depending on the size of your group and how references are handled, you may elect to choose Reference Manager and distribute citation management tasks across your team.

Table 7-1 illustrates the difference between the latest versions of EndNote and Reference Manager, and might help you make a decision between both pieces of software should you still want to consider using Reference Manager.

TABLE 7-1 Differences between EndNote X6 and Reference Manager 12 feature sets

Feature	EndNote	Reference Manager
Version	X6	12
Store and cite images and objects	Yes	No
Find full text articles automatically	Yes	No
Annotate stored PDFs	Yes	No
Automatically search for updated reference info	Yes	No
Import filters for online databases	700+ predefined; create your own	430+ predefined; create your own
Operating system	Mac operating system X & Windows	Win
Access to references	Desktop & Network	Desktop, Network & web browser (via web publisher)
Multiuser access (network or web)	No	Yes
Number of output styles	5000+ predefined; create your own	1,300+ predefined; create your own
Max number of fields	52	37
Max number of Reference Types	46	35
Create table and figure lists	Yes	No
Create a list of "favorite" styles	Yes	No
Reference grouping	Yes	Use keywords or multiple databases
Create Smart Groups for instant sorting	Yes	No
Advanced searching capabilities	Yes	No
Search across multiple databases	Cite While You Write	Databases & Cite While You Write
Construct document with Microsoft Word templates	Yes	No
Unicode compliant	Yes	No

How to format references

Maintaining the proper formatting of references according to publisher requirements is a daunting task because there are literally thousands of formats. Although the style files discussed in this chapter reduce the total amount of formatting efforts and the output quality, inexperienced writers tend to make a large number of formatting mistakes when they cite literature, simply because they are completely unaware of the existing conventions. Some of these conventions are quite universal, and some apply only to narrow fields of specialization. Because the number of formatting rules is so large and they vary so much, a writer should develop a certain intuition about formatting requirements. The following examples intend to provide initial training on this subject for inexperienced writers.

Find typesetting and stylistic mistakes in the following hypothetical text:

- A comprehensive overview of interdigital sensors and transducers is provided in [1].

- One of the earliest examples of using patrolling robots for sensing properties of electric power cables (2) demonstrated technical feasibility of autonomous mobile sensing for maintenance of distributed infrastructures.

- Computationally intensive algorithms that provide a high rate of automated detection and discrimination of a broad range power quality events [e.g. those described in [3,4] can now be implemented in hand-held diagnostic devices.

Find typesetting and formatting mistakes in the following references:

- [1] A. V. Mamishev, K. Sundara-Rajan, F. Yang, Y. Q. Du, and M. Zahn, "Interdigital Sensors and Transducers," *Proceedings of the IEEE,* vol. 92, no. 5, pp. 808-845, May 2004.

- [2] C. P. Hsu, N. E. Jewell-Larsen, I. A. Krichtafovitch, S. W. Montgomery, J. T. Dibene II, and A. V. Mamishev, "Miniaturization of Electrostatic Fluid Accelerators," *Journal of Microelectromechanical Systems*, vol. 16, no. 4, pp. 809-815, Aug. 2007.

- [3] M. Wang and A. V. Mamishev, "Classification of Power Quality Events Using Optimal Time-Frequency Representations -- Part 1: Theory," IEEE Transactions on Power Delivery, 2003.

- [4] M. Wang, Rowe, G. I., and A. V. Mamishev, "Classification of Power Quality Events Using Optimal Time-Frequency Representations -- Part 2: Application," IEEE Transactions on Power Delivery, 2003.

Answers

In text:

- Reference [2] in the second sentence is enclosed in parentheses, whereas the standard is to enclose it in square brackets. Parentheses are used for equation numbers.

- Insertion of reference (2) in the middle of the sentence needlessly interrupts the flow of thought.

- In the third sentence, space is needed between "in" and [3,4].

In the list of references:

- Spacing between the number of the reference and the first initial of the first author is inconsistent.

- The last name "Jewell-Larsen" in reference 2 appears in Arial font. This switching of fonts is a common typesetting mistake when Reference Manager is used. It typically happens when the database line entry is copied from somewhere and the original font setting is preserved. To prevent that from happening, one can strip the font settings from text, for example, by using the command **Paste Special**, **Unformatted Text**.

- References [3] and [4] lack details, such as volume number and page numbers.

- The italics in the journal titles are inconsistent between references [1] and [2] versus [3] and [4].

Exercises

Exercise 7.1

1. Create a *master database* for your group by using EndNote.

2. Populate the master database with literature citations, numbered from 1 to 50.

3. Create a clone database (same content, different file name).

4. Populate the clone database with entries from 101 to 125.

5. Synchronize the clone and the master databases.

Exercise 7.2

1. Create a user-defined field

2. Create three categories in this field

3. Assign groups of papers to these categories

Recap

After completing this chapter, you should have chosen a suitable citation management solution and be capable of the fundamental procedures for working with citations within that suite. You should be able to construct an accurate bibliography for your research papers, and you should be able to use your software of choice to update it automatically as the structure and content of your document changes, minimizing the time you spend fine-tuning the details.

By now, you should be able to

- Add new citations to your database

- Modify citations you have previously added to your database

- Remove citations from your database that are no longer needed

- Insert citations in your paper

- Construct a bibliography for your paper's citations

- Import citations from your database to your paper

- Export your database

- Copy citations from your database into another database

Becoming a Microsoft Word 2013 power user

To get the most out of Microsoft Word 2013, you should learn how to customize the toolbar, keyboard shortcuts, and other settings. This section will guide you in managing the settings most pertinent to the design of research papers and their templates. For more generalized advice, we recommend *http://www.streamtoolsonline.com*, or use your favorite search engine to locate a suitable tutorial.

How to personalize the Word 2013 ribbon

Personalizing the ribbon is quite simple; however, it can be difficult to foresee which customizations will yield the greatest long-term benefits, often in terms of time savings. The following instructions will help you customize your ribbon to best suit the tasks associated with writing research proposals and other academic documents.

To add buttons to the ribbon

1. Right-click anywhere on the ribbon, and click **Customize the Ribbon**.

2. Under the **Choose Commands from** drop-down list, select a group of commands (for example, **Commands Not in the Ribbon**).

3. Locate the command (button) you would like to add to the ribbon.

> **Note** Because commands can only be added to custom groups, you must create a custom group to proceed. If you would like to add a command to an existing group, you must replace that group with a custom group that contains the default commands. Simply follow the next steps to create a custom group, and repeat the steps to add all of the default commands.

4. Under **Customize the ribbon**, locate the tab to which you would like to add the command, and select it.

5. Click **New Group**.

6. Click **Rename**, type a name for the group, and then click **OK**.

7. Click the up and down buttons on the right side of the customize the ribbon box to set the position of the group where you want it.

8. Drag the command you want to the group. Alternatively, make sure both the command and the group are selected, and click the **Add** button.

9. Repeat this process as necessary until you have added all of the commands you want to your preferred groups.

> **Note** If you accidently add a command and want to remove it, either right-click the command and click **Remove**, or select it and click the **Remove** button. You can use this procedure for entire groups, as well.
>
> If you find that you have accidentally deleted a default group and would like to restore the tab to its original state, simply click the **Reset** button and choose **Reset only selected Ribbon tab**. If you would like to restore the ribbon to its default state, choose instead **Reset all customizations**. Keep in mind that you will lose any customizations that you have created.

To hide tabs

1. Right-click anywhere on the ribbon, and click **Customize the Ribbon**.

2. Under the **Customize the Ribbon** box on the right side, locate the tab you would like to hide and clear the check box next to its name.

3. Click **OK**.

To add custom tabs

1. Right-click anywhere on the ribbon, and click **Customize the Ribbon**.

2. Click **New Tab**.

3. Select **New Tab (Custom)** in the **Customize the Ribbon** box, and then click the button labeled **Rename**. Type in a name for your tab in the **Display Name** box, and then click **OK**.

4. Use the up and down buttons on the right side of the **Customize the Ribbon** box to position your tab as needed.

5. Follow the steps in the "To add buttons to the ribbon" procedure to complete the customization of your new tab.

6. Click **OK**.

How to set up Quick Access Toolbar shortcuts

The Quick Access Toolbar contains a customizable list of buttons that you can use to quickly perform many different actions in Word 2013. By default, the toolbar contains **Save**, **Undo**, and **Repeat Typing** (or Redo) commands.

Press the **Alt** key to view the shortcut keys tied to the buttons.

The Quick Access Toolbar allows you to add the commands you use most to the top of the window. You can also trigger these commands by pressing Alt + 1, Alt + 2, and so on.

You can customize this quick access bar to your liking based on the tools and tasks you use most. Click the Customize Quick Access Toolbar button ( ) on the far right side of the toolbar , and then click **More Commands**.

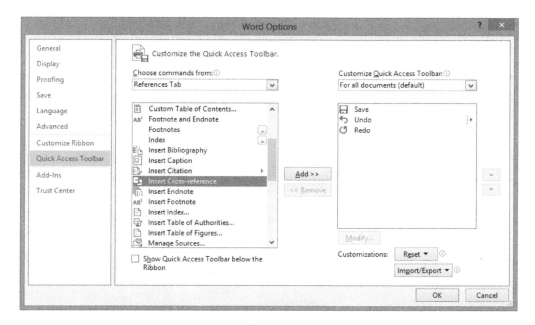

You can add any command to the Quick Access Toolbar through the Word Options dialog box.

For example, you can add **Comment** and **Insert Cross-reference** buttons, so that all you would need to do is press **Alt + 4** or **Alt + 5** when you want to make a comment or insert a reference.

To add a button to the Quick Access Toolbar

1. Click the **Customize Quick Access Toolbar** (▼) button on the far right side of the Quick Access Toolbar.

2. Click **More Commands**.

3. Choose a source tab from the **Choose commands from** drop-down list.

4. Click the command you would like to add.

5. Click **Add**.

6. Click **OK**.

How to use keyboard shortcuts

Numerous keyboard shortcuts are predefined in Word 2013, (the most common of which are listed in Table A-1) and they can greatly reduce the time you spend on basic, repetitive tasks. In addition to using the standard shortcuts, we highly recommended that you define your own shortcuts for common tasks.

Note You will probably discover that you can't create keyboard shortcuts for certain commands. Instead, add the commands to the Quick Access Toolbar, and then you can access them by pressing **Alt** and the corresponding number key (for example, **Alt → 1**).

TABLE A-1 Common keyboard shortcuts in Word 2013

Keyboard shortcuts	Effect
Ctrl + A	Select All
Ctrl + C	Copy selection to Clipboard
Ctrl + X	Cut selection
Ctrl + V	Paste from Clipboard
Ctrl + Shift + C	Copy formatting
Ctrl + Shift + V	Paste formatting
Ctrl + Left Arrow	Move cursor one word to the left
Ctrl + Right Arrow	Move cursor one word to the right
Ctrl + Shift + Left Arrow	Select one word on the right

Keyboard shortcuts	Effect
Ctrl + Shift + Right Arrow	Select one word on the left
End	Move cursor to end of line
Ctrl + End	Move cursor to end of document
Ctrl + B	Make selection bold
Ctrl + I	Make selection italic
Ctrl + U	Underline selection
Ctrl + Shift + A	Capitalize selected text (and vice versa)
Alt + Ctrl + 1	Apply Heading 1 to selected text
Ctrl + Shift + L	Apply bullets
Ctrl + Shift + F5	Create a bookmark
Ctrl + Shift + E	Toggle track changes
Alt → R → J → R	Reject selected changes
Alt → R → A → C	Accept selected changes
Alt → H → I → Enter	Highlight selected text
Alt → H → I → N	Remove highlighting from selection
Ctrl + =	Make selected text a subscript
Ctrl + Shift + =	Make selected text a superscript
Ctrl + J	Justify text
Ctrl + M	Indent
Ctrl + Shift + M	Unindent
Alt → H → L	Open styles list; select style with arrow keys and Enter key
Tab	Insert tab, or jump to next cell or form entry
Shift + Tab	Jump to previous cell or form entry
Ctrl + Tab	Insert a tab (including in tables)
Ctrl + Shift + G	Open Word Count dialog box
Ctrl + S	Save the document
F12	Open the Save As dialog box
Ctrl + F12	Open the Open dialog box
Alt + Shift + R	Link to header or footer from previous section of document
Ctrl + H	Open the Find And Replace dialog box
Ctrl + P	Print
Ctrl + Shift + S	Open the Apply Styles dialog box
Shift + F7	Display the Thesaurus pane
Alt + F7	Move to next misspelling

Note You may have noticed several commands with arrows, such as **Alt → H → I → Enter**. These indicate that you are to press the keys in order, not simultaneously. You should notice that, when you press the **Alt** key, letters appear on the tabs of the ribbon. By pressing the letters that appear, you can navigate the ribbon by using only the keyboard. If you navigate to a drop-down menu, you can usually make a selection by pressing **Enter**. To cancel, press **Alt** again.

Other useful tricks

Warning when saving or printing a file with track changes

The *Track Changes* feature in Word allows the user to add revisions to a document while still preserving the original text. However, track changes are occasionally difficult to notice or easily forgotten. Complications can occur if a document is submitted with undesired track changes when a polished, final draft is expected. Within Word 2013, there is a feature that warns the user that the document contains track changes when saving or printing. To turn on this notification, click **File ⇒ Options ⇒ Trust Center**. Click **Trust Center Settings** and then click **Privacy Options**. Finally, select the check box next to the option **Warn before printing, saving or sending a file that contains tracked messages or comments**.

Using special characters and non-breaking spaces

For inline lists, as well as between numbers and their labels, you should add a non-breaking space to keep them together. Non-breaking spaces tell Word not to allow the words that they separate to split across two lines. The following examples show how these characters work.

Inline list that uses a normal space between the number and the list item:

This is an example sentence with an inline list: (1) this is the first item in the list, (2) this is the second item in the list, and (3) this is the third.

Inline list that uses a non-breaking space between the number and the list item:

This is an example sentence with an inline list: (1) this is the first item in the list, (2) this is the second item in the list, and (3) this is the third.

Number and label that uses a normal space between them:

 This is an example sentence illustrating how normal spaces and non-breaking spaces work 1 m.

Number and label that uses a non-breaking space between them:

 This is an example sentence illustrating how normal spaces and non-breaking spaces work 1 m.

About STREAM Tools

It is worth noting that the techniques described in this book are part of a larger system, which encompasses many aspects of technical writing. STREAM Tools is a writing system that provides a systematic way of moving through the writing process that helps ensure quality content and attractive documents through efficient processes. In order for STREAM Tools to be the most effective for your team, it helps to understand a bit about the writing process as a whole. STREAM Tools seeks to enable and automate parts of the writing process, but it does not substitute for the process itself, which generally follows the stages outlined in the following sections.

The definition stage

This stage marks the beginning of the document creation process, at which point the team outlines initial plans for the project. This stage includes, for example, holding a kick-off meeting to analyze the audience, formulating the purpose, and selecting the right combination of STREAM Tools.

The preparation stage

This stage marks the initial development and skeleton of a document and assigns responsibilities. This stage includes, for example, evaluating historical documents, creating a file repository, drafting an outline of the document, and assigning writing tasks to the team members.

The writing stage

This stage marks the actual writing process, including drafting, combining, and revising sections. This stage includes, for example, entering legacy content, requesting that team members submit staged drafts, verifying that the document is moving in the right direction, compiling the whole document, and revising content.

The completion stage

This stage marks the final steps in the writing process. At this time, the team confirms that it has met the goals outlined in the early stages of the process, and then submits the final document. This stage includes, for example, copyediting, soliciting external reviews, final submission, and analyzing the whole document development process.

There are, of course, entire books published on the writing process and effectively moving through each stage. Different components of STREAM Tools facilitate the writing process, but these tools do not replace the well-designed writing process that skilled writers employ. STREAM Tools helps writers better perform their work.

 More Info To learn more about STREAM Tools, see the book *Technical Writing for Teams: The STREAM Tools Handbook*, by A.V. Mamishev and S.D. Williams (Wiley-IEEE Press, 2010).

File template for a single-column report or paper

File name	BasicTemplate.docx
Description	This template is designed for simple manuscripts (up to 20 pages or so), written in single-column format, with one-level numbering of figures and tables.
	SEPARATE FILE PROVIDED

GenericReport_Template_2010.docx

[Report Title]

Copyright by [Author Name] and [Author Name]

Version 2
October 2012

Abstract

This template document is designed for generating uniform-looking reports and papers using principles of effective document formatting described in the book *Writing for Research Teams: The STREAM Tools Handbook* by Alexander V. Mamishev and Sean D. Williams. The main purpose of this template is to enable multiple co-authors to write documents using automatic formatting features of Microsoft Word. When each co-author uses the same format for each element of their manuscript, features such as numbering and cross-referencing of headings, figures, equations, and references becomes much easier. In addition, this approach allows easy reuse of portions of material in different documents.

2

Table of Contents:

You can update the Table of Contents at any time by pressing **Ctrl-A** (this selects the entire document), then releasing it, and then pressing **F9**. In short: **Ctrl-A, F9**. The Table of Contents is self-generated. The appearance of the Table of Contents can be changed by clicking **Insert, Index and Tables**.

If you need more lists, for example, the List of Figures or the List of Tables, you can insert them and then use similar logic. Better yet, switch to the ThesisOrBook.doc template to have more features needed that you might need for long documents.

3

1. Introduction

This template contains pre-formatted elements of a typical report: table of contents, headings, figures, tables, equations, and literature citations. In order to guarantee seamless integration of all documents generated by a group of writers, each writer should be careful in preserving format settings for all basic elements.

There is one main principle of this approach: in order to create a new entry, the writer should copy and paste an existing entry into a new location, and then overwrite the content at the new location.

2. Implementation (Heading level 1)

2.1 Heading level 2

2.1.1 Heading level 3

2.1.1.1 Heading level 4

Four levels of headings are provided as an initial template. In order to update numbering of all automated entries, click **CTRL-A, F9**. All figures and tables should be numbered.

To create a new figure, copy the existing figure template (with the attached caption) and paste it to a new location. The figure template is designed in such a way that the caption stays with the image.

In order to cross-reference a figure click **Insert, Reference, Cross-Reference, Figure, Only label and number**, then select the figure you want to cross-reference from the list.

An example of auto-formatted text:

Figure 1 shows the conceptual representation of the electrostatic air pump (EAP) technology.

In order to create or cross-reference a table, use the same command sequences as those for figures.

4

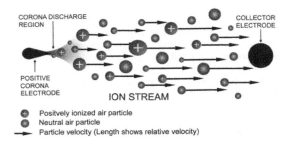

CORONA DISCHARGE REGION

COLLECTOR ELECTRODE

POSITIVE CORONA ELECTRODE

ION STREAM

⊕ Positvely ionized air particle
◉ Neutral air particle
➡ Particle velocity (Length shows relative velocity)

Figure 1. Schematic diagram of ion stream generating from a DC electrohydrodynamic ionic wind pump, where a high voltage is applied between the corona and the collector electrodes [1].

Table 1. This is the template for a table.

a	b	cde
1	2	34

New equations should be created by copying the equation line template below and altering it in a new location. MathType software is recommended for editing equations. MathType is superior to Microsoft Word's built-in equation editor because it has more features and allows exporting to LaTeX.

Example. According to (1), Coulomb's force $\mathbf{f}_C$ acting on an unpaired charge q in electric field $\mathbf{E}$ is equal to

$$f_c = q \times E \tag{1}$$

To cross reference an equation, you first have to create a bookmark by highlighting the equation number, clicking *Insert, Bookmark*, and giving that a unique identifier. For consistency, all equation identifiers should start with "eq". For example, equation (1) is bookmarked as eqColoumbForce.

Several software packages are available for managing literature citations in Microsoft Word. This template relies on software called EndNote. The citations should conform to the requirements of your field or the specific publication source. For example, in the IEEE style, citations should be enclosed in square brackets and look like this [2]. Citations should also be numbered in the order readers encounter them in the text.

5

References:

[1] C. P. Hsu, N. E. Jewell-Larsen, I. A. Krichtafovitch, S. W. Montgomery, J. T. Dibene II, and A. V. Mamishev, "Miniaturization of Electrostatic Fluid Accelerators," *IEEE/ASME Journal of MEMS*, 2007.

[2] J. H. Jeans, *Electricity and Magnetism,* 5th ed., New York, Cambridge University Press, 1927.

6

File template for a double-column paper

File name	BasicTemplateDoubleColumn.docx
Description	This template is designed for double-column, camera-ready papers (up to 10 pages or so), with one-level numbering of headings, figures, and tables.
	SEPARATE FILE PROVIDED

[Report Title]

[Author Name], [Author Name], and [Author Name], *Member, IEEE*

Abstract—This template for a double-column paper was created for the book *Technical Writing for Teams: The STREAM Tools Handbook* according to the instructions for authors contributing papers to the disciplines of the Institute of Electrical and Electronics Engineers (IEEE). The original template provided by the IEEE does not have automated typesetting functions. This, IEEE-Auto template file is preformatted for automatic numbering of manuscript elements. It should be easy to adjust appearance settings (for example, column width), to meet the requirements of other publishers.

Index Terms—About four key words or phrases in alphabetical order, separated by commas. For a list of suggested keywords, send a blank e-mail to keywords@ieee.org or visit the IEEE web site at http://www.ieee.org/organizations/pubs/ani_prod/keywrd98.txt

I. INTRODUCTION

THIS document is a template for Microsoft *Word* versions 14.0 or later, designed according to the IEEE template TRANS-JOUR.DOC, available from the IEEE website http://www.ieee.org/organizations/pubs/transactions/stylesheets.htm so you can use it to prepare your manuscript.

When you open DoubleColumn_Template_2012.docx, select "Page Layout" from the "View" menu in the menu bar (View | Page Layout), which allows you to see the footnotes. Then type over the section of the anuscript and copy the templates of individual manuscript elements to create new elements, such as figures or equations.

The pull-down style menu is at the left of the Formatting Toolbar at the top of your *Word* window (for example, the style at this point in the document is "Text"). Highlight a section that you want to designate with a certain style, then select the appropriate name on the style menu. The style will adjust your fonts and line spacing. **Do not change the font sizes or line spacing to squeeze more text into a limited number of pages.** Use italics for emphasis; do not underline.

To insert images into *Word*, position the cursor at the insertion point and either use Insert | Picture | From File or copy the image to the Windows clipboard and then Edit | Paste Special | Picture (with "Float over text" unchecked).

IEEE will do the final formatting of your paper. If your paper is intended for a conference, please observe the conference page limits.

II. PROCEDURE FOR PAPER SUBMISSION

A. Review Stage

Please check with your editor on whether to submit your manuscript by hard copy or electronically for review. If hard copy, submit photocopies such that only one column appears per page. This will give your referees plenty of room to write comments. Send the number of copies specified by your editor (typically four). If submitted electronically, find out if your editor prefers submissions on disk or as e-mail attachments.

If you want to submit your file with one column electronically, please do the following:

--First, click on the View menu and choose Print Layout.

--Second, place your cursor in the first paragraph. Go to the Format menu, choose Columns, choose one column Layout, and choose "apply to whole document" from the dropdown menu.

--Third, click and drag the right margin bar to just over 4 inches in width.

The graphics will stay in the "second" column, but you can drag them to the first column. Make the graphic wider to push out any text that may try to fill in next to the graphic.

B. Final Stage

When you submit your final version, after your paper has been accepted, print it in two-column format, including figures and tables. Send three prints of the paper; two will go to IEEE and one will be retained by the Editor-in-Chief or conference publications chair.

You must also send your final manuscript on a disk, which IEEE will use to prepare your paper for publication. Write the authors' names on the disk label. If you are using a Macintosh, please save your file on a PC formatted disk, if possible. You may use *Zip* or CD-ROM disks for large files, or compress files using *Compress, Pkzip, Stuffit, or Gzip*.

Also send a sheet of paper with complete contact information for all authors. Include full mailing addresses, telephone numbers, fax numbers, and e-mail addresses. This

Manuscript received [October 9, 2012]. (Write the date on which you submitted your paper for review.) This work was supported in part by the U.S. Department of Commerce under Grant BS123456 (sponsor and financial support acknowledgment goes here). Paper titles should be written in uppercase and lowercase letters, not all uppercase. Avoid writing long formulas with subscripts in the title; short formulas that identify the elements are fine (e.g., "Nd–Fe–B"). Do not write "(Invited)" in the title. Full names of authors are preferred in the author field, but are not required. Put a space between authors' initials.

F. A. Author is with the National Institute of Standards and Technology, Boulder, CO 80305 USA (corresponding author to provide phone: 303-555-5555; fax: 303-555-5555; e-mail: author@ boulder.nist.gov).

S. B. Author, Jr., was with Rice University, Houston, TX 77005 USA. He is now with the Department of Physics, Colorado State University, Fort Collins, CO 80523 USA (e-mail: author@lamar. colostate.edu).

T. C. Author is with the Electrical Engineering Department, University of Colorado, Boulder, CO 80309 USA, on leave from the National Research Institute for Metals, Tsukuba, Japan (e-mail: author@nrim.go.jp).

information will be used to send each author a complimentary copy of the journal in which the paper appears. In addition, designate one author as the "corresponding author." This is the author to whom proofs of the paper will be sent. Proofs are sent to the corresponding author only.

C. Figures

All tables and figures will be processed as images. **However, IEEE cannot extract the tables and figures embedded in your document.** (The figures and tables you insert in your document are only to help you gauge the size of your paper, for the convenience of the referees, and to make it easy for you to distribute preprints.) Therefore, **submit, on separate sheets of paper, enlarged versions of the tables and figures that appear in your document.** These are the images IEEE will scan and publish with your paper.

D. Electronic Image Files (Optional)

You will have the greatest control over the appearance of your figures if you are able to prepare electronic image files. If you do not have the required computer skills, just submit paper prints as described above and skip this section.

1) The Easiest Way: If you have a scanner, the best and quickest way to prepare non-color figure files is to print your tables and figures on paper exactly as you want them to appear, scan them, and then save them to a file in PostScript (PS) or Encapsulated PostScript (EPS) formats. Use a separate file for each image. File names should be of the form "fig1.ps" or "fig2.eps."

2) The Slightly Harder Way: Using a scanner as above, save the images in TIFF format. High-contrast line figures and tables should be prepared with 600 dpi resolution and saved with no compression, 1 bit per pixel (monochrome), with file names of the form "fig3.tif" or "table1.tif." To obtain a 3.45-in figure (one-column width) at 600 dpi, the figure requires a horizontal size of 2070 pixels. Typical file sizes will be on the order of 0.5 MB.

Photographs and grayscale figures should be prepared with 220 dpi resolution and saved with no compression, 8 bits per pixel (grayscale). To obtain a 3.45-in figure (one-column width) at 220 dpi, the figure should have a horizontal size of 759 pixels.

Color figures should be prepared with 400 dpi resolution and saved with no compression, 8 bits per pixel (palette or 256 color). To obtain a 3.45-in figure (one column width) at 400 dpi, the figure should have a horizontal size of 1380 pixels.

For more information on TIFF files, please go to http://www.ieee.org/organizations/pubs/transactions/informati on.htm and click on the link "Guidelines for Author Supplied Electronic Text and Graphics."

3) The Somewhat Harder Way: If you do not have a scanner, you may create noncolor PostScript figures by "printing" them to files. First, download a PostScript printer driver from http://www.adobe.com/support/downloads/pdrvwin.htm (for Windows) or from http://www.adobe.com/support/downloads/ pdrvmac.htm (for Macintosh) and install the "Generic PostScript Printer" definition. In *Word,* paste your figure into a new document. Print to a file using the PostScript printer driver. File names should be of the form "fig5.ps." Use Adobe Type 1 fonts when creating your figures, if possible.

4) Other Ways: Experienced computer users can convert figures and tables from their original format to TIFF. Some useful image converters are Adobe *Photoshop,* Corel *Draw,* and Microsoft *Photo Editor,* an application that is part of Microsoft *Office* (look for C:\Program Files\Common Files \Microsoft Shared\ PhotoEd\ PHOTOED.EXE. (You may have to custom-install *Photo Editor* from your original *Office* disk.)

Here is a way to make TIFF image files of tables. First, create your table in *Word.* Use horizontal lines but no vertical lines. Hide gridlines (Table | Hide Gridlines). Spell check the table to remove any red underlines that indicate spelling errors. Adjust magnification (View | Zoom) such that you can view the entire table *at maximum area* when you select View | Full Screen. Move the cursor so that it is out of the way. Press "Print Screen" on your keyboard; this copies the screen image to the Windows clipboard. Open Microsoft *Photo Editor* and click Edit | Paste as New Image. Crop the table image (click Select button; select the part you want, then Image | Crop). Adjust the properties of the image (File | Properties) to monochrome (1 bit) and 600 pixels per inch. Resize the image (Image | Resize) to a width of 3.45 inches. Save the file (File | Save As) in TIFF with no compression (click "More" button).

Most graphing programs allow you to save graphs in TIFF; however, you often have no control over compression or number of bits per pixel. You should open these image files in a program such as Microsoft *Photo Editor* and re-save them using no compression, either 1 or 8 bits, and either 600 or 220 dpi resolution (File | Properties; Image | Resize). See Section II-D2 for an explanation of number of bits and resolution. If your graphing program cannot export to TIFF, you can use the same technique described for tables in the previous paragraph.

A way to convert a figure from Windows Metafile (WMF) to TIFF is to paste it into Microsoft *PowerPoint,* save it in JPG format, open it with Microsoft *Photo Editor* or similar converter, and re-save it as TIFF.

Microsoft *Excel* allows you to save spreadsheet charts in Graphics Interchange Format (GIF). To get good resolution, make the *Excel* charts *very* large. Then use "Save as HTML" feature (see http://support.microsoft.com/support/ kb/articles/q158/0/79.asp). You can then convert from GIF to TIFF using Microsoft *Photo Editor,* for example.

No matter how you convert your images, it is a good idea to print the TIFF files to make sure nothing was lost in the conversion.

If you modify this document for use with other IEEE journals or conferences, you should save it as type "Word 97-2000 & 6.0/95 - RTF (*.doc)" so that it can be opened by any version of *Word.*

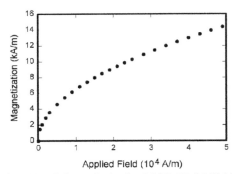

Fig. 1. Magnetization as a function of applied field. Note that "Fig." is abbreviated. There is a period after the figure number, followed by two spaces. It is good practice to explain the significance of the figure in the caption.

E. Copyright Form

An IEEE copyright form should accompany your final submission. You can get a .pdf, .html, or .doc version at http://www.ieee.org/copyright or from the first issues in each volume of the IEEE TRANSACTIONS and JOURNALS. Authors are responsible for obtaining any security clearances.

III. MATH

If you are using *Word,* use either the Microsoft Equation Editor or the *MathType* add-on (http://www.mathtype.com) for equations in your paper (Insert | Object | Create New | Microsoft Equation *or* MathType Equation). "Float over text" should *not* be selected.

IV. UNITS

Use either SI (MKS) or CGS as primary units. (SI units are strongly encouraged.) English units may be used as secondary units (in parentheses). **This applies to papers in data storage.** For example, write "15 Gb/cm^2 (100 Gb/in^2)." An exception is when English units are used as identifiers in trade, such as "3½ in disk drive." Avoid combining SI and CGS units, such as current in amperes and magnetic field in oersteds. This often leads to confusion because equations do not balance dimensionally. If you must use mixed units, clearly state the units for each quantity in an equation.

The SI unit for magnetic field strength H is A/m. However, if you wish to use units of T, either refer to magnetic flux density B or magnetic field strength symbolized as $\mu_0 H$. Use the center dot to separate compound units, e.g., "A·m^2."

V. HELPFUL HINTS

A. Figures and Tables

Because IEEE will do the final formatting of your paper, you do not need to position figures and tables at the top and bottom of each column. In fact, all figures, figure captions,

and tables can be at the end of the paper. Large figures and tables may span both columns. Place figure captions below the figures; place table titles above the tables.

TABLE I
UNITS FOR MAGNETIC PROPERTIES

Symbol	Quantity	Conversion from Gaussian and CGS EMU to SI [a]
Φ	magnetic flux	$1\ \text{Mx} \rightarrow 10^{-8}\ \text{Wb} = 10^{-8}\ \text{V·s}$
B	magnetic flux density, magnetic induction	$1\ \text{G} \rightarrow 10^{-4}\ \text{T} = 10^{-4}\ \text{Wb/m}^2$
H	magnetic field strength	$1\ \text{Oe} \rightarrow 10^3/(4\pi)\ \text{A/m}$
m	magnetic moment	$1\ \text{erg/G} = 1\ \text{emu}$ $\rightarrow 10^{-3}\ \text{A·m}^2 = 10^{-3}\ \text{J/T}$
M	magnetization	$1\ \text{erg/(G·cm}^3) = 1\ \text{emu/cm}^3$ $\rightarrow 10^3\ \text{A/m}$
$4\pi M$	magnetization	$1\ \text{G} \rightarrow 10^3/(4\pi)\ \text{A/m}$
σ	specific magnetization	$1\ \text{erg/(G·g)} = 1\ \text{emu/g} \rightarrow 1\ \text{A·m}^2/\text{kg}$
j	magnetic dipole moment	$1\ \text{erg/G} = 1\ \text{emu}$ $\rightarrow 4\pi \times 10^{-10}\ \text{Wb·m}$
J	magnetic polarization	$1\ \text{erg/(G·cm}^3) = 1\ \text{emu/cm}^3$ $\rightarrow 4\pi \times 10^{-4}\ \text{T}$
χ, κ	susceptibility	$1 \rightarrow 4\pi$
χ_ρ	mass susceptibility	$1\ \text{cm}^3/\text{g} \rightarrow 4\pi \times 10^{-3}\ \text{m}^3/\text{kg}$
μ	permeability	$1 \rightarrow 4\pi \times 10^{-7}\ \text{H/m}$ $= 4\pi \times 10^{-7}\ \text{Wb/(A·m)}$
μ_r	relative permeability	$\mu \rightarrow \mu_r$
w, W	energy density	$1\ \text{erg/cm}^3 \rightarrow 10^{-1}\ \text{J/m}^3$
N, D	demagnetizing factor	$1 \rightarrow 1/(4\pi)$

No vertical lines in table. Statements that serve as captions for the entire table do not need footnote letters.

[a]Gaussian units are the same as cgs emu for magnetostatics; Mx = maxwell, G = gauss, Oe = oersted; Wb = weber, V = volt, s = second, T = tesla, m = meter, A = ampere, J = joule, kg = kilogram, H = henry.

figures; place table titles above the tables. If your figure has two parts, include the labels "(a)" and "(b)" as part of the artwork. Please verify that the figures and tables you mention in the text actually exist. **Please do not include captions as part of the figures. Do not put captions in "text boxes" linked to the figures. Do not put borders around the outside of your figures.** Use the abbreviation "Fig." even at the beginning of a sentence. Do not abbreviate "Table." Tables are numbered with Roman numerals.

Color printing of figures is available, but is billed to the authors (approximately $1300, depending on the number of figures and number of pages containing color). Include a note with your final paper indicating that you request color printing. **Do not use color unless it is necessary for the proper interpretation of your figures.** If you want reprints of your color article, the reprint order should be submitted promptly. There is an additional charge of $81 per 100 for color reprints.

Figure axis labels are often a source of confusion. Use words rather than symbols. As an example, write the quantity "Magnetization," or "Magnetization M," not just "M." Put units in parentheses. Do not label axes only with units. As in Fig. 1, for example, write "Magnetization (A/m)" or "Magnetization (A·m^{-1})," not just "A/m." Do not label axes with a ratio of quantities and units. For example, write "Temperature (K)," not "Temperature/K."

Multipliers can be especially confusing. Write "Magnetization (kA/m)" or "Magnetization (10^3 A/m)." Do not write "Magnetization (A/m) × 1000" because the reader would not know whether the top axis label in Fig. 1 meant 16000 A/m or 0.016 A/m. Figure labels should be legible, approximately 8 to 12 point type.

B. References

Number citations consecutively in square brackets [1]. The sentence punctuation follows the brackets [2]. Multiple references [2], [3] are each numbered with separate brackets [1]–[3]. When citing a section in a book, please give the relevant page numbers [2]. In sentences, refer simply to the reference number, as in [3]. Do not use "Ref. [3]" or "reference [3]" except at the beginning of a sentence: "Reference [3] shows ... ." Unfortunately the IEEE document translator cannot handle automatic endnotes in *Word*; therefore, type the reference list at the end of the paper using the "References" style.

Number footnotes separately in superscripts (Insert | Footnote).[1] Place the actual footnote at the bottom of the column in which it is cited; do not put footnotes in the reference list (endnotes). Use letters for table footnotes (see Table I).

Please note that the references at the end of this document are in the preferred referencing style. Give all authors' names; do not use "*et al.*" unless there are six authors or more. Use a space after authors' initials. Papers that have not been published should be cited as "unpublished" [4]. Papers that have been submitted for publication should be cited as "submitted for publication" [5]. Papers that have been accepted for publication, but not yet specified for an issue should be cited as "to be published" [6]. Please give affiliations and addresses for private communications [7].

Capitalize only the first word in a paper title, except for proper nouns and element symbols. For papers published in translation journals, please give the English citation first, followed by the original foreign-language citation [8].

C. Abbreviations and Acronyms

Define abbreviations and acronyms the first time they are used in the text, even after they have already been defined in the abstract. Abbreviations such as IEEE, SI, ac, and dc do not have to be defined. Abbreviations that incorporate periods should not have spaces: write "C.N.R.S.," not "C. N. R. S." Do not use abbreviations in the title unless they are unavoidable (for example, "IEEE" in the title of this article).

D. Equations

Number equations consecutively with equation numbers in parentheses flush with the right margin, as in (1). First use the equation editor to create the equation. Then select the "Equation" markup style. Press the tab key and write the equation number in parentheses. To make your equations more compact, you may use the solidus (/), the exp function, or appropriate exponents. Use parentheses to avoid ambiguities

in denominators. Punctuate equations when they are part of a sentence, as in

$$\int_0^{r_2} F(r,\varphi)\, dr\, d\varphi = \left[\frac{\sigma\, r_2}{2\,\mu_0}\right] \cdot \int_0^\infty \frac{e^{-\lambda|z_j - z_i|} J_1(\lambda\, r_2) J_0(\lambda\, r_i)\, d\lambda}{\lambda} \tag{1}$$

Be sure that the symbols in your equation have been defined before the equation appears or immediately following. Italicize symbols (T might refer to temperature, but T is the unit tesla). Refer to "(1)," not "Eq. (1)" or "equation (1)," except at the beginning of a sentence: "Equation (1) is ... ."

E. Other Recommendations

Use one space after periods and colons. Hyphenate complex modifiers: "zero-field-cooled magnetization." Avoid dangling participles, such as, "Using (1), the potential was calculated." [It is not clear who or what used (1).] Write instead, "The potential was calculated by using (1)," or "Using (1), we calculated the potential."

Use a zero before decimal points: "0.25," not ".25." Use "cm^3," not "cc." Indicate sample dimensions as "0.1 cm × 0.2 cm," not "0.1 × 0.2 cm^2." The abbreviation for "seconds" is "s," not "sec." Do not mix complete spellings and abbreviations of units: use "Wb/m^2" or "webers per square meter," not "webers/m^2." When expressing a range of values, write "7 to 9" or "7-9," not "7~9."

A parenthetical statement at the end of a sentence is punctuated outside of the closing parenthesis (like this). (A parenthetical sentence is punctuated within the parentheses.) In American English, periods and commas are within quotation marks, like "this period." Other punctuation is "outside"! Avoid contractions; for example, write "do not" instead of "don't." The serial comma is preferred: "A, B, and C" instead of "A, B and C."

If you wish, you may write in the first person singular or plural and use the active voice ("I observed that ..." or "We observed that ..." instead of "It was observed that ..."). Remember to check spelling. If your native language is not English, please get a native English-speaking colleague to proofread your paper.

VI. Some Common Mistakes

The word "data" is plural, not singular. The subscript for the permeability of vacuum μ_0 is zero, not a lowercase letter "o." The term for residual magnetization is "remanence"; the adjective is "remanent"; do not write "remanence" or "remnant." Use the word "micrometer" instead of "micron." A graph within a graph is an "inset," not an "insert." The word "alternatively" is preferred to the word "alternately" (unless you really mean something that alternates). Use the word "whereas" instead of "while" (unless you are referring to simultaneous events). Do not use the word "essentially" to mean "approximately" or "effectively." Do not use the word "issue" as a euphemism for "problem." When compositions are not specified, separate chemical symbols by en-dashes; for example, "NiMn" indicates the intermetallic compound $Ni_{0.5}Mn_{0.5}$ whereas "Ni–Mn" indicates an alloy of some composition Ni_xMn_{1-x}.

---

[1] It is recommended that footnotes be avoided (except for the unnumbered footnote with the receipt date on the first page). Instead, try to integrate the footnote information into the text.

Be aware of the different meanings of the homophones "affect" (usually a verb) and "effect" (usually a noun), "complement" and "compliment," "discreet" and "discrete," "principal" (e.g., "principal investigator") and "principle" (e.g., "principle of measurement"). Do not confuse "imply" and "infer."

Prefixes such as "non," "sub," "micro," "multi," and ""ultra" are not independent words; they should be joined to the words they modify, usually without a hyphen. There is no period after the "et" in the Latin abbreviation "*et al.*" (it is also italicized). The abbreviation "i.e.," means "that is," and the abbreviation "e.g.," means "for example" (these abbreviations are not italicized).

An excellent style manual and source of information for science writers is [9]. A general IEEE style guide, *Information for Authors,* is available at http://www.ieee.org/organizations/pubs/transactions/informati on.htm

VII. EDITORIAL POLICY

Submission of a manuscript is not required for participation in a conference. Do not submit a reworked version of a paper you have submitted or published elsewhere. Do not publish "preliminary" data or results. The submitting author is responsible for obtaining agreement of all coauthors and any consent required from sponsors before submitting a paper. IEEE TRANSACTIONS and JOURNALS strongly discourage courtesy authorship. It is the obligation of the authors to cite relevant prior work.

The Transactions and Journals Department does not publish conference records or proceedings. The TRANSACTIONS does publish papers related to conferences that have been recommended for publication on the basis of peer review. As a matter of convenience and service to the technical community, these topical papers are collected and published in one issue of the TRANSACTIONS.

At least two reviews are required for every paper submitted. For conference-related papers, the decision to accept or reject a paper is made by the conference editors and publications committee; the recommendations of the referees are advisory only. Undecipherable English is a valid reason for rejection. Authors of rejected papers may revise and resubmit them to the TRANSACTIONS as regular papers, whereupon they will be reviewed by two new referees.

VIII. PUBLICATION PRINCIPLES

The contents of IEEE TRANSACTIONS and JOURNALS are peer-reviewed and archival. The TRANSACTIONS publishes scholarly articles of archival value as well as tutorial expositions and critical reviews of classical subjects and topics of current interest.

Authors should consider the following points:

1) Technical papers submitted for publication must advance the state of knowledge and must cite relevant prior work.
2) The length of a submitted paper should be commensurate with the importance, or appropriate to the complexity, of the work. For example, an obvious extension of previously published work might not be appropriate for publication or might be adequately treated in just a few pages.
3) Authors must convince both peer reviewers and the editors of the scientific and technical merit of a paper; the standards of proof are higher when extraordinary or unexpected results are reported.
4) Because replication is required for scientific progress, papers submitted for publication must provide sufficient information to allow readers to perform similar experiments or calculations and use the reported results. Although not everything need be disclosed, a paper must contain new, useable, and fully described information. For example, a specimen's chemical composition need not be reported if the main purpose of a paper is to introduce a new measurement technique. Authors should expect to be challenged by reviewers if the results are not supported by adequate data and critical details.
5) Papers that describe ongoing work or announce the latest technical achievement, which are suitable for presentation at a professional conference, may not be appropriate for publication in a TRANSACTIONS or JOURNAL.

IX. CONCLUSION

A conclusion section is not required. Although a conclusion may review the main points of the paper, do not replicate the abstract as the conclusion. A conclusion might elaborate on the importance of the work or suggest applications and extensions.

APPENDIX

Appendixes, if needed, appear before the acknowledgment.

ACKNOWLEDGMENT

The preferred spelling of the word "acknowledgment" in American English is without an "e" after the "g." Use the singular heading even if you have many acknowledgments. Avoid expressions such as "One of us (S.B.A.) would like to thank ... ." Instead, write "F. A. Author thanks ... ." **Sponsor and financial support acknowledgments are placed in the unnumbered footnote on the first page.**

REFERENCES

[1] G. O. Young, "Synthetic structure of industrial plastics (Book style with paper title and editor)," in *Plastics*, 2nd ed. vol. 3, J. Peters, Ed. New York: McGraw-Hill, 1964, pp. 15–64.
[2] W.-K. Chen, *Linear Networks and Systems* (Book style). Belmont, CA: Wadsworth, 1993, pp. 123–135.
[3] H. Poor, *An Introduction to Signal Detection and Estimation*. New York: Springer-Verlag, 1985, ch. 4.
[4] B. Smith, "An approach to graphs of linear forms (Unpublished work style)," unpublished.
[5] E. H. Miller, "A note on reflector arrays (Periodical style—Accepted for publication)," *IEEE Trans. Antennas Propagat.*, to be published.

[6] J. Wang, "Fundamentals of erbium-doped fiber amplifiers arrays (Periodical style—Submitted for publication)," *IEEE J. Quantum Electron.*, submitted for publication.

[7] C. J. Kaufman, Rocky Mountain Research Lab., Boulder, CO, private communication, May 1995.

[8] Y. Yorozu, M. Hirano, K. Oka, and Y. Tagawa, "Electron spectroscopy studies on magneto-optical media and plastic substrate interfaces(Translation Journals style)," *IEEE Transl. J. Magn.Jpn.*, vol. 2, Aug. 1987, pp. 740–741 [*Dig. 9th Annu. Conf. Magnetics* Japan, 1982, p. 301].

[9] M. Young, *The Techincal Writers Handbook.* Mill Valley, CA: University Science, 1989.

[10] J. U. Duncombe, "Infrared navigation—Part I: An assessment of feasibility (Periodical style)," *IEEE Trans. Electron Devices*, vol. ED-11, pp. 34–39, Jan. 1959.

[11] S. Chen, B. Mulgrew, and P. M. Grant, "A clustering technique for digital communications channel equalization using radial basis function networks," *IEEE Trans. Neural Networks*, vol. 4, pp. 570–578, July 1993.

[12] R. W. Lucky, "Automatic equalization for digital communication," *Bell Syst. Tech. J.*, vol. 44, no. 4, pp. 547–588, Apr. 1965.

[13] S. P. Bingulac, "On the compatibility of adaptive controllers (Published Conference Proceedings style)," in *Proc. 4th Annu. Allerton Conf. Circuits and Systems Theory*, New York, 1994, pp. 8–16.

[14] G. R. Faulhaber, "Design of service systems with priority reservation," in *Conf. Rec. 1995 IEEE Int. Conf. Communications*, pp. 3–8.

[15] W. D. Doyle, "Magnetization reversal in films with biaxial anisotropy," in *1987 Proc. INTERMAG Conf.*, pp. 2.2-1–2.2-6.

[16] G. W. Juette and L. E. Zeffanella, "Radio noise currents n short sections on bundle conductors (Presented Conference Paper style)," presented at the IEEE Summer power Meeting, Dallas, TX, June 22–27, 1990, Paper 90 SM 690-0 PWRS.

[17] J. G. Kreifeldt, "An analysis of surface-detected EMG as an amplitude-modulated noise," presented at the 1989 Int. Conf. Medicine and Biological Engineering, Chicago, IL.

[18] J. Williams, "Narrow-band analyzer (Thesis or Dissertation style)," Ph.D. dissertation, Dept. Elect. Eng., Harvard Univ., Cambridge, MA, 1993.

[19] N. Kawasaki, "Parametric study of thermal and chemical nonequilibrium nozzle flow," M.S. thesis, Dept. Electron. Eng., Osaka Univ., Osaka, Japan, 1993.

[20] J. P. Wilkinson, "Nonlinear resonant circuit devices (Patent style)," U.S. Patent 3 624 12, July 16, 1990.

[21] *IEEE Criteria for Class IE Electric Systems* (Standards style), IEEE Standard 308, 1969.

[22] *Letter Symbols for Quantities*, ANSI Standard Y10.5-1968.

[23] R. E. Haskell and C. T. Case, "Transient signal propagation in lossless isotropic plasmas (Report style)," USAF Cambridge Res. Lab., Cambridge, MA Rep. ARCRL-66-234 (II), 1994, vol. 2.

[24] E. E. Reber, R. L. Michell, and C. J. Carter, "Oxygen absorption in the Earth's atmosphere," Aerospace Corp., Los Angeles, CA, Tech. Rep. TR-0200 (420-46)-3, Nov. 1988.

[25] (Handbook style) *Transmission Systems for Communications*, 3rd ed., Western Electric Co., Winston-Salem, NC, 1985, pp. 44–60.

[26] *Motorola Semiconductor Data Manual*, Motorola Semiconductor Products Inc., Phoenix, AZ, 1989.

[27] (Basic Book/Monograph Online Sources) J. K. Author. (year, month, day). *Title* (edition) [Type of medium]. Volume(issue). Available: http://www.(URL)

[28] J. Jones. (1991, May 10). Networks (2nd ed.) [Online]. Available: http://www.atm.com

[29] (Journal Online Sources style) K. Author. (year, month). Title. *Journal* [Type of medium]. Volume(issue), paging if given. Available: http://www.(URL)

R. J. Vidmar. (1992, August). On the use of atmospheric plasmas as electromagnetic reflectors. *IEEE Trans. Plasma Sci.* [Online]. *21(3)*. pp. 876—880. Available: http://www.halcyon.com/pub/journals/21ps03-vidmar

First A. Author (M'76–SM'81–F'87) and the other authors may include biographies at the end of regular papers. Biographies are often not included in conference-related papers. This author became a Member (M) of IEEE in 1976, a Senior Member (SM) in 1981, and a Fellow (F) in 1987. The first paragraph may contain a place and/or date of birth (list place, then date). Next, the author's educational background is listed. The degrees should be listed with type of degree in what field, which institution, city, state or country, and year degree was earned. The author's major field of study should be lower-cased.

The second paragraph uses the pronoun of the person (he or she) and not the author's last name. It lists military and work experience, including summer and fellowship jobs. Job titles are capitalized. The current job must have a location; previous positions may be listed without one. Information concerning previous publications may be included. Try not to list more than three books or published articles. The format for listing publishers of a book within the biography is: title of book (city, state: publisher name, year) similar to a reference. Current and previous research interests ends the paragraph.

The third paragraph begins with the author's title and last name (e.g., Dr. Smith, Prof. Jones, Mr. Kajor, Ms. Hunter). List any memberships in professional societies other than the IEEE. Finally, list any awards and work for IEEE committees and publications. If a photograph is provided, the biography will be indented around it. The photograph is placed at the top left of the biography. Personal hobbies will be deleted from the biography.

File template for a thesis, book, or long report

File name	ThesisTemplate.docx
Description	This template is designed for long manuscripts, such as theses, dissertations, books, and reports. The template is written in single-column format, with multi-level numbering (for example, "Figure 3.2" as opposed to "Figure 7"). The template also contains extensive elements of front matter and back matter (rarely present in shorter documents) including dedications, acknowledgments, foreword, glossary, and index. Page numbering in the template follows the standard thesis page numbering with front matter using roman numerals, and the rest of the manuscript using arabic numerals.
	SEPARATE FILE PROVIDED

[Ph.D. Dissertation Title]

[Author Name]

A dissertation submitted in partial fulfillment of the requirements for the degree of

Doctor of Philosophy

University of Washington
2012

Program Authorized to Offer Degree: [Department of Electrical Engineering]

University of Washington
Graduate School

This is to certify that I have examined this copy of a doctoral dissertation by

[Author Name]

and have found it complete and satisfactory in all respects,
and that any and all revisions required by the final
examining committee have been made.

Chair of Supervisory Committee:

_____
[Committee Chair]

Reading Committee:

_____
[Committee member 1]

_____
[Committee member 2]

_____
[Committee member 3]

_____
[Committee member 4]

Date: _____

In presenting this dissertation in partial fulfillment of the requirements for a doctoral degree at the University of Washington, I agree that the Library shall make its copies freely available for inspection. I further agree that extensive copying of this dissertation is allowable only for scholarly purposes, consistent with "fair use" as prescribed in the U.S. Copyright Law. Any other reproduction for any purposes or by any means shall not be allowed without my written permission.

Signature_____

Date_____

University of Washington

Abstract

[Dissertation Title]

by [Author Name]

Chair of the Supervisory Committee

Associate Professor [Advisor Name]
Department of Electrical Engineering

This is the abstract of the dissertation. The abstract of a Ph.D. dissertation cannot be longer than *350* words. The abstract section does not go into the table of contents.

TABLE OF CONTENTS

i

LIST OF FIGURES

ii

LIST OF TABLES

iii

ACKNOWLEDGEMENTS

The acknowledgement section goes here. The acknowledge section does not go into the table of contents.

iv

DEDICATION

[this page is optional and does not go into the table of contents]

Chapter 1. Introduction

This is a template document for dissertations, master's theses or other long manuscripts, including books. This document is specific to one institution, but the vast majority of universities use very similar formats.

1.1   Cover Page

The formatting of the cover page and first few pages needs to be followed exactly. There is no space to use creativity in this case. The degree name is strictly "Doctor of Philosophy," instead of "Doctor of Philosophy in Electrical Engineering." In the committee page, make sure you have the exact template as in this dissertation. The chair person should be listed twice, in a separate section and in the committee list. The acknowledgements, abstract, and vita sections should not show up in table of contents.

1.2   Table of Contents

The Table of Contents should be self-generated. The format of it can be changed through Insert-Index and Tables. The same is true for List of Figures. The List of Tables can be generated in the same command window as List of Figures.

In the Table of Contents, the list and pages of "List of Figures," "List of Tables," and "Reference" won't automatically generate. You can bookmark these titles at corresponding pages, and reference their page numbers in Table of Contents. In this way, you could auto generate the list in Table of Contents.

v

Do not forget to keep capitalization consistent in the Table of Contents. There should be at least two entries under each subheading (if you have 2.1, you must have 2. 2). If you don't reconsider your headings and organization scheme.

1.3   Chapter Title and Heading Title Style

Most universities have strict rules on the style of chapter titles and heading titles. The safest way is to follow this template and to consult with the appropriate parties who certify formatting of a thesis or dissertation.

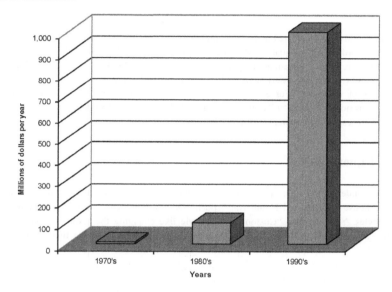

Figure 1.1. Increase in the cost of power quality problems in the United States [1].

1.4   Tables and Figures

Figure titles always go below the figure, while table titles always go above the table. This is a convention to be followed. In order to update numbering of all automated entries, click CTRL-A F9.

All figures should be numbered. To create a new figure, copy the existing figure (with the attached caption) and paste it to a new location. The figure template is designed in such a way that the caption stays with the image. Remember that letter and line thickness of each figure should be sufficiently large in order to be clearly legible in a double-column format.

Figure 1.1 is an example figure. In order to cross reference a figure click Insert-Cross Reference-Figure-Only label and number, then select the appropriate figure. This procedure is the same for tables. Also, the caption of the figure is recommended to have indentation on both sides so to distinguish from normal text.

1.5   Equations

The equations should be created using the template below and MathType software. MathType is superior to Word's built-in equation editor because it allows exporting to LaTeX and is faster.

To cross reference an equation, you must first create a bookmark by highlighting the equation number, clicking Insert-Bookmark, and giving that a unique identifier. All equation identifiers start with "eq". For example, eqColoumbForce. Pay attention to the font of your variables. It is not ok to have "V" in the equation and "V" in text. Auto-numbering of figures and tables that correspond to chapters (e.g. Fig 3.3) is discussed in the next section.

1.6   Chapter Heading

First, you can define the style of headings of a chapter. Right-click on the line of the chapter's title and choose "Bullets and Numbering," push "Outline Numbered" tab, to choose different sample styles. You can also "Customize" the style like changing the "Number Format." For example, you can add "Chapter" in front of the chapter number to make this the format of Heading 1*.

Next time, when writing a new chapter, just type in the chapter title, then choose "Heading 1". Your defined style will automatically appear.

Another method of adding "Chapter" in front of each chapter number is to create "Chapter" character in other software, then copy it as a picture in front of the number.

If you make changes to the title format of one chapter, you can update all other chapters' title format at the same time, instead of redoing them one by one. Just re-click "Heading 1," a window of "Modify Style" pops up. Check "update the style to reflect recent changes."

1.6.1   Include Chapter Number in Figure Caption

To include the chapter number in a figure's caption, click "Insert-Caption" and choose label "Figure." Then click "Numbering," check "include chapter number" and also choose a desired format. Thus, the chapter number will be included.

1.6.2 Include Chapter Number in Equation Numbering

Normally only one number is assigned to one equation, as mentioned above. To include the chapter number, in front of the **original** equation number click "Insert-Cross reference-Heading-Heading number," and then check the corresponding chapter. The chapter number will be present. Don't forget to add a "." between the chapter number and original equation number.

This is a sample equation [2]:

$$a = -b = c \qquad\qquad (1.1)$$

Equation counting does not restart from 1 in a new chapter. To solve this problem, in a new chapter (For example in Chapter 2, please refer to beginning of next chapter), right-click before the **original** equation number, check "Toggle Field Codes," the code will show up like "SEQ eq * MERGEFORMAT," add "2" after "eq" meaning the second (new) series of equation to "SEQ eq2 * MERGEFORMAT," then right-click "Toggle Field Codes" again, the second equation number in this new chapter will start from 1. For equations in the next chapter, just add "3" after "eq."

Also, it is very important to define every variable of the equation in the text nearby. If you use a lot of equations, it pays to learn shortcuts in MathType.

1.7 Section and Page Breaks

When writing a thesis, you are often required to use different styles of numbering for different sections. For example, Roman numerals are often used for preliminary pages, and Arabic numerals are used for text. You can achieve these differences by inserting section breaks: Insert-Break-Next Page (Section break types). After that, you can adjust the numbering style freely in each section. If you just want to start writing a new chapter from the next page in the same section (you want to continue the sequential numbering), you can just insert a Page Break.

1.8 Subsections

Please use the following style for the sub-section heading titles.

1.8.1 Subsection Level 3

This section is just to show you how to make sub-sections.

1.8.1.1   Subsection Level 4

This section is just to show you how to make sub-sections.

1.9   Orphan Control

Orphan control is very important in order to pass the review of graduate school. Make sure that no page ends with a heading title (any level), and make sure the figure title and figure are on the same page. The same concept applies for tables and table titles.

Chapter 2. Complete Your Dissertation

Some professors use *Ph.D. dissertation* and *Ph.D. thesis* interchangeably, while some other professors do not feel comfortable with the wording *Ph.D. thesis*. So make sure you make all of them happy about this throughout your dissertation.

This is a sample equation [2]:

$$P(t, f) = \int_{-\infty}^{\infty} \int_{-\infty}^{\infty} A(\eta, \tau) \; \varphi(\eta, \tau) \; e^{j2\pi\eta t} \; e^{j-2\pi f \tau} \; d\eta \; d\tau \qquad (2.1)$$

where t represents time, f represents frequency, η represents continuous frequency shift, and τ represents continuous time lag. The ambiguity plane $A(\eta, \tau)$ for a given signal $s(t)$ is defined as:

$$A(\eta, \tau) = \int_{\infty}^{\infty} s(t) \; s^*(t + \tau)^{j2\pi\eta t} dt \qquad (2.2)$$

Here $s(t)$ represents the signal at time t, and $s(t + \tau)$ represents the signal at a future time $t + \tau$, and the $s^*(t + \tau)$ means the complex conjugate of $s(t + \tau)$.

Table 2.1 is a sample table.

Table 2.1. A Sample Table Caption

Row 1	Value	Location
Row 2	1.89	Y
Row 3	1.94	N
Row 4	2.33	N
Row 5	1.45	N
Row 6	2.11	N

2.1   References

For literature citations, use EndNote software. The citations and references list should conform to the standards of your discipline.

It is very important to keep the consistency of the reference database file in the writing process, especially when you work on multiple computers.

2.2   Conclusions

This template document will be updated as more and more students start to work on Ph.D. dissertations. Please do note that the requirements for MS thesis and Ph.D. dissertation are slightly different. Although this template may also be helpful for writing a MS thesis, it is important to identify the requirement difference and make appropriate changes.

End Notes

The current solution is to copy the whole reference section over.

References

[1] B. Kennedy, *Power Quality Primer,* McGraw-Hill, 2000.

[2] L. Cohen, *Time-Frequency Analysis,* Prentice-Hall, 1995.

Vita

A short bio of the author is required for a Ph.D. dissertation at the University of Washington. The vita section does not go into the table of content. The formatting style follows the text of the dissertation.

IEEE template with STREAM Tools enabled

File name	IEEETransactionsTemplate_2010.docx
Description	The following sample showcases how an IEEE journal paper enabled with STREAM Tools should be formatted. Please note that individual agency requirements will change over time, so authors are encouraged to closely review their guidelines before submission.
	SEPARATE FILE PROVIDED

Preparation of Papers for IEEE Transactions and Journals (October 2006, STREAM Tools modification February 2012)

[Author Name], [Author Name], and [Author Name], *Member, IEEE*

Abstract—**These instructions give you guidelines for preparing papers for IEEE Transactions and Journals. Use this document as a template if you are using Microsoft *Word* 6.0 or later. Otherwise, use this document as an instruction set. The electronic file of your paper will be formatted further at IEEE. Define all symbols used in the abstract. Do not cite references in the abstract. Do not delete the blank line immediately above the abstract; it sets the footnote at the bottom of this column. This template file has been modified from the original IEEE version, so that it enables the authors to use automatic numbering of figures, tables, equations, and references, as well as fast conversion to single column format for reports, theses, book, etc. The principles behind template modification are described in the book *Technical Writing for Teams*, by A. V. Mamishev and S.D. Williams, and at the website www.streamtoolsonline.com. Section IX. STREAM Tools of this template provides usage details.**

Index Terms—**About four key words or phrases in alphabetical order, separated by commas. For a list of suggested keywords, send a blank e-mail to keywords@ieee.org or visit the IEEE web site at http://www.ieee.org/organizations/pubs/ani_prod/keywrd98.txt**

I. Introduction

THIS document is a template for Microsoft *Word* versions 14.0 or later. If you are reading a paper version of this document, please download the electronic file, TRANS-JOUR.DOC, from http://www.ieee.org/organizations/pubs/transactions/stylesheets.htm so you can use it to prepare your manuscript. If you

Manuscript received [October 9, 2012]. (Write the date on which you submitted your paper for review.) This work was supported in part by the U.S. Department of Commerce under Grant BS123456 (sponsor and financial support acknowledgment goes here). Paper titles should be written in uppercase and lowercase letters, not all uppercase. Avoid writing long formulas with subscripts in the title; short formulas that identify the elements are fine (e.g., "Nd–Fe–B"). Do not write "(Invited)" in the title. Full names of authors are preferred in the author field, but are not required. Put a space between authors' initials.

F. A. Author is with the National Institute of Standards and Technology, Boulder, CO 80305 USA (corresponding author to provide phone: 303-555-5555; fax: 303-555-5555; e-mail: author@ boulder.nist.gov).

S. B. Author, Jr., was with Rice University, Houston, TX 77005 USA. He is now with the Department of Physics, Colorado State University, Fort Collins, CO 80523 USA (e-mail: author@lamar. colostate.edu).

T. C. Author is with the Electrical Engineering Department, University of Colorado, Boulder, CO 80309 USA, on leave from the National Research Institute for Metals, Tsukuba, Japan (e-mail: author@nrim.go.jp).

would prefer to use LATEX, download IEEE's LATEX style and sample files from the same Web page. Use these LATEX files for formatting, but please follow the instructions in TRANS-JOUR.DOC or TRANS-JOUR.PDF.

If your paper is intended for a *conference*, please contact your conference editor concerning acceptable word processor formats for your particular conference.

When you open TRANS-JOUR.DOC, select "Page Layout" from the "View" menu in the menu bar (View | Page Layout), which allows you to see the footnotes. Then type over sections of TRANS-JOUR.DOC or cut and paste from another document and then use markup styles. The pull-down style menu is at the left of the Formatting Toolbar at the top of your *Word* window (for example, the style at this point in the document is "Text"). Highlight a section that you want to designate with a certain style, then select the appropriate name on the style menu. The style will adjust your fonts and line spacing. **Do not change the font sizes or line spacing to squeeze more text into a limited number of pages.** Use italics for emphasis; do not underline.

To insert images in *Word*, position the cursor at the insertion point and either use Insert | Picture | From File or copy the image to the Windows clipboard and then Edit | Paste Special | Picture (with "Float over text" unchecked).

IEEE will do the final formatting of your paper. If your paper is intended for a conference, please observe the conference page limits.

II. Procedure for Paper Submission

A. Review Stage

Please check with your editor on whether to submit your manuscript by hard copy or electronically for review. If hard copy, submit photocopies such that only one column appears per page. This will give your referees plenty of room to write comments. Send the number of copies specified by your editor (typically four). If submitted electronically, find out if your editor prefers submissions on disk or as e-mail attachments.

If you want to submit your file with one column electronically, please do the following:

--First, click on the View menu and choose Print Layout.

--Second, place your cursor in the first paragraph. Go to the Format menu, choose Columns, choose one column Layout, and choose "apply to whole document" from the dropdown menu.

--Third, click and drag the right margin bar to just over 4 inches in width.

The graphics will stay in the "second" column, but you can drag them to the first column. Make the graphic wider to push out any text that may try to fill in next to the graphic.

B. Final Stage

When you submit your final version, after your paper has been accepted, print it in two-column format, including figures and tables. Send three prints of the paper; two will go to IEEE and one will be retained by the Editor-in-Chief or conference publications chair.

You must also send your final manuscript on a disk, which IEEE will use to prepare your paper for publication. Write the authors' names on the disk label. If you are using a Macintosh, please save your file on a PC formatted disk, if possible. You may use *Zip* or CD-ROM disks for large files, or compress files using *Compress, Pkzip, Stuffit, or Gzip.*

Also send a sheet of paper with complete contact information for all authors. Include full mailing addresses, telephone numbers, fax numbers, and e-mail addresses. This information will be used to send each author a complimentary copy of the journal in which the paper appears. In addition, designate one author as the "corresponding author." This is the author to whom proofs of the paper will be sent. Proofs are sent to the corresponding author only.

C. Figures

All tables and figures will be processed as images. **However, IEEE cannot extract the tables and figures embedded in your document.** (The figures and tables you insert in your document are only to help you gauge the size of your paper, for the convenience of the referees, and to make it easy for you to distribute preprints.) Therefore, **submit, on separate sheets of paper, enlarged versions of the tables and figures that appear in your document.** These are the images IEEE will scan and publish with your paper.

D. Electronic Image Files (Optional)

You will have the greatest control over the appearance of your figures if you are able to prepare electronic image files. If you do not have the required computer skills, just submit paper prints as described above and skip this section.

1) Easiest Way: If you have a scanner, the best and quickest way to prepare noncolor figure files is to print your tables and figures on paper exactly as you want them to appear, scan them, and then save them to a file in PostScript (PS) or Encapsulated PostScript (EPS) formats. Use a separate file for each image. File names should be of the form "fig1.ps" or "fig2.eps."

2) Slightly Harder Way: Using a scanner as above, save the images in TIFF format. High-contrast line figures and tables should be prepared with 600 dpi resolution and saved with no compression, 1 bit per pixel (monochrome), with file names of the form "fig3.tif" or "table1.tif." To obtain a 3.45-in figure (one-column width) at 600 dpi, the figure requires a horizontal size of 2070 pixels. Typical file sizes will be on the order of 0.5 MB.

Photographs and grayscale figures should be prepared with 220 dpi resolution and saved with no compression, 8 bits per pixel (grayscale). To obtain a 3.45-in figure (one-column width) at 220 dpi, the figure should have a horizontal size of 759 pixels.

Color figures should be prepared with 400 dpi resolution and saved with no compression, 8 bits per pixel (palette or 256 color). To obtain a 3.45-in figure (one column width) at 400 dpi, the figure should have a horizontal size of 1380 pixels.

For more information on TIFF files, please go to http://www.ieee.org/organizations/pubs/transactions/informati on.htm and click on the link "Guidelines for Author Supplied Electronic Text and Graphics."

3) Somewhat Harder Way: If you do not have a scanner, you may create noncolor PostScript figures by "printing" them to files. First, download a PostScript printer driver from http://www.adobe.com/support/downloads/pdrvwin.htm (for Windows) or from http://www.adobe.com/support/downloads/pdrvmac.htm (for Macintosh) and install the "Generic PostScript Printer" definition. In *Word,* paste your figure into a new document. Print to a file using the PostScript printer driver. File names should be of the form "fig5.ps." Use Adobe Type 1 fonts when creating your figures, if possible.

4) Other Ways: Experienced computer users can convert figures and tables from their original format to TIFF. Some useful image converters are Adobe *Photoshop,* Corel *Draw,* and Microsoft *Photo Editor,* an application that is part of Microsoft *Office 97* and *Office 2000* (look for C:\Program Files\Common Files \Microsoft Shared\ PhotoEd\ PHOTOED.EXE. (You may have to custom-install *Photo Editor* from your original *Office* disk.)

Here is a way to make TIFF image files of tables. First, create your table in *Word.* Use horizontal lines but no vertical lines. Hide gridlines (Table | Hide Gridlines). Spell check the table to remove any red underlines that indicate spelling errors. Adjust magnification (View | Zoom) such that you can view the entire table *at maximum area* when you select View | Full Screen. Move the cursor so that it is out of the way. Press "Print Screen" on your keyboard; this copies the screen image to the Windows clipboard. Open Microsoft *Photo Editor* and click Edit | Paste as New Image. Crop the table image (click Select button; select the part you want, then Image | Crop). Adjust the properties of the image (File | Properties) to monochrome (1 bit) and 600 pixels per inch. Resize the image (Image | Resize) to a width of 3.45 inches. Save the file (File | Save As) in TIFF with no compression (click "More" button).

Most graphing programs allow you to save graphs in TIFF; however, you often have no control over compression or number of bits per pixel. You should open these image files in a program such as Microsoft *Photo Editor* and re-save them using no compression, either 1 or 8 bits, and either 600 or 220 dpi resolution (File | Properties; Image | Resize). See Section II-D2 for an explanation of number of bits and resolution. If your graphing program cannot export to TIFF, you can use the same technique described for tables in the previous paragraph.

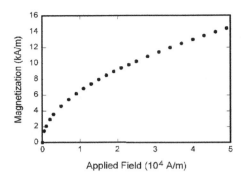

Fig. 1. Magnetization as a function of applied field. Note that "Fig." is abbreviated. There is a period after the figure number, followed by two spaces. It is good practice to explain the significance of the figure in the caption.

A way to convert a figure from Windows Metafile (WMF) to TIFF is to paste it into Microsoft *PowerPoint*, save it in JPG format, open it with Microsoft *Photo Editor* or similar converter, and re-save it as TIFF.

Microsoft *Excel* allows you to save spreadsheet charts in Graphics Interchange Format (GIF). To get good resolution, make the *Excel* charts *very* large. Then use the "Save as HTML" feature (see http://support.microsoft.com/support/kb/articles/q158/0/79.asp). You can then convert from GIF to TIFF using Microsoft *Photo Editor*, for example.

No matter how you convert your images, it is a good idea to print the TIFF files to make sure nothing was lost in the conversion.

If you modify this document for use with other IEEE journals or conferences, you should save it as type "Word 97-2000 & 6.0/95 - RTF (*.doc)" so that it can be opened by any version of *Word.*

E. Copyright Form

An IEEE copyright form should accompany your final submission. You can get a .pdf, .html, or .doc version at http://www.ieee.org/copyright or from the first issues in each volume of the IEEE TRANSACTIONS and JOURNALS. Authors are responsible for obtaining any security clearances.

III. MATH

If you are using *Word,* use either the Microsoft Equation Editor or the *MathType* add-on (http://www.mathtype.com) for equations in your paper (Insert | Object | Create New | Microsoft Equation *or* MathType Equation). "Float over text" should *not* be selected.

TABLE I
UNITS FOR MAGNETIC PROPERTIES

Symbol	Quantity	Conversion from Gaussian and CGS EMU to SI [a]
Φ	magnetic flux	$1 \text{ Mx} \rightarrow 10^{-8} \text{ Wb} = 10^{-8} \text{ V·s}$
B	magnetic flux density, magnetic induction	$1 \text{ G} \rightarrow 10^{-4} \text{ T} = 10^{-4} \text{ Wb/m}^2$
H	magnetic field strength	$1 \text{ Oe} \rightarrow 10^3/(4\pi) \text{ A/m}$
m	magnetic moment	$1 \text{ erg/G} = 1 \text{ emu}$ $\rightarrow 10^{-3} \text{ A·m}^2 = 10^{-3} \text{ J/T}$
M	magnetization	$1 \text{ erg/(G·cm}^3) = 1 \text{ emu/cm}^3$ $\rightarrow 10^3 \text{ A/m}$
$4\pi M$	magnetization	$1 \text{ G} \rightarrow 10^3/(4\pi) \text{ A/m}$
σ	specific magnetization	$1 \text{ erg/(G·g)} = 1 \text{ emu/g} \rightarrow 1 \text{ A·m}^2/\text{kg}$
j	magnetic dipole moment	$1 \text{ erg/G} = 1 \text{ emu}$ $\rightarrow 4\pi \times 10^{-10} \text{ Wb·m}$
J	magnetic polarization	$1 \text{ erg/(G·cm}^3) = 1 \text{ emu/cm}^3$ $\rightarrow 4\pi \times 10^{-4} \text{ T}$
χ, κ	susceptibility	$1 \rightarrow 4\pi$
χ_ρ	mass susceptibility	$1 \text{ cm}^3/\text{g} \rightarrow 4\pi \times 10^{-3} \text{ m}^3/\text{kg}$
μ	permeability	$1 \rightarrow 4\pi \times 10^{-7} \text{ H/m}$ $= 4\pi \times 10^{-7} \text{ Wb/(A·m)}$
μ_r	relative permeability	$\mu \rightarrow \mu_r$
w, W	energy density	$1 \text{ erg/cm}^3 \rightarrow 10^{-1} \text{ J/m}^3$
N, D	demagnetizing factor	$1 \rightarrow 1/(4\pi)$

No vertical lines in table. Statements that serve as captions for the entire table do not need footnote letters.

[a] Gaussian units are the same as cgs emu for magnetostatics; Mx = maxwell, G = gauss, Oe = oersted; Wb = weber, V = volt, s = second, T = tesla, m = meter, A = ampere, J = joule, kg = kilogram, H = henry.

IV. UNITS

Use either SI (MKS) or CGS as primary units. (SI units are strongly encouraged.) English units may be used as secondary units (in parentheses). **This applies to papers in data storage.** For example, write "15 Gb/cm^2 (100 Gb/in^2)." An exception is when English units are used as identifiers in trade, such as "3½ in disk drive." Avoid combining SI and CGS units, such as current in amperes and magnetic field in oersteds. This often leads to confusion because equations do not balance dimensionally. If you must use mixed units, clearly state the units for each quantity in an equation.

The SI unit for magnetic field strength H is A/m. However, if you wish to use units of T, either refer to magnetic flux density B or magnetic field strength symbolized as $\mu_0 H$. Use the center dot to separate compound units, e.g., "A·m^2."

V. HELPFUL HINTS

A. Figures and Tables

Because IEEE will do the final formatting of your paper, you do not need to position figures and tables at the top and bottom of each column. In fact, all figures, figure captions, and tables can be at the end of the paper. Large figures and tables may span both columns. Place figure captions below the figures; place table titles above the tables. If your figure has two parts, include the labels "(a)" and "(b)" as part of the artwork. Please verify that the figures and tables you mention in the text actually exist. **Please do not include captions as part of the figures. Do not put captions in "text boxes" linked to the figures. Do not put borders around the outside of your figures.** Use the abbreviation "Fig." even at the beginning of a sentence. Do not abbreviate "Table." Tables are numbered with Roman numerals.

Color printing of figures is available, but is billed to the authors (approximately $1300, depending on the number of figures and number of pages containing color). Include a note with your final paper indicating that you request color printing. **Do not use color unless it is necessary for the proper interpretation of your figures.** If you want reprints of your color article, the reprint order should be submitted promptly. There is an additional charge of $81 per 100 for color reprints.

Figure axis labels are often a source of confusion. Use words rather than symbols. As an example, write the quantity "Magnetization," or "Magnetization M," not just "M." Put units in parentheses. Do not label axes only with units. As in Fig. 1, for example, write "Magnetization (A/m)" or "Magnetization $(A \cdot m^{-1})$," not just "A/m." Do not label axes with a ratio of quantities and units. For example, write "Temperature (K)," not "Temperature/K."

Multipliers can be especially confusing. Write "Magnetization (kA/m)" or "Magnetization (10^3 A/m)." Do not write "Magnetization (A/m) × 1000" because the reader would not know whether the top axis label in Fig. 1 meant 16000 A/m or 0.016 A/m. Figure labels should be legible, approximately 8 to 12 point type.

B. References

Number citations consecutively in square brackets [1]. The sentence punctuation follows the brackets [2]. Multiple references [2], [3] are each numbered with separate brackets [1]–[3]. When citing a section in a book, please give the relevant page numbers [2]. In sentences, refer simply to the reference number, as in [3]. Do not use "Ref. [3]" or "reference [3]" except at the beginning of a sentence: "Reference [3] shows ... ." Unfortunately the IEEE document translator cannot handle automatic endnotes in *Word*; therefore, type the reference list at the end of the paper using the "References" style.

Number footnotes separately in superscripts (Insert | Footnote).[1] Place the actual footnote at the bottom of the column in which it is cited; do not put footnotes in the reference list (endnotes). Use letters for table footnotes (see Table I).

Please note that the references at the end of this document are in the preferred referencing style. Give all authors' names; do not use "*et al.*" unless there are six authors or more. Use a space after authors' initials. Papers that have not been published should be cited as "unpublished" [4]. Papers that have been submitted for publication should be cited as "submitted for publication" [5]. Papers that have been accepted for publication, but not yet specified for an issue should be cited as "to be published" [6]. Please give affiliations and addresses for private communications [7].

Capitalize only the first word in a paper title, except for proper nouns and element symbols. For papers published in translation journals, please give the English citation first, followed by the original foreign-language citation [8].

C. Abbreviations and Acronyms

Define abbreviations and acronyms the first time they are used in the text, even after they have already been defined in the abstract. Abbreviations such as IEEE, SI, ac, and dc do not have to be defined. Abbreviations that incorporate periods should not have spaces: write "C.N.R.S.," not "C. N. R. S." Do not use abbreviations in the title unless they are unavoidable (for example, "IEEE" in the title of this article).

D. Equations

Number equations consecutively with equation numbers in parentheses flush with the right margin, as in (1). First use the equation editor to create the equation. Then select the "Equation" markup style. Press the tab key and write the equation number in parentheses. To make your equations more compact, you may use the solidus (/), the exp function, or appropriate exponents. Use parentheses to avoid ambiguities in denominators. Punctuate equations when they are part of a sentence, as in

$$\int_0^{r_2} F(r,\varphi)\, dr\, d\varphi = \left[\frac{\sigma\, r_2}{2\,\mu_0}\right] \cdot \int_0^{\infty} \frac{e^{-\lambda|z_j - z_i|}\, J_1(\lambda\, r_2) J_0(\lambda\, r_i) d\lambda}{\lambda} \qquad (1)$$

Be sure that the symbols in your equation have been defined before the equation appears or immediately following. Italicize symbols (T might refer to temperature, but T is the unit tesla). Refer to "(1)," not "Eq. (1)" or "equation (1)," except at the beginning of a sentence: "Equation (1) is ... ."

E. Other Recommendations

Use one space after periods and colons. Hyphenate complex modifiers: "zero-field-cooled magnetization." Avoid dangling participles, such as, "Using (1), the potential was calculated." [It is not clear who or what used (1).] Write instead, "The potential was calculated by using (1)," or "Using (1), we calculated the potential."

Use a zero before decimal points: "0.25," not ".25." Use "cm^3," not "cc." Indicate sample dimensions as "0.1 cm × 0.2 cm," not "0.1 × 0.2 cm^2." The abbreviation for "seconds" is "s," not "sec." Do not mix complete spellings and abbreviations of units: use "Wb/m^2" or "webers per square meter," not "webers/m^2." When expressing a range of values, write "7 to 9" or "7-9," not "7~9."

A parenthetical statement at the end of a sentence is punctuated outside of the closing parenthesis (like this). (A parenthetical sentence is punctuated within the parentheses.) In American English, periods and commas are within quotation marks, like "this period." Other punctuation is "outside"! Avoid contractions; for example, write "do not" instead of "don't." The serial comma is preferred: "A, B, and C" instead of "A, B and C."

If you wish, you may write in the first person singular or plural and use the active voice ("I observed that ..." or "We observed that ..." instead of "It was observed that ..."). Remember to check spelling. If your native language is not English, please get a native English-speaking colleague to proofread your paper.

---

[1] It is recommended that footnotes be avoided (except for the unnumbered footnote with the receipt date on the first page). Instead, try to integrate the footnote information into the text.

VI. Some Common Mistakes

The word "data" is plural, not singular. The subscript for the permeability of vacuum μ_0 is zero, not a lowercase letter "o." The term for residual magnetization is "remanence"; the adjective is "remanent"; do not write "remnance" or "remnant." Use the word "micrometer" instead of "micron." A graph within a graph is an "inset," not an "insert." The word "alternatively" is preferred to the word "alternately" (unless you really mean something that alternates). Use the word "whereas" instead of "while" (unless you are referring to simultaneous events). Do not use the word "essentially" to mean "approximately" or "effectively." Do not use the word "issue" as a euphemism for "problem." When compositions are not specified, separate chemical symbols by en-dashes; for example, "NiMn" indicates the intermetallic compound $Ni_{0.5}Mn_{0.5}$ whereas "Ni–Mn" indicates an alloy of some composition Ni_xMn_{1-x}.

Be aware of the different meanings of the homophones "affect" (usually a verb) and "effect" (usually a noun), "complement" and "compliment," "discreet" and "discrete," "principal" (e.g., "principal investigator") and "principle" (e.g., "principle of measurement"). Do not confuse "imply" and "infer."

Prefixes such as "non," "sub," "micro," "multi," and ""ultra" are not independent words; they should be joined to the words they modify, usually without a hyphen. There is no period after the "et" in the Latin abbreviation "*et al.*" (it is also italicized). The abbreviation "i.e.," means "that is," and the abbreviation "e.g.," means "for example" (these abbreviations are not italicized).

An excellent style manual and source of information for science writers is [9]. A general IEEE style guide, *Information for Authors,* is available at http://www.ieee.org/organizations/pubs/transactions/informati on.htm

VII. Editorial Policy

Submission of a manuscript is not required for participation in a conference. Do not submit a reworked version of a paper you have submitted or published elsewhere. Do not publish "preliminary" data or results. The submitting author is responsible for obtaining agreement of all coauthors and any consent required from sponsors before submitting a paper. IEEE Transactions and Journals strongly discourage courtesy authorship. It is the obligation of the authors to cite relevant prior work.

The Transactions and Journals Department does not publish conference records or proceedings. The Transactions does publish papers related to conferences that have been recommended for publication on the basis of peer review. As a matter of convenience and service to the technical community, these topical papers are collected and published in one issue of the Transactions.

At least two reviews are required for every paper submitted. For conference-related papers, the decision to accept or reject a paper is made by the conference editors and publications committee; the recommendations of the referees are advisory only. Undecipherable English is a valid reason for rejection. Authors of rejected papers may revise and resubmit them to the Transactions as regular papers, whereupon they will be reviewed by two new referees.

VIII. Publication Principles

The contents of IEEE Transactions and Journals are peer-reviewed and archival. The Transactions publishes scholarly articles of archival value as well as tutorial expositions and critical reviews of classical subjects and topics of current interest.

Authors should consider the following points:

1) Technical papers submitted for publication must advance the state of knowledge and must cite relevant prior work.
2) The length of a submitted paper should be commensurate with the importance, or appropriate to the complexity, of the work. For example, an obvious extension of previously published work might not be appropriate for publication or might be adequately treated in just a few pages.
3) Authors must convince both peer reviewers and the editors of the scientific and technical merit of a paper; the standards of proof are higher when extraordinary or unexpected results are reported.
4) Because replication is required for scientific progress, papers submitted for publication must provide sufficient information to allow readers to perform similar experiments or calculations and use the reported results. Although not everything need be disclosed, a paper must contain new, useable, and fully described information. For example, a specimen's chemical composition need not be reported if the main purpose of a paper is to introduce a new measurement technique. Authors should expect to be challenged by reviewers if the results are not supported by adequate data and critical details.
5) Papers that describe ongoing work or announce the latest technical achievement, which are suitable for presentation at a professional conference, may not be appropriate for publication in a TRANSACTIONS or JOURNAL.

IX. Stream Tools

This Microsoft Word file has been preset for compatible use with the STREAM Tools template designed for creating well-formatted reports and papers using the automatic formatting features of Microsoft Word. The principles behind the template is fully explained in *Technical Writing for Teams: The STREAM Tools Handbook* by A. V. Mamishev and S.D Williams and at www.streamtoolsonline.com. Basic idea is to strive to achieve LaTeX-like functionality in Microsoft Word. This template is one of a set. Depending on the document you are creating, you may switch to templates for single-column reports, books, etc..

A. Headings

To add a new heading to your document:

1. Choose the placeholder heading in this whose heading level matches the heading you wish to add. Four heading levels are provided.

2. Copy this placeholder heading and paste it in the desired location. The newly pasted heading will take on the appropriate heading number.

3. Replace the placeholder text with your own heading text

B. Figures and Captions

To add a new figure and caption to your document:

4. Select and copy the placeholder figure (see below) and its accompanying caption.

5. Paste to the desired location in your document.

6. Copy and paste the figure you wish to add to the **Clipboard**.

7. Select the placeholder figure so that you will overwrite it when you paste in your figure.

8. On the **Edit** menu, click **Paste Special.**

9. In the **Paste Special** dialog box click **Picture (Windows Metafile)** and click **OK.**

10. Replace the placeholder caption text with your own caption text.

11. If desired, update all your figure numbers with the **Global Update** command: Press **CTRL+A** to select the entire document and then **F9** to update all updatable components.

C. Cross References for Figures and Tables

There are many occasions when you need to refer the reader from the text of your document to the caption of a figure or table.

To add a cross reference to a figure or table:

12. Place the mouse pointer at the location where you wish to add the cross reference.

13. On the **Insert** menu, click **Reference** and then **Cross Reference.**

14. In the **Cross Reference** dialog box, click the caption to which you are building the text reference.

15. In the case of a figure, under **Reference Type** click **Figure** and under **Insert Reference To**, click **Only Label and Number.**

OR

In the case of a table, under Reference Type click Table and under Insert Reference To, click Only Label and Number.

16. Click **Insert.**

An autonumbered cross reference (such as **Figure 13** or **Table 4**) will appear in the text. Remove the boldfacing and write the figure or table cross reference text manually.

17. If desired, update all your table numbers with the **Global Update** command: Press **CTRL+A** to select the entire document and then **F9** to update all updatable components.

18. Remember not to use text boxes — unfortunately, automatic numbering fails when one uses them.

X. CONCLUSION

A conclusion section is not required. Although a conclusion may review the main points of the paper, do not replicate the abstract as the conclusion. A conclusion might elaborate on the importance of the work or suggest applications and extensions.

APPENDIX

Appendixes, if needed, appear before the acknowledgment.

ACKNOWLEDGMENT

The preferred spelling of the word "acknowledgment" in American English is without an "e" after the "g." Use the singular heading even if you have many acknowledgments. Avoid expressions such as "One of us (S.B.A.) would like to thank ... ." Instead, write "F. A. Author thanks ... ." **Sponsor and financial support acknowledgments are placed in the unnumbered footnote on the first page.**

REFERENCES

[1] G. O. Young, "Synthetic structure of industrial plastics (Book style with paper title and editor)," in *Plastics*, 2nd ed. vol. 3, J. Peters, Ed. New York: McGraw-Hill, 1964, pp. 15–64.

[2] W.-K. Chen, *Linear Networks and Systems* (Book style). Belmont, CA: Wadsworth, 1993, pp. 123–135.

[3] H. Poor, *An Introduction to Signal Detection and Estimation*. New York: Springer-Verlag, 1985, ch. 4.

[4] B. Smith, "An approach to graphs of linear forms (Unpublished work style)," unpublished.

[5] E. H. Miller, "A note on reflector arrays (Periodical style—Accepted for publication)," *IEEE Trans. Antennas Propagat.*, to be published.

[6] J. Wang, "Fundamentals of erbium-doped fiber amplifiers arrays (Periodical style—Submitted for publication)," *IEEE J. Quantum Electron.*, submitted for publication.

[7] C. J. Kaufman, Rocky Mountain Research Lab., Boulder, CO, private communication, May 1995.

[8] Y. Yorozu, M. Hirano, K. Oka, and Y. Tagawa, "Electron spectroscopy studies on magneto-optical media and plastic substrate interfaces(Translation Journals style)," *IEEE Transl. J. Magn.Jpn.*, vol. 2, Aug. 1987, pp. 740–741 [*Dig. 9th Annu. Conf. Magnetics* Japan, 1982, p. 301].

[9] M. Young, *The Techincal Writers Handbook*. Mill Valley, CA: University Science, 1989.

[10] J. U. Duncombe, "Infrared navigation—Part I: An assessment of feasibility (Periodical style)," *IEEE Trans. Electron Devices*, vol. ED-11, pp. 34–39, Jan. 1959.

[11] S. Chen, B. Mulgrew, and P. M. Grant, "A clustering technique for digital communications channel equalization using radial basis function networks," *IEEE Trans. Neural Networks*, vol. 4, pp. 570–578, July 1993.

[12] R. W. Lucky, "Automatic equalization for digital communication," *Bell Syst. Tech. J.*, vol. 44, no. 4, pp. 547–588, Apr. 1965.

[13] S. P. Bingulac, "On the compatibility of adaptive controllers (Published Conference Proceedings style)," in *Proc. 4th Annu. Allerton Conf. Circuits and Systems Theory*, New York, 1994, pp. 8–16.

[14] G. R. Faulhaber, "Design of service systems with priority reservation," in *Conf. Rec. 1995 IEEE Int. Conf. Communications*, pp. 3–8.

[15] W. D. Doyle, "Magnetization reversal in films with biaxial anisotropy," in *1987 Proc. INTERMAG Conf.*, pp. 2.2-1–2.2-6.

[16] G. W. Juette and L. E. Zeffanella, "Radio noise currents n short sections on bundle conductors (Presented Conference Paper style)," presented at the IEEE Summer power Meeting, Dallas, TX, June 22–27, 1990, Paper 90 SM 690-0 PWRS.

[17] J. G. Kreifeldt, "An analysis of surface-detected EMG as an amplitude-modulated noise," presented at the 1989 Int. Conf. Medicine and Biological Engineering, Chicago, IL.

[18] J. Williams, "Narrow-band analyzer (Thesis or Dissertation style)," Ph.D. dissertation, Dept. Elect. Eng., Harvard Univ., Cambridge, MA, 1993.

[19] N. Kawasaki, "Parametric study of thermal and chemical nonequilibrium nozzle flow," M.S. thesis, Dept. Electron. Eng., Osaka Univ., Osaka, Japan, 1993.

[20] J. P. Wilkinson, "Nonlinear resonant circuit devices (Patent style)," U.S. Patent 3 624 12, July 16, 1990.

[21] *IEEE Criteria for Class IE Electric Systems* (Standards style), IEEE Standard 308, 1969.

[22] *Letter Symbols for Quantities*, ANSI Standard Y10.5-1968.

[23] R. E. Haskell and C. T. Case, "Transient signal propagation in lossless isotropic plasmas (Report style)," USAF Cambridge Res. Lab., Cambridge, MA Rep. ARCRL-66-234 (II), 1994, vol. 2.

[24] E. E. Reber, R. L. Michell, and C. J. Carter, "Oxygen absorption in the Earth's atmosphere," Aerospace Corp., Los Angeles, CA, Tech. Rep. TR-0200 (420-46)-3, Nov. 1988.

[25] (Handbook style) *Transmission Systems for Communications*, 3rd ed., Western Electric Co., Winston-Salem, NC, 1985, pp. 44–60.

[26] *Motorola Semiconductor Data Manual*, Motorola Semiconductor Products Inc., Phoenix, AZ, 1989.

[27] (Basic Book/Monograph Online Sources) J. K. Author. (year, month, day). *Title* (edition) [Type of medium]. Volume(issue).   Available: http://www.(URL)

[28] J. Jones. (1991, May 10). Networks (2nd ed.) [Online]. Available: http://www.atm.com

[29] (Journal Online Sources style) K. Author. (year, month). Title. *Journal* [Type of medium]. Volume(issue), paging if given.   Available: http://www.(URL)

[30] R. J. Vidmar. (1992, August). On the use of atmospheric plasmas as electromagnetic reflectors. *IEEE Trans. Plasma Sci.* [Online]. *21(3).* pp. 876—880.   Available: http://www.halcyon.com/pub/journals/21ps03-vidmar

First A. Author (M'76–SM'81–F'87) and the other authors may include biographies at the end of regular papers. Biographies are often not included in conference-related papers. This author became a Member (M) of IEEE in 1976, a Senior Member (SM) in 1981, and a Fellow (F) in 1987. The first paragraph may contain a place and/or date of birth (list place, then date). Next, the author's educational background is listed. The degrees should be listed with type of degree in what field, which institution, city, state or country, and year degree was earned. The author's major field of study should be lower-cased.

The second paragraph uses the pronoun of the person (he or she) and not the author's last name. It lists military and work experience, including summer and fellowship jobs. Job titles are capitalized. The current job must have a location; previous positions may be listed without one. Information concerning previous publications may be included. Try not to list more than three books or published articles. The format for listing publishers of a book within the biography is: title of book (city, state: publisher name, year) similar to a reference. Current and previous research interests ends the paragraph.

The third paragraph begins with the author's title and last name (e.g., Dr. Smith, Prof. Jones, Mr. Kajor, Ms. Hunter). List any memberships in professional societies other than the IEEE. Finally, list any awards and work for IEEE committees and publications. If a photograph is provided, the biography will be indented around it. The photograph is placed at the top left of the biography. Personal hobbies will be deleted from the biography.

NIH template with STREAM Tools enabled

File name	NIHTemplate_2010.docx
Description	The following sample showcases how an NIH document enabled with STREAM Tools should be formatted. Please note that individual agency requirements will change over time, so authors are encouraged to closely review their guidelines before submission.
	SEPARATE FILE PROVIDED

[GRANT PROPOSAL TITLE]

[PI's First Name] [PI's Last Name]
[Organization]

[Key Personnel's First Name] [Key Personnel's Last Name]
[Organization]

Table of Contents

Note: When new headings or sections are added to the document, the table of contents can be updated by pressing **Ctrl + A**, and then **F9**.The table of contents included here is for internal use and should **not** be included in an attachment submitted to the NIH. The NIH login and submission system automatically generates their own table of contents based on the submitted document, which the proposer cannot edit. When submitting the finalized proposal, **be sure to delete the table of contents** in favor of the auto-generated version.

It should also be noted that submission through the NIH R01 mechanism occurs through the SF424 PDF form package. This document has compiled many of the required attachments and combined them into a single word document for your convenience. In order to submit, you will need to divide each component in this word document into a separate PDF file (file names may only use standard characters: A-Z, 0-9, and underscore), and then attach them into the specified SF424 locations.

Legend for the text of the proposal:
        Agency instructions will appear highlighted in yellow.
        Sample proposal text in the proper format (white)

PROJECT SUMMARY

The Project Summary must contain a summary of the proposed activity suitable for dissemination to the public. It should be a self-contained description of the project and should contain a statement of objectives and methods to be employed. It should be informative to other persons working in the same or related fields and insofar as possible understandable to a scientifically or technically literate lay reader. This Summary must not include any proprietary/confidential information.

The **Project Summary** is meant to serve as a succinct and accurate description of the proposed work when separated from the application. State the application's broad, long-term objectives and specific aims, making reference to the health relatedness of the project (i.e., relevance to the **mission of the agency**). Describe concisely the research design and methods for achieving the stated goals. This section should be informative to other persons working in the same or related fields and insofar as possible understandable to a scientifically or technically literate reader. Avoid describing past accomplishments and the use of the first person. Finally, please make every effort to be succinct.

This section must be no longer than 30 lines of text, and follow the required font and margin specifications. An abstract which exceeds this allowable length may be flagged as an error by the agency upon submission. This would require a corrective action before the application will be accepted.

This template provides instructions for preparing grant proposals in accordance with the June 18, 2012 National Institutes of Health's (NIH) SF424 General Guide guidelines and regulations. These regulations change frequently, so it is encouraged that applicants carefully review the guidelines and regulations. This template provides directions on how to structure and format an NIH proposal. The auto-formatting and technical directions are written specifically for Microsoft Word 2010, but any version of Microsoft Word later than 2007 should be suitable.

The project summary is a self-contained description of the activities that would ensue should the project be funded. It must be suitable for publication, and no more than one page in length. The summary should be written in the third person and include a statement of objectives and the methods to be employed.

PROJECT NARRATIVE

Provide Project Narrative in accordance with the announcement and/or agency-specific instructions. **For NIH and other PHS agencies applications, this attachment will reflect the second component of the Project Summary.** The second component of the Project Summary/Abstract (i.e., "Description") is **Relevance.** Using no more than two or three sentences, describe the relevance of this research to public health. In this section, be succinct and use plain language that can be understood by a general, lay audience.

Using no more than two or three sentences, this section should concisely outline how the project is relevant to public health.

SPECIFIC AIMS

State concisely the goals of the proposed research and summarize the expected outcome(s), including the impact that the results of the proposed research will exert on the research field(s) involved. List succinctly the specific objectives of the research proposed, e.g., to test a stated hypothesis, create a novel design, solve a specific problem, challenge an existing paradigm or clinical practice, address a critical barrier to progress in the field, or develop new technology. The Specific Aims attachment is required unless otherwise specified in the FOA. Specific Aims are limited to one page.

RESEARCH STRATEGY

Organize the Research Strategy in the specified order and using the instructions provided below. Start each section with the appropriate section heading – Significance, Innovation, Approach. Cite published experimental details in the Research Strategy section and provide the full reference in the Bibliography and References Cited section

A. Significance

- Explain the importance of <u>the problem or critical barrier to progress</u> in the field that the proposed project addresses.
- Explain how the proposed project will <u>improve scientific knowledge, technical capability</u>, and/or clinical practice in one or more broad fields.
- Describe how the concepts, methods, technologies, treatments, services, or preventative interventions that drive this field will be changed if the proposed aims are achieved. Explain the <u>project's potential to lead to a marketable product, process or service</u>.

The body of the text is called the "Research Strategy" in NIH regulations and will be referred to as such hereafter. The Research Strategy should concisely outline all of the important criteria found in the bulleted lists above and below, and should be prepared with the care and thoroughness of a paper submitted for publication. It should also be completely self-contained. This means that URLs should not be included in the proposal. The reviewers are under no obligation to look at website links, and website links can be seen as an attempt to circumvent the page limitations.

The applicant may include as many second-level sections as needed, so long as they do not exceed the twelve page limit. Generally, the only three required headings under which the entire proposal should fit are: 1) Significance, 2) Innovation, and 3) Approach. All other headings may be added, modified, or removed to fit the needs of a relevant proposal. It should be noted that the second-level headings provided below (i.e., A.1. Technical Guidelines) are to be used as guidelines for formatting your template; these second-level headings are not required for an NIH submission.

A.1. Technical Guidelines

At this time, page numbers should not be included to the body of the proposal, as the SF424 application package automatically adds its own page numbering system to each file. The project description should be no longer than twelve pages, including graphs, charts, maps, tables, and other pictorial representation. A comprehensive list of all references used are not included in the twelve page limit. Unless otherwise specified in an NIH program solicitation, page extensions can only be obtained by the written approval of the cognizant NIH assistant Director/Office Head or some other designee. Additionally, the NIH encourages proposers to use the Metric System in all of their calculations, where applicable.

A.1.1. Font Sizing and Pagination

The NIH requests a black font of either Arial, Helvetica, Platino Linotype, or Georgia typeface. The proposal font must be size 11 or larger. Additionally, all margins must be at least one-half inch in size.

A.1.2. Figures and Tables

Any number of figures or tables can be included in the proposal, but must all appear within the project description and count toward the twelve page limitation. Figures may be in color, but be aware that reviewers are not required to print in color. Ensure that every figure can be read both in color and in black-and-white; in other words, color-sensitive figures should use shades of gray that stand out. Text inside a figure or table for the purpose of labeling may be smaller than 11 point font; however, the font must still be readable and the text may not be used as a means for circumventing the 11 page font limitation.

Several figure and table samples are provided below. To insert new figures and tables, you should begin by copy and pasting these existing elements into your proposal. Modify the text, but do not delete the table or figure numbers, When you are finished, press Ctrl+A, and then F9 to automatically update the numbering for your figures and tables.

Table 1. An example table.

A	B	C
D	E	F
G	H	I

To create a new table, simply copy the existing one, replace the title, and input any data. The process is similar for figures, copy the current figure, replace the picture and edit the caption. To update the numbering, press **Ctrl + A** and then **F9**. This should update the numbering of all headings, tables, and figures.

Figure 1. *This is an example figure of the NIH logo. Note that the word Figure is completely written out, and that a period (.) follows the number.*

Figure 2. *This is an example figure of the University of Washington seal. It should be noted that these two figures appear side-by-side, but the page remains in single column format.*

Figure 3. *This is an example figure of the Department of State Seal. To avoid Double Column formatting, both figures have been placed in a two-column, one-row table, and the lines have been removed.*

To cross-reference a table or figure, on the **Insert** tab, click **Cross-reference**, select either **Table** or **Figure** from the dropdown menu, uncheck **Insert as hyperlink**, and select **Only label and number** from the second dropdown menu. Then press **OK**. This sentence contains an example of a cross reference to **Figure 1**. Place the cursor within the preceding "**Figure 1**" and it will appear with a gray background, indicating that it is autotext. Ideally, when preparing a proposal, your figures will be first mentioned in the text before they appear.

Figure 4. *This is an example of a floating figure template.*

A.1.3. Equations

All equations should be numbered in the order that they appear in the text.

$$y = mx + b \qquad\qquad (1)$$

To insert an equation, simply copy the existing equation and number, and paste it into the new location. Then, retype a new equation in place of the old text. To update the numbering press **CTRL + A** and then **F9**.

To create a cross reference to an equation, you must first create a bookmark for it. Select equation number to the right of the equation. Next, on the **Insert** tab, clock **Bookmark**, and create a name for your equation. It is highly recommended that all of your equation bookmarks should start with "eq" for identification purposes. Next, on the **Insert** tab, click **Cross reference.** In the dialog box, choose **Bookmark** and **Bookmark Text** from the dropdown lists, and click **OK**. This sentence contains an example cross reference to Equation 1.

B. Innovation

- Explain how the application challenges and seeks to shift current research or clinical practice paradigms.
- Describe any novel theoretical concepts, approaches or methodologies, instrumentation or interventions to be developed or used, and any advantage over existing methodologies, instrumentation, or interventions.
- Explain any refinements, improvements, or new applications of theoretical concepts, approaches or methodologies, instrumentation, or interventions.

C. Approach

- Describe the overall strategy, methodology, and analyses to be used to accomplish the specific aims of the project. Provide a tentative sequence or timetable for the project. Unless addressed separately in Item 15 (Resource Sharing Plan), include how the data will be collected, analyzed, and interpreted as well as any resource sharing plans as appropriate.
- Discuss potential problems, alternative strategies, and benchmarks for success anticipated to achieve the aims.
- If the project is in the early stages of development, describe any strategy to establish feasibility, and address the management of any high risk aspects of the proposed work.
- Point out any procedures, situations, or materials that may be hazardous to personnel and precautions to be exercised. A full discussion on the use of select agents should appear in Item 11, below.

If an applicant has multiple Specific Aims, then the applicant may address Significance, Innovation and Approach for each Specific Aim individually, or may address Significance, Innovation and Approach for all of the Specific Aims collectively.

As applicable, also include the following information as part of the Research Strategy, keeping within the three sections listed above: Significance, Innovation, and Approach.

Preliminary Studies for New Applications: For new applications, include information on Preliminary Studies. Discuss the PD/PI's preliminary studies, data, and or experience pertinent to this application. Except for Exploratory/Developmental Grants (R21/R33), Small Research Grants (R03), and Academic Research Enhancement Award (AREA) Grants (R15), preliminary data can be an essential part of a research grant application and help to establish the likelihood of success of the proposed project. Early Stage Investigators should include preliminary data (however, for R01 applications, reviewers will be instructed to place less emphasis on the preliminary data in application from Early Stage Investigators than on the preliminary data in applications from more established investigators).

FACILITIES & OTHER RESOURCES

This information is used to assess the capability of the organizational resources available to perform the effort proposed. Identify the facilities to be used (Laboratory, Animal, Computer, Office, Clinical and Other). If appropriate, indicate their capacities, pertinent capabilities, relative proximity and extent of availability to the project. Describe only those resources that are directly applicable to the proposed work. Provide any information describing the Other Resources available to the project (e.g., machine shop, electronic shop) and the extent to which they would be available to the project.

No special form is required but this section must be completed and attached for submissions to NIH and other PHS agencies unless otherwise noted in an FOA. Describe how the scientific environment in which the research will be done contributes to the probability of success (e.g., institutional support, physical resources, and intellectual rapport). In describing the scientific environment in which the work will be done, discuss ways in which the proposed studies will benefit from unique features of the scientific environment or subject populations or will employ useful collaborative arrangements.

For Early Stage Investigators, describe institutional investment in the success of the investigator, e.g., resources for classes, travel, training; collegial support such as career enrichment programs, assistance and guidance in the supervision of trainees involved with the ESI's project, and availability of organized peer groups; logistical support such as administrative management and oversight and best practices training; and financial support such as protected time for research with salary support.

If there are multiple performance sites, describe the resources available at each site. Describe any special facilities used for working with biohazards or other potentially dangerous substances.

EQUIPMENT

List major items of equipment already available for this project and, if appropriate identify location and pertinent capabilities.

BIBLIOGRAPHY & REFERENCES CITED

Provide a bibliography of any references cited in the Project Narrative. Each reference must include the names of all authors (in the same sequence in which they appear in the publication), the article and journal title, book title, volume number, page numbers, and year of publication. Include only bibliographic citations. Applicants should be especially careful to follow scholarly practices in providing citations for source materials relied upon when preparing any section of the application.

Unless otherwise noted in an FOA, this section is required for submissions to NIH and other PHS agencies. This section (formerly "Literature Cited") should include any references cited in the PHS 398 Research Plan component(see Section 5.5 for details on completing that component). When citing articles that fall under the Public Access Policy, were authored or co-authored by the applicant and arose from NIH support, provide the NIH Manuscript Submission reference number (e.g., NIHMS97531) or the PubMed Central (PMC) reference number (e.g., PMCID234567) for each article. If the PMCID is not yet available because the Journal submits articles directly to PMC on behalf of their authors, indicate "PMC Journal – In Process." A list of these journals is posted at: http://publicaccess.nih.gov/submit_process_journals.htm.

Citations that are not covered by the Public Access Policy, but are publicly available in a free, online format may include URLs or PubMed ID (PMID) numbers along with the full reference (note that copies of publicly available publications are not accepted as appendix material). The references should be limited to relevant and current literature. While there is not a page limitation, it is important to be concise and to select only those literature references pertinent to the proposed research.

[1]   Mamishev, Alexander, and Sean Williams. *Technical Writing for Teams: The STREAM Tools Handbook.* 1st ed. Hoboken, NJ: IEEE Press, 2010. Print.

Index

Symbols & Numbers

A

B

C

R

radicals, editing, 154
Reference Manager, 171, 184–185. *See also* citations
references. *See* citations
renumbering figures, 94–95
resizing
    figures, 44, 90, 97
    tables, 87
resolution, photo, 96
Reveal Formatting pane, 12
Roman pagination, selecting, 38
ruler, displaying, 51

S

sans serif fonts, 98, 148
saving, figures, as .png files, 97
scaling, figures, 97
section breaks
    inserting, 32, 66
    restarting numbering after, 66
section headings, 4
sections
    creating tables of contents for, 73–74
    inserting blank pages between, 34
selecting
    all contents, 15
    in math zones, 130–131
    tables, 86
selection objects in math zones, 130–131
serif fonts, 98
shading
    headings, 64
    tables, 111
sizing figures, 19
soft line breaks, 150
soft page breaks, inserting, 65
spacing in equations, 130, 136, 151, 159
standard templates, 14
STREAM Tools, templates compatible with, finding, 13
structures gallery, 126
structuring documents, 31–33
Style gallery, 6, 7, 42
Style Inspector, 11
style-less tables, 109–113
Style Separators, 143

styles
    adding and removing from Style gallery, 7, 42
    applying to text, 6
    automatically updating, 43
    built-in, 113–114
    changing, 95
    for citations, 172
    creating, 9–11, 49, 87, 104, 133
    deleting from document, 7, 8
    displaying, 11
    for front matter, 67
    for headings, 6, 61, 77
    inheritance of, 10–11
    modifying, 9, 42–43, 61
    naming, 9
    overview of, 6–8
    revealing formatting of, 12
    for tables, 22, 49, 104
    for tables of contents, 70
    updating, automatically, 61
    updating, from changed text, 10
subheadings, creating, 43
subscripts
    creating, 136
    formatting, 166
    in linear notation, 128–129
    prescripts for, 152
summations, entering, 129
superscripts
    creating, 135
    formatting, 166
    in linear notation, 128–129
    prescripts for, 152
Symbol dialog box, 125
symbols
    inserting, 124, 125, 126, 161
    keyboard shortcuts for, 159

T

tables
    adding rows/columns, 22
    aligning, 86
    aligning on page, 46, 110
    autofitting to contents, 87
    borders and shading, 47, 48, 50, 104, 110, 119
    built-in styles, applying, 113
    captions, editing, 23
    captions, inserting, 46, 112

U

V

variables
    defining, 166
    sizing consistently, 165

W

wrapping text
    around figures, 45
    in tables, 46
writing equations with pen or mouse, 154

Y

yellow text, 2

About the authors

ALEXANDER MAMISHEV, PHD, is a Professor of Electrical Engineering, Adjunct Professor of Mechanical Engineering, and Director of the Sensors, Energy, and Automation Laboratory at University of Washington. As author of more than 100 articles and papers, four books, and four patents, he is keenly attuned to the challenges of writing technical documents, particularly when working in teams.

MURRAY SARGENT, PHD, is a Partner Software Design Engineer at Microsoft. He has written more than 100 articles and six books, and currently focuses on the editing engine and math editing and display capabilities in Microsoft Office.

Now that you've read the book...

Tell us what you think!

Was it useful?
Did it teach you what you wanted to learn?
Was there room for improvement?

Let us know at http://aka.ms/tellpress

Your feedback goes directly to the staff at Microsoft Press,
and we read every one of your responses. Thanks in advance!

 Microsoft